Yeats's Shakespeare

RUPIN W. DESAI

YEATS'S
SHAKESPEARE

1971

Northwestern University Press

EVANSTON

Material from the following works is reprinted with
permission of The Macmillan Company of New York,
Macmillan & Company Ltd. of London, and M. B.
Yeats.: *The Variorum Edition of the Plays of William
Butler Yeats,* ed. Russell K. Alspach. Copyright © by
Russell K. Alspach and Bertha Georgie Yeats, 1966.
Copyright 1903, 1904, 1907, 1908, 1912, 1921, 1924,
1928, 1934, 1935, 1951 by The Macmillan Company.
Copyright 1911, 1938 by William Butler Yeats.
Copyright 1940 by Georgie Yeats. Copyright renewed
1940, 1949, 1950, 1952, 1962 by Bertha Georgie
Yeats. Copyright renewed 1956 by Georgina Yeats.
Copyright renewed 1935, 1936, 1938 by William Butler
Yeats. *The Variorum Edition of the Poems of William
Butler Yeats,* ed. Peter Allt and Russell K. Alspach.
Copyright 1906 by The Macmillan Company, renewed
1934 by William Butler Yeats. Copyright 1916, 1919,
1924, 1933, 1934 by The Macmillan Company,
renewed 1944, 1947, 1952, 1961, 1962 by Bertha
Georgie Yeats. Copyright 1928 by The Macmillan
Company, renewed 1956 by Georgie Yeats. Copyright
1940 by Georgie Yeats, renewed 1968 by Bertha
Georgie Yeats, Michael Butler Yeats, and Anne Yeats.

Material from the following works is reprinted with
permission of New Directions Publishing Corporation
and Faber and Faber Ltd.: *The Classic Noh Theatre
of Japan,* by Ezra Pound and Ernest Fenollosa,
copyright © 1959 by New Directions Publishing
Corporation; and *Canto LXXX,* from *The Cantos,*
by Ezra Pound, copyright 1948 by Ezra Pound.

Rupin W. Desai is Reader in English
at the University of Delhi, India

TO EVELYN AND ANTIPAS

Shakespearean fish swam the sea, far away from land;
Romantic fish swam in nets coming to the hand;
What are all those fish that lie gasping on the strand?
—Yeats, "Three Movements"

Contents

Acknowledgments

IN THE writing of this book my debt to Professor Richard Ellmann is incalculable. His guidance and advice at every stage of my research, combined with his great knowledge of Yeats, have saved me from many errors and made this work more readable than it was originally. In return I can, in the words of Jaques, only render him the beggarly thanks.

Professors Moody E. Prior and Donald T. Torchiana have taken valuable time from their own very busy schedules to read through the entire manuscript and suggest many improvements. Professor Torchiana's unshakable faith in the importance of my subject has sustained me through the numerous stages of vision and revision that the manuscript passed. I am thankful to Professor Samuel Schoenbaum for reading chapter 2 of the manuscript and giving me, in the form of several useful suggestions, the benefit of his familiarity with Shakespearean criticism.

The staffs of the Rare Book Room and the Reference Room at Deering Library, Northwestern University, headed by Richard Olson and Noel Owens, respectively, have been indispensable, and I must thank them for their attention and courtesy. Marjorie Carpenter of the Inter-Library Loan Department made special efforts to track down certain obscure references of Yeats; I am grateful to her for her tireless energy in this pursuit. I must also acknowledge with appreciation the help rendered me by Margaret Buth, who has extended herself considerably in supplying me with essential Yeats material after my return to India.

When making a study of an author who died just three decades ago, one inevitably turns to those persons now connected with the institutions with which he was associated during his lifetime. I am indebted to Dr. R. W. Reynolds, the present headmaster of The High School, Dublin, where Yeats was a student from 1881 to 1883; to Maurice Wilkins, son of William Wilkins, who was headmaster of The High School in Yeats's time; to Dr. Charles C. Duggan, a student at the school thirteen years after Yeats had left; and to the Department of Education at Dublin, all of whom have provided me with information on Yeats's early exposure to Shakespeare. Dr. Levi Fox, director of the Shakespeare Birthplace Trust at Stratford, James Livock, secretary of the Maddermarket Theatre at Norwich, and Paul Myers, curator of the Theatre Collection in the New York Public Library, have shed useful light on Yeats's acquaintance with performances of Shakespeare. I am thankful to them for their prompt replies to my queries.

My wife and I remember with nostalgia the friendship and affection of Truman and Elnora Metzel of Winnetka, Illinois, that we experienced throughout our stay in the United States, and the encouragement that their unabating interest in this book afforded time and again.

I am grateful to the United States government for a Fulbright Scholarship (1964–65), which made it possible for me to go to the United States from my homeland, India, and begin research on Yeats, and to the Rockefeller Foundation for its handsome grant (1965–68), which enabled me to complete this book. In particular, I would like to record my gratitude to Mr. K. S. Nair, Indian Scholars Officer of the United States Educational Foundation in New Delhi, and to Mr. Jesse P. Perry, Fellowship Officer of the Rockefeller Foundation in New York, for their kind and unfailing solicitude.

It is pleasant to recall the training I received, as a graduate student, from Principal S. S. Chawla, then of the University of Delhi, in whose tutorial classes, insubordinate to the restraint of the clock, I first came to understand and then enjoy the poetry of Yeats.

I am grateful to my wife, chief aider and abettor in the enterprise, for her help in ways too numerous to recount here, and to our son Antipas for his consideration in making fewer demands on my time than would be expected from a boy devoted to cricket and baseball.

R.W.D.

Introduction

Shakespeare [was] not more in our fathers' minds than
[he is] in ours.

Yeats, *Letters to DW*

A<small>LTHOUGH</small> Yeats's regard for Shakespeare has been considered in a few articles and in sections of certain books, mine is the first full investigation of the subject. Yeats admired Shakespeare from early childhood. Yet he could also be critical of Shakespeare, especially on discovering in the plays evidence of a scattering rather than a concentration of talent. At times Yeats considered his own effort to revive poetic drama in twentieth-century Ireland to be, in fact, a revival of Shakespearean drama. But at other times he seems to have felt that Shakespeare, in catering to the taste of a motley audience, weakened his art with elements extraneous to great drama.

Of course, Yeats's double attitude is by now easily seen as a traditional view of Shakespeare. For since Shakespeare has become a legend, perhaps no English dramatist has been free of an uneasy awareness of his commanding presence; what Cassius said of Caesar could well be applied to Shakespeare:

> Why, man, he doth bestride the narrow world
> Like a Colossus.

But seventeenth-century writers, close enough to Shakespeare not to be

awed by his as yet modest fame, did not consider it sacrilegious to casti-
gate him for what Dryden called his bombast and disregard of the
unities. Dryden's attempts to recast Shakespeare, along with the adaptations of Nahum Tate, an Irishman, demonstrate the direction in which
response to Shakespeare was tending. Despite the noble tribute that Dryden's Neander pays to Shakespeare, he chooses Ben Jonson's *The Silent
Woman* as "the pattern of the perfect play," ruling out Shakespeare's
and Fletcher's works for their lack of discipline in plot construction.
He is careful to accord to Shakespeare distinction only in "poesy."
Granting that in this particular feature he is Ben Jonson's "equal, perhaps his superior," Neander nevertheless concludes with the celebrated
declaration, "I admire him [Jonson] but I love Shakespeare."[1] Here,
despite the sentimental attachment expressed for Shakespeare, Shakespeare clearly comes off only second-best, for love, unlike admiration,
is based on personal preference, not on universally acknowledged excellence.

Thomas Rymer's unmitigated denunciation of Shakespeare, Nahum
Tate's adaptations of the plays, Dryden's qualified praise, and Dr. Johnson's strictures on the lapses in Shakespeare's moral sense and his verbal
grossness, all reflect seventeenth- and eighteenth-century discontent with
Shakespeare and a refreshing freedom from the bardolatry that was soon
to prevail. Wrong-headed and absurd though these critics often were,
they at least refused to be cowed by Shakespeare. And combined with
their discontent was a genuine appreciation of Shakespeare's genius as
poet and even as dramatist, along with a disregard for Shakespeare as a
biographical subject. Yeats too, as we shall see, stubbornly accepted and
rejected Shakespeare according to his own poetic and theoretical, not
to mention Irish, determinations.

In the early part of the nineteenth century the incisive criticism of
Goethe, Schlegel, Coleridge, Hazlitt, and Lamb rescued Shakespeare
from the stifling atmosphere that the eighteenth-century neoclassicists
firmly believed was an exhalation from classical drama. Shakespeare now
came to be regarded as the creator of a world separate in many ways

---

1 "An Essay of Dramatic Poetry," *Essays of John Dryden,* ed. W. P. Ker
(Oxford, 1900), I, 79, 82–83.

from that of real life. His plays were no longer required to conform to the strict dictates of nature, but were regarded as distinct entities, as artistic wholes defying the crippling bondage of realism. This splendid emancipation from realism and its demands could not, however, last indefinitely. Inevitably, Shakespeare the moralist was molded and fashioned in the image of the age, and by the mid-nineteenth century, he was considered the custodian of humanity's ethical and moral values. G. G. Gervinus and Edward Dowden, both of whom Yeats regarded with distaste for their Shakespearean criticism, were perhaps the most formidable spokesmen for this equally formidable Shakespeare. Gervinus is convinced that if Othello and Desdemona had only consulted Brabantio, their marriage would have turned out differently. He maintains that Shakespeare builds a system of morality on nature and reason, and the view was shared by numerous (and vociferous) admirers who let loose a gush of Shakespearean eulogy.

Fulsome and trite, this praise had damaging repercussions. With Shakespeare now enthroned on the pinnacle of perfection, the nineteenth-century playwright could not escape his ever-lengthening shadow; the paucity of even tolerably good plays during that period may, in part, be attributed to a haunting sense of inferiority to Shakespeare that effectively crippled any urge to experiment or innovate. In the nineteenth century "the worn-out conventions of English poetic drama," as Yeats aptly called them, were no longer Shakespeare, but rather a Shakespeare stultified and mummified.[2] It was not enough to produce plays in blank verse and apply the misnomer "poetic drama" to these bankruptcies; rather, what was needed was a revival of Shakespeare's exuberance coupled with a stern insistence on the artistic restraint of the Greeks that, Yeats felt, was unfortunately less conspicuous in Shakespeare.

Yeats was perhaps the first modern writer of note to point out the flaws in what he recognized to be Shakespeare's magnificent art and to show that his very greatness made these flaws all the more regrettable.

---

2 *Ex*, p. 80. For a thorough study of the uneasiness of nineteenth-century authors when faced with Shakespeare's greatness, see Moody E. Prior, *The Language of Tragedy* (New York, 1947), chapter 4.

Thus Yeats revived the boldness that had marked eighteenth-century commentators on Shakespeare and made it possible for himself and his contemporaries to formulate new dramatic techniques that, though clearly influenced by Shakespeare, were no longer slavish imitations. As examples of this liberated spirit, one has only to think of Shaw's audacious diatribes against Shakespeare, and of T. S. Eliot who, alone among modern critics, has been a stout defender of Rymer's notorious attack on *Othello* as a bloody farce devoid of justice, reason, law, or humanity. By endeavoring to report on Yeats's varied responses to Shakespeare, the observer risks exposing himself to the predicament in which Claudius' unfortunate spies, Rosencrantz and Guildenstern, found themselves. Hamlet's sardonic observation is a warning:

> 'Tis dangerous when the baser nature comes
> Between the pass and fell incenséd points
> Of mighty opposites.

Yeats and Shakespeare are, in one sense, mighty opposites, and to referee their sparring is a hazardous undertaking. Nevertheless, I shall take the risk. The sense of uneasiness that Yeats experienced in trying to reconcile Shakespeare's genius with his disregard for a rigorous dramatic form is epitomized in his exalting Shakespeare's subjective individualism in "The Tragic Generation" of his *Autobiography,* only to revise this attitude a few years later in *A Vision* and depict him on the verge of splintering into fragments. The qualities that Shakespeare lacked Yeats found in Greek drama, whose "elaborate unity" he commended. His translations of Sophocles' *King Oedipus* and *Oedipus at Colonus* are evidence of this appreciation.

Unlike Cassius, Yeats was a lover of plays. He must have seen many more Shakespearean performances than I have been able to establish, but even the list presented here is enough to show how familiar he was with Shakespeare on the stage. In spite of his outspoken disgust for techniques of production that relied on lavish realism, he continued to go to Shakespearean performances, and—perhaps to demonstrate how Shakespeare should appear on the stage—he seriously considered taking over one of the London theaters for a season in order to produce Shakespeare, along with several other plays, on his own.

Yeats was well versed in Shakespearean criticism. The second half of the nineteenth century saw an unprecedented outpouring of work on Shakespeare, notable more for its quantity than quality. A preoccupation with Shakespeare's ability to create the experience of actual life by peopling his plays with characters who had seemingly stepped out of the familiar world tended to obscure much of his symbolical purpose. But Yeats, vigorously opposed to the realists' approach to Shakespeare, held that the plays could not rightly be treated as having been accidentally written in verse rather than in prose. Instead, they created phenomenological worlds of their own, governed by laws that were as much literary as natural, "a kind of vision of reality," as he wrote to his father describing the relationship between art and life. Moreover, their reality would have been for Yeats more than physical, for "the arts are founded on the life beyond the world," and they come into their own when "the world has been consumed and become a vision."[3] Transcending reality, the Shakespearean universe defied the canons of the everyday world and promulgated its own laws.

By placing Shakespeare on a historical map in *A Vision*, Yeats could study and appraise both his defects and his greatness in a framework that was not purely arbitrary. For Yeats, historical necessity dictated the shape that Shakespearean drama took as much as did Shakespeare's individual genius. Thus Yeats disapproves of the Renaissance for its being a time when foreign influences disrupt an erstwhile unity; and he complains of Shakespeare's readiness to entertain hospitably such influences. During a period when Yeats felt strongly that an Irish national literature was something badly needed, it was understandable for him to question Shakespeare's eclecticism. Of course Yeats was being unfair to Shakespeare, but his lack of humility indicates a refusal to approach him as a suppliant, a refreshing contrast to the posture of his age.

Although Yeats criticized Shakespeare for his cosmopolitan art, only four years later, in 1905, when Synge's *The Shadow of the Glen* was assailed for owing its plot to some ancient Greek writer and not to Irish antecedents, Yeats spiritedly came to his defense by pointing out

3 *Letters*, p. 588; *E&I*, p. 184.

that "he [Synge] would have precedents to encourage him. Shakespeare laid the scene of *Cymbeline* in his own country, but he found the story in the *Decameron*."[4] Evidently Yeats's attitude toward Shakespeare was not that of a bigot. Just as he was constantly revising earlier themes and experimenting with new ones in his own work, so was he constantly renewing his relationship with Shakespeare, like Jacob who compelled his antagonist to bless him ere he would let him depart.

In fact, at the end of his career, Yeats appears to have been identifying himself with Shakespeare, but at the same time evolving in his plays a structure and a syntax that were intentionally as un-Shakespearean as possible. Paradoxically, we may at times detect Shakespeare's presence only because Yeats is determined to exclude him. On the other hand, more obviously, several of his poems, plays, and observations suggest a close kinship with Shakespeare, and Shakespearean echoes occur with greater frequency than before. The sense of struggle with Shakespeare diminishes. Yeats begins to see himself undergoing the mental turmoil and passionate striving of his violent heroes—men like Timon and Lear. At this point the dynamic energy of Shakespeare interests him more than nice considerations of unity and disunity. From his early enthusiasm for the *Hamlet* he saw as a boy—an enthusiasm that remained with him till the end—to the electric presence of certain Shakespearean characters who step directly into his later poems, Yeats's absorption in Shakespeare was deep and continuous. In the following pages I have recorded that absorption.

Chapters 1 and 2 survey Shakespearean productions that Yeats knew, his readings in Shakespeare, and his familiarity with Shakespearean criticism. Yeats as a Shakespearean critic has rarely been given the recognition that he deserves; yet Yeats is quite at ease among such men as Johnson, Coleridge, Hazlitt, and Goethe. When we read them, Shakespeare as well as the critics are illuminated. Yeats on Shakespeare likewise illuminates both Shakespeare and himself. Since John Butler

---

4 W. B. Yeats, "J. M. Synge's 'The Shadow of the Glen,'" *The United Irishman* (January 28, 1905); quoted in Colton Johnson, "Yeats's Prose Contributions to Periodicals: 1900–1939" (Ph.D. diss., Northwestern University, 1968).

Yeats's letters to his son W. B. are filled with references to Shakespeare, whom he admired for his benign humanity, I accent the father's philosophy that in so many ways shaped his son's attitudes toward Shakespeare.

Chapter 3 outlines Yeats's fluctuating opinions on Shakespeare over a period of three decades, after which came a more settled stance. Viewed within the framework of the historical survey in *A Vision*, Yeats's stance is remarkably consistent with his broader perspective of Western civilization from the rape of Leda to the brink of World War II. Yeats himself tells us—far from apologetically—that his essay "Dove or Swan," in *A Vision*, is based chiefly on his recollection of the history he studied at school, and on what he had "since learned from the plays of Shakespeare or the novels of Dumas."[5]

Chapter 4 considers Yeats's reasons for placing Shakespeare at Phase 20 in *A Vision*, a location that he seems to have decided on after some uncertainty. Did Shakespeare possess an assertive or a retiring personality? If the former, how did he so successfully submerge it in his work and allow the personae of the plays an autonomous existence? These are some of the questions that seem to have engaged Yeats as he sought to explain the paradox that Shakespeare's vehement dramatic creations are products of an unassertive and self-effacing personality.

Accordingly, in chapters 5 and 6 certain Yeatsian concepts (the daimon, death, ecstasy, personality, and character) which have particular reference to Shakespeare are examined. Not unexpectedly, Yeats seems to have come to feel that his own work was produced under the guiding hand of Shakespeare's daimon, that the spirit influence of Shakespeare's genius presided over his own efforts to revive poetic drama in Ireland. For obvious reasons, however, Yeats nowhere states this explicitly, though as I shall show, the suggestion is implicit in certain of his reflections.

I have reserved for the last two chapters a discussion of some Shakespearean echoes in Yeats's plays. Steeped as Yeats was in Shakespeare, it is not surprising that his own work should reflect at moments,

5   *Ex*, p. 291.

in the configuration of detail, in the interplay of character, a Shake-spearean motif employed by him—often, it seems, consciously—to enforce a particular effect. But the greatest writers channel out new riverbeds even when they accept inflows from their predecessors; they imbibe from their forbears but refuse to abnegate their own authority. As we shall see, Hamlet is present in two of Yeats's late poems, but he is as much Yeats's Hamlet as Shakespeare's. The impress of Yeats's personality on this Hamlet brands him as no longer Shakespeare's exclusive property. Yet it would be difficult to deny that this Hamlet was also present in Shakespeare's mind when he wrote the play. Here in fact is an example of one major writer assimilating the work of another while not allowing himself to be engulfed, but rather establishing yet more firmly his own individuality.[6] Ezra Pound's praise of Yeats, though deliberately excessive, is not altogether facetious:

> Neath Ben Bulben's buttocks lies
> Bill Yeats, a poet twoice the size
> Of William Shakespear, as they say
> Down Ballykillywuchlin way.

Influence study is complex and often dubious. Recognizing that it is often so subtle as to be ineffable, I have restricted myself to a detailed examination of nine plays of Yeats and a handful of his poems. In addition I glance at certain other plays of his where Shakespearean undertones seem present. In these, I think, Shakespeare's influence is not only traceable, but also discussable. Beyond them lies a rolling landscape in which Shakespearean contours may be glimpsed, but the scene is too overpoweringly Yeatsian to permit my establishing any Shakespearean lines of demarcation. Thus, in Appendix 3, I record these glimpses—with extreme caution. The first two appendixes list in chrono-logical order Yeats's direct references to Shakespeare and his plays.

For my reconstruction of Yeats's Shakespeare, in addition to Yeats's own writings as listed in the appendixes, I have drawn upon several works on Yeats that contain hitherto unpublished Yeats ma-

6   See, e.g., Richard Ellmann, *Eminent Domain: Yeats among Wilde, Joyce, Pound, Eliot, and Auden* (New York, 1967), chapter 1.

terial. Doubtless, as additional primary material comes to light, fresh insights into Yeats's attitudes toward Shakespeare will become possible. But I do not think that these will affect Yeats's final relationship with Shakespeare, for in this, as in much else that he arrived at, Yeats

> toiled long years and at length
> Came to so deep a thought.

List of Abbreviations

Vis	*A Vision.* 2d ed., 1937; reissued London: Macmillan, 1962.
Vis (1925)	*A Vision.* London: Macmillan, 1925.
Yeats and TSM	*W. B. Yeats and T. Sturge Moore: Their Correspondence, 1901–1937.* Edited by Ursula Bridge. London: Routledge and Kegan Paul, 1953.

BOOKS ABOUT YEATS

Henn	T. R. Henn. *The Lonely Tower: Studies in the Poetry of W. B. Yeats.* 1950; reprinted London: Methuen, 1966.
Hone	Joseph Hone. *W. B. Yeats, 1865–1939.* 2d ed., 1962; reprinted London: Macmillan, 1965.
Identity	Richard Ellmann. *The Identity of Yeats.* 2d ed. New York: Oxford University Press, 1964.
Man and Masks	———. *Yeats: The Man and the Masks.* New York: E. P. Dutton, 1948.
Man and Poet	A. Norman Jeffares. *W. B. Yeats: Man and Poet.* 2d ed., 1961; reprinted New York: Barnes and Noble, 1966.
Stallworthy	Jon Stallworthy. *Between the Lines: Yeats's Poetry in the Making.* London: Oxford University Press, 1963.
Torchiana	Donald T. Torchiana. *W. B. Yeats and Georgian Ireland.* Evanston: Northwestern University Press, 1966.

Citations from the plays and poems of Yeats are to *Variorum Plays* and *Variorum Poems.*

Citations from Shakespeare are to *The London Shakespeare.* Edited by John Munro. 6 vols. New York: Simon and Schuster, 1957.

Yeats's Shakespeare

1

Points of Contact

He [Yeats] several times said to me that the only
dramatist he cared for was Shakespeare.
—Lennox Robinson, "The Man and the Dramatist"

YEATS was introduced to Shakespeare when he was a boy under
the guidance of his father, J. B. Yeats. Yeats recalled in "Reveries
over Childhood and Youth" (1915) that when he was ten or twelve his
father took him to see Henry Irving play Hamlet and that the performance left a deep impression on his mind, Hamlet becoming "for
many years . . . an image of heroic self-possession for the poses of youth
and childhood to copy, a combatant of the battle within myself." This
may sound strange, since Hamlet is far from being imperturbable: his
soliloquies are full of tormented introspection, he verges on the hyster-
ical in his mother's bedchamber, and he grapples with Laertes in
Ophelia's grave. Whether he assumes a pose of madness, or whether he
actually goes mad are matters that have engaged the attention of all
readers of the play. Yet Yeats sees him as an example of heroic self-
possession, perhaps having in mind the last act of the play where
Hamlet's mood is one of steely resignation. In 1909, after seeing
the play, he described this phase of Hamlet's development as being a
point in the play where his delight always began anew, an indication

of the kind of equilibrium that he strove to achieve in his own life.[1]

Yeats tells us that when a boy he tried his best to imitate Irving's peculiar stride in his role as Hamlet, but the fascination that Irving's rendering of Hamlet exercised over him does not seem to have stopped with the passing of adolescence, for as long after as 1936, the deliberately casual line "There struts Hamlet" in "Lapis Lazuli" is perhaps a recapitulation of Irving's characteristic gait. Again, in 1938, Yeats recalled that he had even walked down the streets of Dublin displaying Irving's "strut" as Hamlet, a strut that Gordon Craig compared to a movement in a dance, Yeats informs us.[2] The boyish Yeats being enamored of Irving's grandeur is understandable and interesting, but that Yeats, nearly sixty years later, should be still picturing Hamlet as Irving portrayed him is indeed significant. Hamlet must have been, for Yeats, a symbol of his own isolation in an increasingly hostile and degenerate world. His couplet written in August, 1938, in "A Nativity," celebrates Irving's performance as Hamlet.

> What brushes fly and moth aside?
> Irving and his plume of pride.

The verbs "strut" and "brushes" with reference to Hamlet are unusual; they hint at Yeats's dominant impression of Hamlet's aristocratic indifference to the inferiors who baited him.

Hamlet's ability to counter the numerous attempts made by Claudius and his lackeys to discover his innermost thoughts impressed Yeats. A philosopher at the beginning of the play, Hamlet later reveals a hardness and resoluteness quite unexpected. For Yeats, the urge to become something other than what he was may be seen in the report Yeats gives us many years later of his forcing himself as a young man, timid and retiring, to attend a club whose members were exceptionally obstreperous, so that he might become self-possessed as Hamlet was, capable of facing his enemies with unquivering eyelash.[3] Evidently Yeats

---

1   *Au*, pp. 29, 318.
2   *Au*, p. 50; W. B. Yeats, "I Became an Author," *The Listener* (August 4, 1938). Yeats's reference here is to Gordon Craig, *Henry Irving* (New York, 1930), p. 74.
3   *Au*, p. 57.

has here in mind Hamlet's biting, yet exaggeratedly polite, letter to Claudius in which he begs leave to see his "kingly eyes." In fact, Hamlet's attitude toward his erstwhile friends now turned spies is full of scorn and disdain: "'Sblood, do you think I am easier to be played on than a pipe?" This was the kind of self-assurance that Yeats cultivated assiduously.

> There one that ruffled in a manly pose
> For all his timid heart,

he tells us in "Coole Park, 1929." Hamlet, his anti-self, was everything that he would have liked to become, and, in fact, later did become. So also, in his old age, he longed to remake himself in the mold of Timon and Lear, foolish, passionate old men who refuse to give up their individuality in the face of persecution.

At the club that Yeats forced himself to attend, argument and personal recrimination ran rife, without the restraints of decorum normally associated with public debate. Attending these meetings must have been a heady experience, and despite his determination to hold up Hamlet as a model of equanimity, Yeats confesses that he was often swept away by the excitement of the moment. Far from helping him achieve Hamlet's detachment, the experience at the club, he admits, made him feel wretched; he then adds wistfully that his efforts were misdirected, for Hamlet's self-possession was not derived from schooling, but from "indifference" and "passion-conquering sweetness."[4] When he made these observations on Hamlet, he was fifty years old, and a note of weariness is audible in several of the poems in *The Wild Swans at Coole,* which belongs to this period in his life. The heroic detachment of the protagonist in "The Gyres," a much later poem, who can exclaim jubilantly, "What matter though numb nightmare ride on top," and of the poet himself who can urge the curious horseman to pass by his place of burial is an attitude of indifference that was still remote from him when he ascribed it to Hamlet.

Other Shakespearean plays besides *Hamlet* left such vivid impressions on Yeats's boyhood mind that they too persisted in asserting them-

4 *Au,* p. 57.

selves in his works long afterward. Since Yeats was educated chiefly by his father, who taught him "to set certain passages in Shakespeare above all else in literature," his many references to *Coriolanus,* for example, are understandable, for they seem to derive in great measure from his father's impassioned recitation of the most dramatic scenes from the play, particularly the one where Coriolanus tells the impudent servants of Aufidius that his home is under the canopy "I' the city of kites and crows," a scene that Yeats declares was always more real to him than the many stage versions of the play that he saw later. Yeats also tells us that his fierce old grandfather William Pollexfen coalesced in his boyhood imagination with King Lear, and that whenever he subsequently read the play, his grandfather's image—one of passionate intensity—was always before him.[5] These characters and scenes are dramatically realized by Yeats in some of his plays, and behind his own passionate heroes lurk several Shakespearean archetypes that had become entrenched in his boyhood imagination.

Since Yeats's early impressions of Shakespeare are so vivid, we may well wonder whether, besides his father's infectious enthusiasm for the plays, he had any formal exposure to Shakespeare. When he was sixteen, he began to attend the Erasmus Smith High School on Harcourt Street in Dublin and continued to do so till the age of eighteen, that is, from October, 1881, to December, 1883.[6] He must have sat for the Middle Grade Examination set by the Intermediate Education Board in 1882 (normally taken by students at the age of seventeen) and for the Senior Grade Examination in 1883. According to the Department of Education at Dublin, *As You Like It* and *Macbeth* were the plays prescribed for the Middle and Senior Grade examinations in those two years.[7] But curiously enough, neither of these two plays—not even *Macbeth*—seems to have made an imaginative impact on Yeats. An explanation for this may be found in his complaint against the kind of exposure to Shakespeare that he had at the High School on Harcourt Street: "I was worst of all at literature," he says,

5   *Boiler,* p. 14; *Au,* pp. 39, 5.
6   *Man and Masks,* p. 27. See also *Au,* p. 34.
7   August 1, 1968: personal communication.

"for we read Shakespeare for his grammar exclusively."[8] Most probably this is an overstatement, particularly the word "exclusively," but it reveals Yeats's exasperation with the accepted scholastic method of studying Shakespeare, which preserved the letter but destroyed the spirit of the plays.

In contrast to what Yeats felt Shakespeare was reduced to at school were his father's animated opinions on the plays and the individual characters. J. B. Yeats's emphasis on certain characteristics in Shakespeare—his passion and intensity on one hand and a capacity for reverie on the other—to make up a multitudinous personality was the basis for Yeats's own attitude toward Shakespeare. Although later there were occasional disagreements, what he imbibed from his father was both considerable and important; in later years many of his ideas derived their keenness from having been sharpened by an interplay between him and his father. J. B. Yeats advocated the efflorescence of the human personality as against a rigid and binding code of conduct. Flexibility in all things was the great virtue. "Shakespeare was great because of his vast humanity," he wrote to a correspondent, and the age of Shakespeare was, for him, the ideal, because then "everybody was happy."[9] Yeats, as we shall see, was always tempted by this theory, but along with his attraction toward the Renaissance went a feeling of mistrust, for it seemed to him to be a period in which the fracturing of sensibility, accompanied by the triumph of the intellect over the emotions, became uncomfortably pronounced. Thus, along with Yeats's refusal to allow Shakespeare's metaphorical vision to be reduced to the matter-of-fact world of grammar and dull reality, went his refusal to pay a too simplistic homage to Shakespeare and his age as being the El Dorado of Western man's history.

For the period of his schooling in Dublin, there is no record of Yeats's having seen a Shakespeare play on the stage. In fact, before 1900, the only Shakespearean play that we know he saw on the professional stage was Irving's *Hamlet,* which his father took him to see in 1874. Yeats does mention, however, a Board School continuation class pro-

8   *Au,* p. 34.
9   Hone, p. 34; J. B. Yeats, *Early Memories* (Dundrum, Cuala, 1923), p. 37.

duction of *Hamlet,* which he must have seen before 1902. In May, 1900, he invited Lady Gregory to a production of *Richard II,* presented by Benson's company. In April, 1901, he visited Stratford-on-Avon and saw Shakespeare's English History Plays performed "in their right order, with all the links that bind play to play unbroken," he writes in his essay "At Stratford-on-Avon," which was the outcome of this visit. There were several other Shakespeare plays presented at Stratford during the season, and it is possible that Yeats saw them.[10]

In 1902 he wrote to Henry Newbolt that he had come to Stratford "for the Shakespeare Cycle." On this occasion Ellen Terry played Queen Katharine in *Henry VIII.* He went to Stratford again, for the Shakespeare festival, in the spring of 1904. It was the Silver Jubilee of the Memorial Theatre and an exceptionally long program was presented: thirteen Shakespearean plays and the Orestean trilogy of Aeschylus, but Yeats was not impressed by the way in which the trilogy was rendered. During his visit to America early in 1904, he saw *Romeo and Juliet* with Julia Marlowe in the title role; her performance has been eulogized in the semihumorous poem "His Phoenix." In November of that same year he saw Beerbohm Tree's production of *The Tempest* in London and thoroughly disapproved of Tree's ornate settings and extravagant techniques. In 1905 he saw *The Merchant of Venice* in London and felt that it too was very poorly done.[11]

Yeats attended another Stratford Shakespeare festival in 1905. Benson's announcement that Henry Irving would play Shylock could well have been an added attraction that drew him there. But illness prevented Irving from coming to the Memorial Theatre, for he was then very sick and in the last six months of his life. On March 14, 1908, Yeats saw *Romeo and Juliet* at the Lyceum. Although he did not disparage the production, he was disgusted with the inability of those in

10 *E&I,* p. 382; *Letters,* p. 342; *E&I,* pp. 96–97 (The part of this essay in which Yeats comments on the performances of individual actors is not included in *Essays and Introductions.* It appeared in *The Speaker* (May 11, 1901), section III, p. 159). For a complete list of plays presented at Stratford, see T. C. Kemp and J. C. Trewin, *The Stratford Festival: A History of the Shakespeare Memorial Theatre* (London, 1953).

11 *Letters,* p. 366; *Ex,* pp. 174–75; *Letters,* pp. 443, 465–66.

the gallery to appreciate the poetry of the balcony scene. This experience must have been instrumental in convincing him that poetic drama of the twentieth century, being incomprehensible to a larger public, should be confined to only a small and select audience. About this time he observed in a letter that the "modern audience has lost the habit of careful listening," a remark suggestive of his disenchantment with the growing trend toward substituting for the auditory appeal of drama mere spectacle.[12]

In 1908, for the fifth time, Yeats visited Stratford. He wrote to Florence Farr on April 21 that he was going there to see Sara Allgood play Isabella in *Measure for Measure*. Miss Allgood, an Irish actress associated with the Abbey Theatre, had been loaned to William Poel, who was producing *Measure for Measure* at Stratford. Poel, founder and director of the Elizabethan Stage Society, had all his life led the crusade against realism in the staging of Shakespeare, and he had met Yeats and Synge when his company performed in Dublin. Some of the rehearsals for *Measure for Measure* had been held there, and Poel himself was to play Angelo. This would explain Yeats's interest in seeing the play performed at Stratford. There was considerable uneasiness in Stratford over the staging of the play because of its undisguised sexual theme, but Yeats's response to the play was positive. He declared that he was astonished at Miss Allgood's performance, which was full of simplicity and power.[13]

Yeats's desire to see Poel's production must also have been prompted by his own interest in verse delivery, his theory being perhaps as controversial as was that of Poel. Yeats apparently never agreed with Poel's method of verse-speaking, which was to pick out certain key words and phrases in a speech and then instruct the actor to emphasize these. Yeats felt that such a method would inevitably shatter the illusion

---

12 *Letters*, p. 449; Kemp and Trewin, *Stratford Festival*, p. 68; W. B. Yeats, *Four Plays for Dancers* (London, 1921), p. 88 (For the dating of the production, see J. C. Trewin, *Shakespeare on the English Stage: 1900–1964* [London, 1964], p. 261); *Letters*, p. 482.

13 *Letters*, p. 508; Robert Speaight, *William Poel and the Elizabethan Revival* (London, 1954), p. 95; W. B. Yeats, Editorial, *Samhain* (November, 1908), p. 4.

that poetic drama, "the proud fragility of dreams," should create. As early as 1902, in his essay "Speaking to the Psaltery," Yeats had explained his method for speaking verse, but it was only with his *Four Plays for Dancers,* written much later, that he gave to his theory a local habitation and a name. In *A Vision,* Daniel O'Leary goes to see *Romeo and Juliet* immediately after the Great War, expecting to find the realist mode of verse delivery ousted by the Yeatsian technique of a rhythmical chant, as Yeats had described it to George Russell and Robert Bridges, but to his intense chagrin finds "those well-known persons Mr . . . and Miss . . . at their kitchen gabble." Unable to stand their performance any longer, he unlaces his boots, flings them at the targets of his disgust, and wisely decamps. This production of *Romeo and Juliet,* which Yeats obviously saw, was given at the Lyric on April 12, 1919, and the well-known persons were Doris Keane as Juliet and Basil Sydney, her husband, as Romeo. That Daniel O'Leary was not being overly captious is clear from J. C. Trewin's account, which corroborates O'Leary's impression of the production, that Miss Keane's delivery of the verse was feeble and inaudible, whereas Ellen Terry as the nurse dominated the production.[14]

In the spring of 1909 Yeats was again in Stratford, and he probably stayed for the Festival; later, in October of that year, he saw *Hamlet* acted in Dublin, and the production stirred him, as his observations on the play seem to indicate. For Yeats, however, despite his occasional appreciation of Shakespeare productions, dissatisfaction with the methods of production was always close to the surface, ready to erupt. He wrote to Lady Gregory in March, 1916, that he, Charles Ricketts, and Edmund Dulac were negotiating with the management of the Aldwych Theatre to run it for one season: "If it comes off there will be no compromise—romance, fine scenery, the whole *Hamlet, Volpone* and some Molière plays staged strangely and beautifully." Yeats's wish to produce an uncut *Hamlet* is interesting. Poel had presented in January, 1914, a *Hamlet*

---

14 See Speaight, *William Poel,* pp. 62–70, 95; William Poel, *Shakespeare in the Theatre* (London, 1913), pp. 17–20, 57–60; W. B. Yeats, Preface, *Plays for an Irish Theatre* (London and Stratford-on-Avon, 1911), p. ix; *E&I,* pp. 13–27; *Letters,* pp. 327, 354; *Vis,* pp. 33–34; Trewin, *Shakespeare,* pp. 84–85, 264.

showing "scenes never acted in versions on the modern stage," and in April, 1916, about the same time that Yeats was projecting his uncut *Hamlet,* the Old Vic under Ben Greet acted the full text of the Second Quarto. But Poel's *Hamlet* was a badly mangled affair. He omitted the "To be, or not to be" soliloquy and the grave-diggers' scene, a liberty that must have roused Yeats's ire and been instrumental in prompting him to consider producing the whole *Hamlet.*[15] Perhaps resentful of the stage tradition that had bowdlerized *Hamlet,* Yeats seems to have resolved that his production would not perpetuate such a travesty.

At this point it would be well to consider briefly the state of Shakespeare production in England during the first two decades of the twentieth century. Beerbohm Tree's meretricious realism, along with the attendant necessity for ruthlessly cutting and transposing scenes to allow time for setting up an elaborate spectacle, was on its way out. The techniques of William Poel, Edward Gordon Craig, Harley Granville-Barker, and Nugent Monck were the counterpoises to Tree's banalities. All four men advocated a complete breakaway from the tedious realism that had been imposed on Shakespeare, and a return to the clean simplicity of the Elizabethan stage. Yeats's appreciation for Craig's production methods is evident in his essay "At Stratford-on-Avon," where he decries "naturalistic scene-painting" and recommends in its place "decorative scene-painting," which would succeed in establishing a new and autonomous artistic reality unhindered by the intrusion of the outside world. As an example of this, he points to Craig's scenery, "the first beautiful scenery our stage has seen." Elsewhere in his writings, too, Yeats was full of enthusiasm for Craig's methods and declared that he had banished a whole world that had wearied him and was undignified. He wrote to Craig that his work was always a great inspiration to him. But Yeats's generous tributes to other men of the theater who were courageous innovators should not be allowed to obscure the fact that he was himself a pioneer in the campaign against established stage

---

15 *Au,* pp. 315, 318; *Letters,* p. 612; "Hamlet: *Stage History,*" *The Reader's Encyclopedia of Shakespeare,* ed. Oscar James Campbell (New York, 1966); Speaight, *William Poel,* p. 223; Winifred F. E. C. Isaac, *Ben Greet and the Old Vic* (London, n.d.), pp. 136, 137.

practice, that he was not so much a follower as a setter of trends that poetic drama could be expected to take. In 1911 he concluded his address to the Dramatic Club of Harvard University with the warning that the methods of production for a Galsworthy play and a Shakespeare play would have to be radically different.[16] Suggestion and symbolism, rather than trite realism, were for Yeats the right instruments with which the producer of Shakespeare could hope to touch the secret of his plays.

Granville-Barker's techniques also won Yeats's commendation. Granville-Barker insisted on presenting an uncut Shakespeare text, along with a continuous flow of rapid action untrammeled by the cumbersome devices of the naturalistic stage. In 1912 his production of *The Winter's Tale,* sadly neglected on the London stage, created a sensation. The reaction was a mixed one, for to audiences long accustomed to a leisurely presentation of Shakespeare, a swift delivery of his verse with scenes succeeding each other with barely a pause was all but unintelligible. For such audiences this was a new and demanding Shakespeare, whose language they had to attend to with keen concentration or confess that his was a language beyond their comprehension. Yet there were many who applauded Granville-Barker's efforts to revive the Shakespearean tempo of the blank verse, and, in the same year, when Granville-Barker's *Twelfth Night* was presented, it was received with almost unanimous acclaim by audience and critics alike. Yeats must have seen both productions, because in a letter dated March, 1913, to his publisher A. H. Bullen, he instructed him to bring out immediately a new issue of his *Collected Works,* beginning with his dramatic criticism. By coinciding with the Granville-Barker productions of Shakespeare, it would be well timed. How conscious Yeats was of his own decisive role in the shaping

16 See M. St. Clare Byrne, "Fifty Years of Shakespearian Production," *Shakespeare Survey,* ed. Allardyce Nicoll (Cambridge, 1949), II, 1–20; *E&I,* p. 100; W. B. Yeats, "The Tragic Theatre," *The Mask,* III (Florence, 1910–11), 81; Donald Oenslager, "Edward Gordon Craig: Artist of the Theater: 1872–1966," *Bulletin of the New York Public Library,* LXXI (September, 1967), 439; W. B. Yeats, "The Theater of Beauty," *Harper's Weekly* (November 11, 1911), p. 11. See also *Letters,* pp. 366, 555, 579; Yeats's letter in the *Times* (September 13, 1912), in which he praises Craig's screens; and Yeats's Preface, *Plays for an Irish Theatre* (London and Stratford-on-Avon, 1911), pp. ix–xiii.

and reforming of theatrical taste is apparent from the tone of the letter. Here Yeats welcomes enthusiastically the growing tendency toward adopting the "new decorative method" of stage setting and scenery and points out that his essay would "contain the only serious criticism of the new craft of the Theatre"; he adds: "It is the exact moment for it."[17] Shakespeare was now beginning to be produced in a manner that Yeats had suggested more than a decade earlier.

Nugent Monck, actor and producer, and the fourth name among those who emancipated Shakespeare from the gloomy prison house of realism, was influenced greatly by Poel. From 1911 on, he made strenuous attempts to establish a theater in which a return to the austere Elizabethan stage would be possible. Yeats seems to have been well acquainted with Monck: in 1911 he spent a week with him at Norwich, and later, Monck's company, known as the Norwich Players, presented some of Yeats's plays with settings and costumes designed by Gordon Craig. Monck's unremitting efforts to have his own theater bore fruit finally, and on September 23, 1921, the Maddermarket Theatre in Norwich was inaugurated by Yeats. On the opening night the Norwich Players presented *As You Like It*. Monck, in an account of the history of the Maddermarket, states triumphantly: "During the interval at 9 P.M. W. B. Yeats formally opened the theatre. So the first practical model of a sixteenth century stage since Shakespeare's day came into being with this performance of *As You Like It*."[18] The following report of the event appeared in a local newspaper:

> During the single interval which Mr. Nugent Monck usually allows the Norwich Players in a Shakespearean production, Mr. W. B. Yeats, the distinguished Irish poet and playwright, spoke to last night's audience of the importance of the occasion. He explained that for the first time since Oliver Cromwell closed the theatres we have, in the Maddermarket Theatre, a stage similar in all essentials to that on which the plays of Shakespeare were originally produced. Mr. Yeats pointed out with an apt allusion that the modern theatre, by reason of its vastness and the

17 C. E. Purdom, *Harley Granville-Barker: Man of the Theater, Dramatist, and Scholar* (Cambridge, Mass., 1956), pp. 139–43; *Letters*, p. 579.

18 Hone, p. 255; Nugent Monck, "The Maddermarket Theatre and the Playing of Shakespeare," *Shakespeare Survey*, ed. Allardyce Nicoll (Cambridge, 1959), XII, 72.

consequent remoteness of the actors from the audience, is not suited to the creation of that illusion which, according to the speaker, is necessary in poetic drama.[19]

How close Yeats felt the Shakespearean vision came to his own is evident from the brief report of his remarks on that occasion. Yeats, in his own poetic drama, strove to overcome the remoteness of the actors from the audience by making the drawing room a fit setting for his plays; and his having consented to inaugurate the theater is an indication of his interest in encouraging the increasing trend—a trend that he was instrumental in effecting—toward presenting Shakespeare's plays, not through the minute particulars of eye and ear, but in keeping with their symbolic purpose that must touch the imagination of the spectator if the plays are to have value.

Yeats must have continued to see Shakespeare's plays from 1921 to 1929, but no evidence of this has as yet been found. Then in 1930 he saw *King Lear* at the Abbey Theatre in Dublin but reacted unfavorably to the production. Writing to Lady Gregory, he describes his extreme irritation with the play, which was "but half-visual and badly acted by everybody." He goes on to say that he was too tired to see it through, but it is interesting to note that in spite of his adverse appraisal of the play, he was determined to see the entire production, for he added that he would see the second half the following night. Out of sheer disgust with the inadequate representation of the drama by the actors, he then declares that an elaborate verse play is beyond the capacity of the Abbey Theatre actors, and that if he dared, he "would put *King Lear* into modern English and play it in full light throughout—leaving the words to suggest the storm," a statement indicative of his conviction that the self-generated energy of Shakespearean drama could sustain the play without the aid of puerile stage devices.[20] On Shakespeare's stage, of course, full light prevailed throughout the performance, and Yeats seems to be advocating a return to that technique. Granville-Barker, in his *Prefaces*, had only a few years earlier refuted

---

19 F. W. Weldon, "Norwich Players in *As You Like It:* A Distinguished Guest," *Eastern Daily Press* (September 27, 1921).

20 *Letters*, p. 778. The production that Yeats saw was a revival. *King Lear* had been produced at the Abbey Theatre on November 26, 1928 (T. L. Dume, "William Butler Yeats: A Survey of His Reading," [Ph.D. diss., Temple University, 1950], p. 286).

Lamb's and Bradley's objection that the play was too huge for the stage, by maintaining that Lear, Kent, and the rest must act the storm. Although Yeats would agree with his assertion, he also felt that a verse play made demands that the modern actor was congenitally incapable of fulfilling.

In October, 1934, a feeble *Macbeth* at the Abbey Theatre distressed Yeats. Too much reliance was placed on "black-outs." In "Lapis Lazuli," written two years later, he maintains that the drama exists somewhere beyond its stage representation; "black-out" and other stage effects cannot augment the tragedy. Then in January, 1936, *Coriolanus* was staged at the Abbey. Yeats was in Majorca, but it is likely that his lifelong interest in the play occasioned the production.

Finally, in September, 1937, he saw *Richard II* with Gielgud in the title role but was very disappointed with the performance. The significance of Richard to Yeats we shall examine later; here it should be said that Yeats's identification with the character, who was by worldly standards a failure, combined with his detestation for Bolingbroke and Henry V, both models of energetic success, is an important attitude that manifests itself as early as 1901 in "At Stratford-on-Avon." Many years later his attitude had not changed: "Why must I think the victorious cause the better?" he asks, and adds, "I prefer that the defeated cause should be more vividly described than that which has the advertisement of victory."[21] Likewise, in the poem "What Was Lost," the poet declares paradoxically that he sings what was lost and dreads what was won and takes sides with the "lost king," not the winning king. The exaltation of defeat is both in Yeats and in Shakespeare a motif that they employ with extraordinary power. Richard, Hamlet, Timon, Coriolanus, and Lear, defeated heroes whom Yeats salutes, have been summoned forth by him in the guise of Cuchulain, the tragic hero who goes down before the wily Conchubar.

II

Throughout his life Yeats continued to see Shakespeare's plays and to allude to them. As might be expected, his reading of Shakespeare

21 *Ah, Sweet Dancer,* ed. Roger McHugh (London, 1970), p. 26; *Irish Times* (October 26, 1934); Gerard Fay, *The Abbey Theatre* (Dublin, 1958), pp. 176, 177; *Letters,* p. 899 (see also Trewin, *Shakespeare,* p. 273); *Ex,* p. 398.

was no less zealous, and here the idiosyncrasies of producers and the inadequacies of actors could not obtrude. A. H. Bullen, the Elizabethan scholar and editor of the ten-volume *Stratford Town Shakespeare,* invited Yeats in 1905 to contribute an article on Shakespeare for the last volume, which contained several articles by well-known Shakespearean scholars. Unfortunately, Yeats declined, because he felt that at the time his mind was not on Shakespeare but on Chaucer. Seeing some of the plays, he suggested, might turn his thoughts to Shakespeare, "but one can't count on such things," he told Bullen. A year later, in 1906, he mentioned to Bullen that he had not "read the Elizabethans for fifteen years, except Shakespeare and Spenser." Later, in 1919, when Bullen was unable to make certain stipulated payments to Yeats, Yeats suggested that he "pay in kind." "Perhaps you could spare a set or two of the Stratford Shakespeare," he wrote Bullen. In the same letter he facetiously advises that a set of Shakespeare be presented to his brother-in-law so that it "might mitigate certain theological asperities."[22] Perhaps Yeats felt that Shakespeare's humanizing influence would serve to mellow his brother-in-law's strong theological views.

Then in 1930, he declared with characteristic vehemence that when his wife's automatic writing started in 1917, "all the history I knew was what I had remembered of English and Classical history from school days, or had since learned from the plays of Shakespeare or the novels of Dumas." And in the same year he wrote a semihumorous letter to an imaginary teacher of his son sternly enjoining that hapless individual not to teach the boy "a word of history. I shall take him to Shakespeare's history plays. . . . If you will not do what I say . . . may your soul lie chained on the Red Sea Bottom." Yeats felt that Shakespeare's history plays contained all the fundamental patterns of political behavior to which human beings were prone. As such, they were paradigms that embodied the eternal conflict between subjectivity and objectivity, the twin poles on which history turned. After watching Shakespeare's history plays performed at Stratford in 1901, Yeats described the spectacle as "that strange procession of kings and queens, of warring nobles, of

22 *Letters,* pp. 456–57, 479, 659.

insurgent crowds, of courtiers, and of people of the gutter," a fantastic cross section of Elizabethan society and of human nature condensed into a few hours' traffic on the stage. Long after, writing on the Abbey Theatre, Yeats could define the role that he felt it should play in the life of Ireland, in language that could well apply to his understanding of Shakespeare's stage and audience: "A nation should be like an audience in some great theatre . . . watching the sacred drama of its own history; every spectator finding self and neighbour there, finding all the world there, as we find the sun in the bright spot under the burning glass."[23]

During Yeats's last visit to the United States, in 1932, when somebody asked him about the books that had most moved him, he replied that Shakespeare came first, then the *Arabian Nights,* William Morris, and Balzac. Because most educated replies would place Shakespeare first, Yeats's doing so may not appear particularly significant, until we notice that here Yeats is doing so by deliberate choice and not as a predictable reflex; the other authors he lists are not as widely acclaimed as, for example, Chaucer or Spenser or Milton, in whose writings he was well read. Evidently he chose all four names and placed Shakespeare first with care, and not at random. Then when Yeats visited Pound at Rapallo in 1934 he informed him that he had been "re-reading Shakespeare," a disclosure that Yeats's later works with their Shakespearean overtones confirm.[24]

III

Yeats's attitude toward Shakespeare should be considered against the background of Anglo-Irish tension that reached its climax during his lifetime. His active involvement in the Irish struggle for independence is well known. It may seem astonishing, therefore, that Yeats nowhere resents Shakespeare's obvious pride in England's conquests abroad; he completely overlooks the pulsating fervor for Eng-

---

23 *Ex,* pp. 291, 321; *E&I,* p. 97; *Variorum Poems,* p. 836.
24 *E&I,* p. 447; W. B. Yeats, *King of the Great Clock Tower* (Dublin, 1934), p. vi.

land's supremacy in the history plays. But this nonrecognition springs from a realization that, for Shakespeare, the wholeness of his vision demanded that he be the spokesman for English patriotism inasmuch as he also reveals its futility and emptiness. And Yeats must have felt that, in the ultimate analysis, Shakespeare's sympathy and understanding for the oppressed was a truer index of his feelings than the turgid homage to England for her victories over her weaker neighbors, a homage which was undoubtedly intended to cater to the appetite of a popular audience.

In 1937, depressed and angry at the British government's attempt to malign Roger Casement, one of the heroes of the Easter uprising, Yeats wrote to Dorothy Wellesley, denouncing bitterly the canard. He described the "utter solitude" he had then experienced and identified himself with Shakespeare's sense of isolation as portrayed in Sonnet 66: "I kept repeating the sonnet of Shakespeare's about 'captain good.'" This sonnet that haunted him was the same one that he had quoted in full thirty-six years earlier in "At Stratford-on-Avon." After Yeats's ballad "Roger Casement" was published, he had a letter from an Irish woman revolutionist who wrote "approving of what she supposes to be my hatred of England," Yeats told Lady Wellesley, adding, "It has shocked me for it has made me fear that you think the same. I have written to my correspondent, 'How can I hate England, owing what I do to Shakespeare, Blake and Morris. England is the only country I cannot hate.'" And in a slightly later letter to Lady Wellesley, Yeats distinguishes between hate and indignation: "Hate is a kind of 'passive suffering' but indignation is a kind of joy. . . . We that are joyous need not be afraid to denounce." And denounce is precisely what Yeats does in his fiery pamphlet *On the Boiler*. Here he associates himself with "that old Shakespearean contempt" for the vulgar taste of the common people while condemning the democratic desire for popularity epitomized in the mayor of Dublin.[25]

Yeats's denunciation of England was always limited to its post-Shakespeare age of imperialism when John Bull went to India and entrenched himself. Yeats's poem "The Curse of Cromwell" is a ruthless

25 *Letters to DW*, pp. 123, 111, 114 (see also *Letters*, p. 872) ; *Boiler*, p. 10.

exposure of the leveling forces that Cromwell unleashed and which Yeats saw operating with undiminished vigor in his own time, under the deceptively innocuous labels of socialism and democracy. In his essay on Spenser (1902), Yeats makes Cromwell's regime the dividing line between "Merry England that was about to pass away," and modern England that nourished "the Puritan and the merchant." Yeats regarded Shakespeare as the consummation of all that was excellent in Merry England, an attitude very different from that of many fervently patriotic Englishmen who, perhaps pardonably, saw their bard as the eloquent mouthpiece for the imperialistic exploits that Britannia was bracing herself for after Cromwell's murderous crew had shown the way. In a letter to Mrs. Olivia Shakespear written many years later, Yeats asserts that he "rejected England and France" because they, following Newton rather than Dante, had lost the old insouciance.[26]

Yeats was fully conscious of the fact that his belonging to "the indomitable Irishry" was a factor that must in many ways have affected his relationship with English literature. But the vehemence of his antagonism toward imperial England was always softened by the thought that Shakespeare too belonged to that England; in the following statement an ambivalence toward modern England that Yeats's honesty refuses to conceal is evident:

> The "Irishry" have preserved their ancient "deposit" through wars which, during the sixteenth and seventeenth centuries, became wars of extermination; no people . . . have undergone greater persecution, nor did that persecution altogether cease up to our own day. No people hate as we do in whom that past is always alive, there are moments when hatred poisons my life. . . . Then I remind myself that though mine is the first English marriage I know of in the direct line, all my family names are English, and that I owe my soul to Shakespeare, to Spenser and to Blake, perhaps to William Morris . . . my hatred tortures me with love, my love with hate.

But Yeats regarded Shakespeare and Spenser as belonging to an England that had long since disappeared; Blake, Yeats had claimed as being of Irish descent; and the debt to William Morris, who was undeniably a modern Englishman, he now acknowledges with the qualifier "perhaps." Increasingly, Yeats seems to be including himself among a coterie of writers remote in every way from his contemporaries. His drift toward a

26   *E&I*, p. 364; *Letters*, p. 807.

repudiation of twentieth-century England is corroborated by what Joseph Hone relates, that after the Casement episode he "was astonished by the ferocity of his [Yeats's] feelings. He almost collapsed after reading the verses and had to call for a little port wine."[27]

Might not Yeats's sympathy for Richard and his scorn for Henry be something instinctive, born of the acrimonious nature of Anglo-Irish relations during Yeats's lifetime? Perhaps Yeats admired and was so deeply moved by the failure and rejection of Richard because this deposed king, with his poetic and impractical temperament, became for Yeats a kind of symbol of Ireland that had for seven hundred years been victimized by a succession of Henry the Fifths. By the same token, he heartily despised the success story of Bolingbroke, along with the grandeur of achievement that most Shakespearean critics ascribed to Henry the Fifth. Worst of all was the fact that Edward Dowden, an Irishman and an influential Shakespearean critic, "first made these emotions eloquent and plausible," Yeats bitterly points out. Not only was Richard's rejection a symbolic expression of Ireland's own tragically moving history, but even Shakespeare's *Richard II* could no longer find a sympathetic representation on the modern stage, where acting and dramatic technique were incapable of portraying the mood that the play embodied. In telling imagery, pugnacious and caustically witty, which Auden could not have bettered, Yeats recounted to Dorothy Wellesley his feelings after seeing the play acted on the London stage in 1937: "I have no news except that I went to *Richard II* last night, as fine a performance [as] possible, considering that the rhythm of all the great passages is abolished. The modern actor can speak to another actor, but he is incapable of reverie. On the advice of Bloomsbury he has packed his soul in a bag and left it with the bar-attendant. Did Shakespeare in *Richard II* discover poetic reverie?" Although there was an element of mysticism in the Bloomsbury concept of art, it was, for Yeats, too heavily weighted by a judicious regard for reason and logic.[28]

---

27   *E&I*, pp. 518–19; *The Works of William Blake*, ed. E. J. Ellis and W. B. Yeats (London, 1893), I, 2–3; Hone, p. 450, n. 1 (see also *Letters to DW*, p. 177).
28   *E&I*, p. 104; *Letters*, p. 899; J. K. Johnstone, *The Bloomsbury Group* (London, 1954).

Reverie was for Yeats essentially an inner contemplativeness free from pragmatism, and in Richard he saw this best exemplified. In the poem "Meditations in Time of Civil War," Yeats laments the departure of "self-delighting reverie" as violence and bloodshed grip the land, and he conceives of Phase 15 of *A Vision* as being one in which "thought has been pursued, not as a means but as an end—the poem, the painting, the reverie has been sufficient of itself." The song that the moon sings in the little poem "He and She," with the triple iteration of "I," expresses this efflorescence of the soul as opposed to the restraining logic of the sun:

> "I am I, am I;
> The greater grows my light
> The further that I fly,"
> All creation shivers
> With that sweet cry.

And in "The Old Stone Cross" Yeats declares: "But actors lacking music / Do most excite my spleen." Thus, a delineation of Richard bereft of this essential music—the instrument of reverie—would be a meaningless foray into an area alien to the rational temper of the present age. In Richard's "contemplative virtue," "lyrical fantasy," and "dreamy dignity," Yeats saw the embodiment of all that was contrary to contemporary England's noisy assertiveness; and the defeat and overthrow of Richard by Bolingbroke and then by Henry was, for him, the inevitable triumph of muscular ability or objectivity over poetic reflectiveness or subjectivity.[29] Likewise, Phase 15, though a perfect phase because Unity of Being or complete equilibrium has been attained, cannot long survive; inevitably the subjective yields to the objective, the exquisite to the utilitarian, and decline proceeds apace. Thus Shakespeare's *Richard II* seems to have been for Yeats, not only a deeply moving play, but also a reflection of his own innermost convictions, a metaphor for the antagonism of opposites that was always fundamental to his vision.

The prevalent notion that worldly efficiency was superior to meditativeness continued to engage and anger Yeats. Over three decades

29 *E&I*, p. 106.

after stating his views on Richard and Henry (in "At Stratford-on-Avon"), he was still concerning himself in several sections of his pamphlet, *On the Boiler,* with the inferiority attributed to the Irish emigrant to America when compared with other Western European emigrants. Arguing that the Irishman's ignorance and lack of worldly wisdom are simply the consequence of his not belonging to "a civilisation dominated by towns" and that therefore he is "nearer than the English to the Mythic Age," Yeats goes on to say spiritedly that the Irish are not disinterested observers, being much taken up with their own thoughts and emotions. He clinches the argument with the declaration, "The English are an objective people; they have no longer a sense of tragedy." Long before this, in a lecture delivered in 1909, he spoke of "the old writers as busy with their own sins and of the new writers as busy with other people's," and he ranked Shakespeare with the old, and Milton with the new. And in "The Statues," the Irish, like Shakespeare, Spenser, and Yeats himself, are of the old nation but have been "thrown upon this filthy modern tide / And by its formless spawning fury wrecked." As Yeats had claimed Blake to be of Irish descent and even a fellow member of the Golden Dawn, so in his essay "The Celtic Element in Literature" he had no hesitation in explaining that much of Shakespeare's finest poetry was due to the Celtic influence that he had imbibed.[30]

Consistent with this attitude was Yeats's refusal to consider either Shakespeare or Spenser as products of post-Renaissance England. He boldly asserted that "Shakespeare, with his delight in great persons, with his indifference to the State, with his scorn of the crowd, with his feudal passion, was of the old nation, and Spenser . . . was of the old nation too." Evidently the keen historical sense that Yeats was later to display so brilliantly in the pages of *A Vision* was not a sudden pyrotechnic, but had frequently shown itself, less overtly, long before. He wrote to his father in 1910 that in his lecture tour of the Midlands, he "had put Shakespeare among the old writers and Milton with the new." It is interesting to observe how carefully Yeats draws the dividing line

30 *Boiler,* pp. 16–21; *Identity,* pp. 55–56; *E&I,* pp. 176–77.

between the two, placing Shakespeare at the end of an epoch, and Milton at the beginning of a new epoch. Sir Oliver Elton, who was in the audience, said to Yeats later that he had heard the voice of J. B. Yeats in Yeats's lecture, an instance of the intellectual closeness between father and son.[31]

Yeats's disavowal of his English fellow poets as successors to the Shakespearean tradition of the old writers comes forcefully to light over twenty-five years later in his Introduction to *The Oxford Book of Modern Verse* where, despite his conciliatory acknowledgment of "much that is moving in symbol and imagery" in the poetry of T. S. Eliot, Yeats maintains that he cannot put him "among those that descend from Shakespeare and the translators of the Bible." His exhortation to Irish poets, in "Under Ben Bulben," to learn their trade from the poets of earlier times is a rejection of contemporary literary movements, rootless and devoid of a tradition:

> Irish poets, learn your trade,
> Sing whatever is well made,
> Scorn the sort now growing up
> All out of shape from toe to top,
> Their unremembering hearts and heads
> Base-born products of base beds.
> Sing the peasantry, and then
> Hard-riding country gentlemen,
> The holiness of monks, and after
> Porter-drinkers' randy laughter;
> Sing the lords and ladies gay
> That were beaten into the clay
> Through seven heroic centuries;
> Cast your mind on other days
> That we in coming days may be
> Still the indomitable Irishry.

Yeats seems to have here in mind the contrast between the drab pessimism of his fellow poets and the laughing extravagance of Shakespeare's age with its exuberant vitality and passion for life. Elsewhere, in "Lapis Lazuli," the poet sees Hamlet and Lear as gay in the face of death and defeat, unlike the modern poet faced by these realities, who exhibits a

31 *E&I*, p. 365; *Letters*, pp. 554–55.

morbid gloom. For Yeats, Shakespeare and those that descend from Shakespeare are a family apart.

Yeats felt that he himself did not belong to the rising school of realist poets to which Eliot, Auden, and Graves belonged, but to the tradition of "Milton, Shakespeare, Shelley." As one left behind by his own times, he identified with Richard—a surrogate for Shakespeare himself. In a letter to Dorothy Wellesley, he wrote, "Being the crowd-scorned creatures we always murmur in the end 'Let us sit upon the ground / And tell sad stories of the death of kings.' Do you not feel there the wide-open eyes?"[32] Yeats tacitly shares his own feeling of alienation with Shakespeare, and, like the artist who compels his audience to accept the world he creates as both valid and real, Yeats endows his Shakespeare with qualities that may, in some sense, be more strikingly Yeatsian than Shakespearean.

But this in no way invalidates Yeats's interpretation of Shakespeare. For even when boldly claiming Shakespeare as one who possessed the Celtic way of looking at life, Yeats was careful to state that this insight originated with Matthew Arnold, an Englishman. Clearly Yeats had anticipated the charge of subjectivity, or of an Irishman's idiosyncrasy, being brought against him in his analysis of Shakespeare, and by this observation took the precaution of precluding it. And Yeats's resentment toward the popular drive to interpret Shakespeare as a chauvinist was far from being simply Irish spitefulness; Kipling, in his poem "Recessional," with the image of Britannia holding "dominion over palm and pine," was but giving utterance to a feeling that had become fairly pervasive. That Thomas Carlyle could speak of the Stratford peasant being the grandest thing the English nation had produced, adding that the British would rather relinquish their Indian empire than part with him, is in itself an indication of the way in which empire building and Shakespeare had somehow coalesced in the English national consciousness.[33]

---

32 *Letters to DW*, pp. 58–59.

33 For Yeats's opinion of Kipling, see Hone, p. 371; Carlyle, *Heroes, Hero-Worship, and the Heroic in History* (London, 1841), pp. 104–5.

2

Yeats among Shakespearean Critics

I cannot get it out of my mind that this age of criticism
is about to pass, and an age of imagination, of emotion,
of moods, of revelation, about to come in its place.
—Yeats, "The Body of the Father
Christian Rosencrux"

YEATS both read and knew personally some of the foremost
Shakespearean scholars of his time. Two questions arise: What
Shakespearean criticism did he know? To what extent, if any, was he
affected by it? Since, as we have seen, Yeats was invited by Bullen to contribute an article on Shakespeare for his edition of the plays, it is clear
that Yeats's authorship would have been considered valuable. His brilliant essay, "At Stratford-on-Avon," in which he had argued that Shakespeare was being praised for the wrong things, had appeared just a few
years earlier, and, evidently, his right to speak with authority on Shakespeare was now recognized. In the essay, Yeats states that when at Stratford in 1901, he spent all his time reading the plays and the many critical
books on Shakespeare, good or bad, in the library of the theater. While
there, he wrote to Lady Gregory telling her that he was "working very
hard, reading all the chief criticisms of the plays," adding that he was
too busy to even accept an invitation to go up the river by boat.[1]

1 *Letters,* p. 456; *E&I,* pp. 96, 103; *Letters,* p. 349.

In his writings Yeats mentions several Shakespeare critics by name.[2]
Edward Dowden's book, *Shakspere: A Critical Study of His Mind and
Art,* generally regarded as being one of the most influential in Shakespearean criticism, had appeared in 1875. Dowden was professor of
English literature at Trinity College, Dublin, and a personal friend of
Yeats's father. Yet he was quite unlike J. B. Yeats. Stolid and respectable
as far as innovations in Irish literary matters were concerned, he tended
to distrust the emotions for being too flamboyant and much preferred
the intellect as a guide for conduct. One example of his guarded approach to any untried enterprise was his lack of enthusiasm for an Irish
theme as the choice of Irish authors, and his suggesting that Thomas à
Becket be preferred instead. Yeats was full of indignation and denounced
his timidity and lack of patriotism. Even though the Irish Dramatic
Movement had been launched with Dowden as onlooker, he was quite
incapable of sensing its importance and significance. Others from distant
lands, alive to the new currents flowing, were quick to recognize the
fresh vitality engendered in out-of-the-way Ireland, but Dowden remained imperceptive, sadly shaking his head over the folly of these

---

2 For a brief but useful account of the state of Shakespearean criticism at
the turn of the century, see William M. Schutte, *Joyce and Shakespeare* (New
Haven, 1957), pp. 153–57; Augustus Ralli, *A History of Shakespearian Criticism*
(New York, 1965), II, 1–117; Arthur M. Eastman, *A Short History of Shakespearean
Criticism* (New York, 1968), chapters 6 and 7; and M. C. Bradbrook, *Elizabethan
Stage Conditions* (Cambridge, 1968). Yeats must have known, among others, the
work of Edmond Malone, the famous Irish Shakespeare scholar; Georg Brandes,
William Shakespeare (London, 1899); Sidney Lee, *A Life of William Shakespeare*
(London, 1898): see *Letters,* p. 449; Swinburne's three books on Shakespeare;
Arthur Symons' essays on the individual plays; Granville-Barker's *Prefaces to Shake-
speare,* 5 series (London, 1927–47); A. C. Bradley, *Shakespearean Tragedy* (Lon-
don, 1904); Bradley's essays on Shakespeare in his *Oxford Lectures on Poetry*
(London, 1909); Frank Harris, *The Man Shakespeare and His Tragic Life-Story*
(New York, 1909); John Masefield, *William Shakespeare* (London, 1911); Wyndham
Lewis, *The Lion and the Fox: The Role of the Hero in the Plays of Shakespeare*
(London, 1927). Yeats was familiar with George Bernard Shaw's Shakespearean
idiosyncrasies: see *Ex,* p. 276; *J. B. Yeats: Letters to His Son W. B. Yeats and
Others, 1869–1922,* ed. Joseph Hone (New York, 1946), p. 205. Yeats also read
Paul Verlaine's essay "Shakespeare and Racine," *Fortnightly Review,* CXII (Septem-
ber, 1894), 440–47: see *E&I,* p. 270. Yeats may have seen a book by Sir D. Plunket
Barton, Senator of the National University of Ireland and Member of the Royal Irish
Academy, *Links Between Ireland and Shakespeare* (Dublin, 1919).

young and immature enthusiasts.[3] Still, despite differences of opinion and friction between the Yeats family and Dowden, friendship between them was never dissolved, perhaps more because of Dowden's accommodating nature than a sparing use of ammunition on the other's part.

Dowden's book on Shakespeare seems to have been almost the starting point for Yeats's firmly enunciated attitude toward Shakespeare in "At Stratford-on-Avon," an attitude diametrically opposed to the position Dowden had taken. Today Dowden's work is dated: after the insights of men like L. C. Knights, Dover Wilson, E. E. Stoll, and G. Wilson Knight, we hesitate to regard any single character as a mouthpiece for Shakespeare, to deduce Shakespeare the man from his plays, or to stress that his mind and art went hand in hand. Yet Yeats, over sixty years ago, had objected to all of these assumptions in Dowden's book and went further by not only denying that Shakespeare's work was a simple reflection of his personality, but also maintaining temerariously that Shakespeare, in fact, unlike Ben Jonson, lacked personality, and therefore could not be identified conveniently with any single character or characters of his creation. Such a disparagement of their idol would have been nothing short of anathema to many faithful Victorians, but for Yeats, who theorized that the best artists' work had to be the opposite of what the artists were in life, Shakespeare's example was excellent support. In "At Stratford-on-Avon," Yeats admits to having carefully read Dowden's book but then goes on to disparage Dowden's critical approach, which reduces Shakespeare's ideal to a single formula: Henry V the supreme hero because able and efficient; Richard II the antithesis because sentimental, weak, and selfish. Exasperation with Dowden was not only Yeats's feeling; elsewhere he called it "a family exasperation with the Dowden point of view, which rather filled Dublin in my youth. There is a good deal of my father in it." In fact, J. B. Yeats was delighted with the stand that his son had taken on Shakespeare and declared that Yeats's essay was "the best article" on Shakespeare he had

3 See *Man and Masks*, pp. 14, 47; Torchiana, pp. 12–14; Kathryn Miller Ludwigson, "Transcendentalism in Edward Dowden" (Ph.D. diss., Northwestern University, 1963), chapter 1.

ever read.[4] Yeats points out that Dowden, contrasting England's spectacular achievements with conditions in Ireland, "where everything has
failed," naturally admired attainments that seemed beyond his own
countrymen. Thus, while accusing Dowden, Yeats also ironically excuses
him but will himself have nothing to do with a theory that makes art
a commentary on life. Later we shall see how Yeats, insisting on the
independence of art from life, maintained that the immaterial had an
intenser reality than the material. He hailed Berkeley as the protagonist
of this approach and compared his theory to Coleridge's observations on
Shakespeare's phenomenological world of art.

Dowden's object was to present Shakespeare as having two facets:
a desire to probe the mystery of the soul, and a hard-headed desire to
attain worldly success. A combination of these two provided for fulfillment, an imbalance for failure. Romeo and Hamlet, incapable of balancing their emotional sensibilities against the outside world, inevitably
fail. But Henry V is Shakespeare's hero because he is both practical and
idealistic. Brutus is too idealistic, Polonius too pragmatic; both perish.
It is easy to see why Yeats found Dowden's analysis repugnant. Working
with so obvious a scale, Dowden had evolved a formula that was too
superficial for Yeats. He wrote to Lady Gregory that the more he read
of the critics in the library at Stratford, "the worse does the Shakespeare
criticism become and Dowden is about the climax of it. It came out of
the middle class movement and I feel it my legitimate enemy."[5] By exalting Henry, Dowden discounted all that was excellent in Richard.
Yeats likens this abasing of Richard to what "schoolboys do in perse-
cuting some boy of fine temperament, who has weak muscles and a

---

4 Inscription by Yeats in Vol. VI of his *Collected Works:* see Allan Wade,
A Bibliography of the Writings of W. B. Yeats (London, 1958), p. 88; *Letters*, p.
352.

5 *Letters*, p. 349; Swinburne, Sidney Lee, and Brandes (see n. 2 above) too
have fulsome praise for Henry and call him the prototype of those Englishmen who
were later to colonize the world. The critic who "wrote that Shakespeare admired
this one character alone out of all his characters," but whose name Yeats could not
remember (*E&I*, pp. 104–5), is probably Sidney Lee. Lee says of Henry V: "Alone
in Shakespeare's gallery of English monarchs does Henry's portrait evoke a joyous
sense of satisfaction in the high potentialities of human character and a feeling of
pride among Englishmen that one of his mettle is of English race."

distaste for school games." It was the old conflict between poet and man of action, which Yeats was to develop in several of the plays he wrote shortly thereafter.

After contrasting Bolingbroke's "true and manly patriotism" with Richard's "sentimental favours" when he returns to England and salutes the English earth that he stands on, Dowden then contrasts Henry with Richard by stating that whereas to Richard life was a graceful and shadowy ceremony containing beautiful and pathetic situations, to Henry life was a stern reality demanding practical measures shorn of sentiment and rhetoric. Yeats accepts this contrast but evaluates it in altogether different terms. He too contrasts Richard first with Bolingbroke, next with Henry. Bolingbroke is "unjust" and "violent," a "common man," whereas Richard is "that sweet lovely rose." Turning then to Henry, Yeats says that the posing of character against character was an essential element in Shakespeare's art, and so, having made the vessel of porcelain in the person of Richard, he had to make the vessel of clay in the person of Henry. Henry is Richard's opposite: he is remorseless and undistinguished, whereas Richard is sensitive and poetic. Disdainful of Henry and his fervent admirers, Yeats brackets them together by saying that Henry's character, when contrasted with that of Richard, "lets out a little of Shakespeare's secret, and all but the secret of his critics."[6]

Whereas Dowden judges Shakespeare's people with the same judgment that he would exercise in assessing a colleague, Yeats maintains that Shakespeare's world is not the world of real affairs—"Shakespeare cared little for the State, the source of all our judgments"—but an inner world of poetic sensibilities of which the outer world is but a symbol or a metaphor. Shakespeare possessed "that untroubled sympathy for men as they are, as apart from all they do and seem," and "the world was almost as empty in his eyes as it must be in the eyes of God." Twenty years later he was to state this attitude in more explicit terms, but the beginnings of it are present in "At Stratford-on-Avon." Yeats's Shake-

6 W. B. Yeats, "At Stratford-on-Avon," *The Speaker* (May 11, 1901), p. 159. For a lucid summary of Yeats's views on Richard and Henry, see J. Kleinstuck, "Yeats and Shakespeare," in *W. B. Yeats, 1865–1965: Centenary Essays on the Art of W. B. Yeats*, ed. D. E. S. Maxwell and S. B. Bushrui (Ibadan, 1965), pp. 4–6.

speare is neither moralist nor reformer, but, rather, a benign observer
whose sympathies are with poets and dreamers, outcasts and the down-
trodden. Richard and Hamlet, absorbed in an inner world of thought
and contemplation, are overthrown by the exigencies of the actual world,
which encroaches on them, but for Yeats, their defeat is superficial, for
it takes place only on the level of "the trivial game of life."

Yeats, then, would regard a Shakespearean play as a framework
for revealing inner states of being; he would clearly have no sympathy
with William Archer, for example, who argued that *Othello* was based
on a series of improbabilities, one of which was the fact that Cassio
could not possibly have been alone with Desdemona before the morning
when Othello saw them together.[7] Many years later, Yeats commented
on *Othello* in an extraordinary exchange of letters with Sturge Moore
dealing with the reality or otherwise of the black cat that Frank Harris
reported Ruskin had picked up and deposited outside his window, but
which, strangely enough, no one else saw. Yeats argued that the cat
was indeed a sense-object, though invisible to the others present in the
room. Sturge Moore, a materialist, maintained that it was an illusion
and compared it to the delusion under which Othello labored: that
Desdemona was guilty of an adulterous affection for Cassio. Yeats
brusquely dismissed Sturge Moore's analogy, saying that there was "no
relation between Ruskin's cat and Desdemona's guilt," because Ruskin's
cat was a "sense-datum" having weight, color, shape, whereas Desdemona's guilt was "false reasoning."[8] Thus to Yeats, Othello's delusion
was based on his false reasoning and not on several external situations
of which he was simply a helpless victim. In fact, one can confidently
state that Yeats must have regarded Iago as being not so much the
cause of the rift between Othello and Desdemona as the symbol of that
rift. Opposed to the realistic mode of interpreting drama, Yeats was one
of the first to insist that Shakespeare be considered a dramatist and not
a historian, sociologist, or behaviorist.

In "At Stratford-on-Avon," Yeats's purpose is to lift Shakespeare

7 William Archer, "Is *Othello* a Fit Play for the Modern Stage?" *St. James's
Magazine*, XLIX (September, 1881), 222–25.

8 Frank Harris, *My Life and Loves* (New York, 1963), pp. 442–43; *Yeats
and TSM*, p. 64.

out of the domain of realism into which many well-meaning nineteenth-century critics had thrust him. He brings his argument on this issue to a close by quoting Goethe: "Art is art, because it is not nature." This statement was made during a conversation with Johann Peter Eckermann in which Goethe pointed out that although several features in a picture by Rubens were flagrantly in opposition to the laws of nature, the picture, great art that it was, could flout these laws, transcend them, and establish its own sovereign domain. Yeats, concurring with Goethe's stand, refuses to recognize Shakespeare's plays as carbon copies of nature. As examples of Shakespeare's art carving out its own territorial jurisdiction, he cites the ghosts that haunt Richard, and the arrangement of Richard's and Richmond's tents side by side, at the end of *Richard III*. Yeats has chosen splendid examples to illustrate his point, for in the play as Shakespeare wrote it, the spirits of Richard's victims address him and Richmond alternately, tormenting the one and reassuring the other—a situation that must make any modern producer quail at the ever-present danger of straining his audience's credulity so far as to reduce the whole scene to a bizarre procession of ghosts bobbing from one tent to another. In fact Benson—like many producers today—distorted the scene so as to make the ghosts' imprecations on Richard's head and their benedictions on Richmond's head more credible, but Yeats protests against this falsification of Shakespeare. He believed that no producer had the right to tamper with Shakespeare and so condemned Benson for his presumptuousness.

In Eckermann's *Conversations of Goethe,* Yeats must also have noted Goethe's uneasy but frank recognition of Shakespeare's looming shadow, which no dramatist could escape or ignore. Goethe had declared that any dramatist after Shakespeare must, inescapably, suffer from an acute consciousness of his own inferiority; that in view of this it might be well for him to refrain from reading too much Shakespeare; and that his *Goetz* and *Egmont* were attempts to resist and quell Shakespeare's smothering influence. Heretical as this may sound, Yeats would probably have felt that Goethe's wariness was justified, for he too cautioned his fellow Irish dramatists against trying to imitate "Shakespeare's luxurance."

It is possible to view some of Yeats's plays as his attempts to free

himself from Shakespeare's supremacy. Yeats must also have been aware
of Goethe's well-known comparison of Hamlet, burdened by the task of
revenge, with the planting of an oak in a delicate vase. In "At Stratford-
on-Avon," Yeats, in subtle references to Hamlet, seems to imply that he
shares Goethe's interpretation of the character. But several years later,
Yeats's attitude toward Hamlet underwent a radical change, which we
shall consider in chapter 3. Situated at the other extreme to Goethe's
sensitive Hamlet is Dowden's Hamlet.

Having condemned Richard, Dowden does not spare Hamlet
either. Impressed by Henry's energy and efficiency, he contrasts him
with "the Danish Prince, who is 'fat and scant of breath,' " a procrastinator and slothful. But Yeats, in his essay, puts Hamlet on the side of
Richard, and Henry on the side of Fortinbras: the philosophers as opposed to the activists. He also calls Richard "that unripened Hamlet."
Twenty years later, Yeats seems to have recalled Dowden's thrust at
Hamlet for being fat and scant of breath, for he points out that Shakespeare also made him agile with rapier and dagger, thus depicting him
as a combination of both dreamer and man of action.

Thus, by refusing to make success and failure Shakespeare's criteria
for distributing praise or blame, Yeats takes up a position that comes
very close to what Walter Pater had defined in his *Appreciations* (1889).
Yeats had read Pater with much attention and admiration and in his
essay refers with approval to Pater's concept of Richard as "a wild
creature." Yeats sees Richard as "lovable and full of capricious fancy."

Pater's *Appreciations* contains three essays on Shakespeare: *"Love's
Labour's Lost," "Measure for Measure,"* and "Shakespeare's English
Kings." In this last Pater maintains that Shakespeare's attitude toward
his kings, including Richard, is one of irony; but Yeats's emphasis is on
showing Richard to be a tragic character and not simply an ironical
portrait of the pains of kingship. To Pater, Shakespeare's kings are only
"average human nature," struggling ineffectually with events too large
for their comprehension. Shakespeare's purpose in these plays is not to
romanticize English history, but, rather, to set forth the inescapable
failure that attends the human condition. For, after all, even kings are
but ordinary mortals. To Pater these are not heroes, only men who rise,

struggle, and fall. Yeats's attitude is obviously quite the converse as his revival of the Cuchulain myth indicates. His approval of Standish O'Grady's narration of the "story of Cuchulain that he might bring back an heroic ideal"[9] was also a statement of his own purpose in showing

> Character isolated by a deed
> To engross the present and dominate memory,

as he informs us in "The Circus Animals' Desertion." Moreover, Yeats regards Shakespeare's Richard as a tragic hero, incomparably superior to his crass opponents, who destroy him. Although Yeats, like Pater, reasons that Shakespeare saw "in Richard II the defeat that awaits all, whether they be artist or saint," Richard's defeat is not a proof of the futility of all human endeavor, but is, in fact, for Yeats, its justification. True, Pater too had called Richard "an exquisite poet," but it is also clear that he is slightly contemptuous of this deposed king, for he goes on to exclaim: "No! Shakespeare's kings are not, nor are meant to be, great men: rather, little or quite ordinary humanity, thrust upon greatness." In Yeats's view, on the other hand, the very defeat of Richard insured his victory, for the terms in which Yeats would define defeat and victory were not the accepted ones, but came in fact close to the Aristotelian notion of Harmatia, which A. C. Bradley was to elaborate three years after Yeats's essay appeared. Bradley too reasons that the tragic hero's defeat is in reality his triumph, that his death at the play's end, far from being ignominious, is an assertion of his complete personality. Yet Bradley did not dare proclaim—as Yeats later did in "Lapis Lazuli"— that Hamlet and Lear, in the last scenes of their respective plays, are gay, and that their gaiety transfigures all that dread. Yeats's Hamlet and Lear here embody an emotion that no actor could represent in visual terms on a stage, yet it is possible to argue that in depicting them thus, Yeats has grasped a fundamental truth in Shakespeare's tragic vision that no critic has hitherto had the courage to develop.

Despite differences between Yeats's and Pater's positions, they are in agreement over the folly of some of the German critics. Pater speaks disparagingly of "some German commentators," and Yeats singles out

9 *Ex,* p. 371.

G. G. Gervinus for castigation, bracketing him with Dowden as being unduly preoccupied with values alien to Shakespeare, who "had no nice sense of utilities, no ready balance to measure deeds, like that fine instrument, with all the latest improvements, Gervinus and Professor Dowden handle so skilfully." Gervinus, in his *Shakespeare Commentaries* (1849–50), asserts that Shakespeare's art is based on morality. Like Dowden, he concerns himself wholly with the actions of Shakespeare's people, confuses morality with beauty, and judges the plays in the light of contemporary Victorian standards of right and wrong. Yeats must have glanced through the pages of his book, in keeping with his statement that he had turned over many books while in the library at Stratford, but he could not claim familiarity with these books. Yeats's insistence on Shakespeare's detachment from his characters, and his refusal to regard the plays as a demonstration of an overt moral scheme, can be related to his father's views on Shakespeare, which were so instrumental in shaping those of his son.

In 1909, in a letter to W. B. from America, J. B. Yeats called his son's talent "benign" and pointed out that Shakespeare too "was at his best when most benign," but, he added, "Wordsworth was malign, so was Byron and so is Swinburne. These people could not get away from their self-importance. They must denounce and scold." Then, with excusable paternal pride, J. B. Yeats intones, "This benign quality you get from me; I say this remembering my father's family. They all of them in every fibre of their being were 'the Good people'. . . . For that reason people loved them but did not fear them, so they passed making no mark."[10] Yeats's eclecticism, as seen in his interest in divers faiths and beliefs, and in his preoccupation with the very human dilemma of frustration in love, along with a recoiling from old age and bodily decay, corroborates his father's analysis. Like Shakespeare, Yeats possesses a largeness of vision that encompasses humanity and transcends social, religious, or national affiliations. And, like Shakespeare, Yeats never tired of exalting the peasantry and the aristocracy.

Yeats, as we shall see in a later chapter, denied that Shakespeare

10 *J. B. Yeats: Letters,* ed. Hone, p. 117.

possessed an assertive personality, but as early as 1901, in "At Stratford-on-Avon," he had adumbrated such a hypothesis by saying that after Shakespeare's death the inhabitants of Stratford did not memorialize him, because he was himself a retiring and undemonstrative man, and because the age of legendary magnificence was giving way to Puritanism.

This interesting hypothesis by Yeats was echoed in an article by J. J. Jusserand, the French critic, that appeared in the Bullen edition of Shakespeare to which Yeats had declined the invitation to contribute an article. The edition was published in 1907, and Yeats must have seen the article and found that it confirmed his own theory that Shakespeare's personality was almost one of anonymity. Jusserand, in his article "Ben Jonson's Views on Shakespeare's Art,"[11] points out that "Shakespeare is the exact reverse and counterpart of Jonson": whereas Shakespeare had an aversion for quarrels, Jonson reveled in them; whereas Shakespeare kept aloof from others and avoided scandal, Jonson was gregarious, noisy, audacious; and whereas such terms as "gentle," "mellifluous," and "honeytongued" were applied to him, contemporary descriptions of Jonson made free use of such terms as "gall," "copperas," "wormwood and sulphur." After observing that it is "no wonder great Will's personality looms so indistinctly before us," Jusserand concludes by noting that, in spite of the "assured immortality" Shakespeare claimed for his sonnets, "he attached no more importance to them than to his plays; he never printed any, and when a pirate printed them, he said nothing."

In his analysis of Shakespeare as an example of Phase 20 of *A Vision,* Yeats is clearly in agreement with Jusserand's account of Shakespeare and Jonson. Here Yeats too contrasts the two men in very similar details: he points out that "sweet" and "gentle" were the adjectives applied to Shakespeare by his contemporaries, that his "actual personality seemed faint and passionless," that, unlike Jonson, "he fought no duels" and "dominated no Mermaid Tavern," and that he did not even com-

---

11 In *The Works of William Shakespeare,* ed. A. H. Bullen (Stratford-on-Avon, 1907), X, 297–319. Perhaps Yeats also knew Jusserand's *A Literary History of the English People,* 3 vols. (1904; reprinted London: Fisher Unwin, 1925–26); *English Wayfaring Life in the Middle Ages* (London, 1889); *Shakespeare en France sous l'ancien regime* (1898 [Eng. tr. London, 1899]): see *Ex,* p. 190.

plain "when somebody pirated his sonnets." It is important to note that Jusserand's article merely provided Yeats with evidence with which to buttress his argument advanced six years before, that Shakespeare's personality was unspectacular while his works displayed his artistic genius.

Yeats's reading of Ralph Waldo Emerson too seems to have had a share in determining the phase to which he assigned Shakespeare. Yeats refers to Emerson's essay "Shakespeare; or, the Poet" only once in his works,[12] but it is possible that the essay exercised some influence on him, particularly noticeable in his having given Napoleon (of all persons) as a companion to Shakespeare in Phase 20 of *A Vision*. Improbable though the juxtaposition of these strange bedfellows may appear to us, Yeats's explanation traces the underlying similarity between the two men and thus plausibly brings them within a common fold. He probably found Emerson's two essays "Shakespeare; or, the Poet" and "Napoleon; or, the Man of the World," in *Representative Men* (1841), pertinent to his analysis of the type of person at Phase 20. His examination of Napoleon comes close to Emerson's detailed description of the man.

Yeats's reasons for putting Napoleon and Shakespeare in the same phase may be stated briefly: in a scene of diversity or fragmentation, Unity of Being having long since vanished with the passing of the Renaissance, both men seek to project a dramatization of themselves, which helps to bring about a semblance of the old unity, but it is only a semblance. Shakespeare dramatizes himself through the personae of his plays, whereas Napoleon becomes a dramatic character in his own life. He sees "himself as Alexander moving to the conquest of the East," and, being "a man of action," he desires to accomplish great things, to achieve success, to make a name for himself. Yeats's emphasis is on Napoleon's externalization of himself. Lacking an inner life, he has only a public image. And this obsessive self-dramatization alters his own personality, for he gradually becomes the mask that he has donned.

In Emerson's view the outstanding feature of Napoleon is his ambition: he is callous and inhuman, not bloodthirsty, but "pitiless."

12 *E&I*, p. 368.

Having once fixed his sights on a particular object, he must obtain it regardless of the human suffering involved. His passion for stage-effect makes him see himself as a luminary in the heavens: "I must dazzle and astonish" is his constant self-reminder. Although influenced by Emerson's essay, Yeats, in his examination of Napoleon, is not conditioned by the moral implication of his deeds. To Emerson, Napoleon is totally unscrupulous, selfish, perfidious, and an impostor and a rogue. Yeats's Napoleon may or may not be any of these, because Yeats is not concerned with pronouncing moral judgment on the people who illustrate his scheme.

Yeats's depiction of Shakespeare as belonging to Phase 20 owes something to Emerson, but the resemblances are not as pronounced as they are in his treatment of Napoleon. Yeats, after all, did not need to go to Emerson in order to formulate an opinion on Shakespeare. For Emerson, Shakespeare is the product of his times. He is not original (as, for Emerson, no great poet is) but writes out of a tradition and a common heritage intelligible to all. He provided his age with what it wanted. The people wanted plays, and so he gave them plays. Thus his Shakespeare is almost featureless, more a result than a cause, his greatness not an individual possession but a collective outcome. Yeats too, as we have noted, emphasizes the lack of personality in Shakespeare but points out that while effacing his own personality, Shakespeare at the same time creates himself anew in his dramatic projections, and, like Napoleon, who saw himself as another Alexander, he exults in "an outward flowing, that drenches all with grease and oil" so that we have few biographical facts concerning him. Emerson had likewise declared that "Shakespeare is the only biographer of Shakespeare; and even he can tell nothing, except to the Shakespeare in us."

As is customary with Emerson, he concludes his essay on Shakespeare with a list of complaints against him. After stating that Shakespeare "loves virtue, not for its obligation, but for its grace"—a handsome compliment—Emerson quite inexplicably accuses him of having failed to explore "the virtue which resides in these symbols." He goes on to say that Shakespeare "converted the elements which waited on his command, into entertainments. He was master of the revels to mankind."

Emerson then likens Shakespeare to one who wields power over the planets, but who uses this power simply to entertain a crowd that has come to witness a fireworks display. When Yeats quotes Emerson's pronouncement on Shakespeare as "master of the revels to mankind," he agrees with it, but his argument is qualified by the clause, "as Emerson thought Shakespeare was," implying that, to Yeats, Shakespeare was actually much more. Emerson's tone is derogatory. Shakespeare to him is a disappointment, and the world still awaits its poet-priest, its Shakespeare and Swedenborg in one man. Emerson's discontent with Shakespeare's personality, which lacked the reformer's zeal, is quite unlike Yeats's acceptance and even approval of it. For though Yeats contrasts Shakespeare's retiring nature with Ben Jonson's belligerence, his sympathy and admiration are reserved for Shakespeare who "created the most passionate art that exists" and who "was the greatest of modern poets."[13] Clearly, J. B. Yeats's designation of his son's talent being "benign" was not a father's empty boast.

Yeats was familiar with Jonson's own works, was greatly interested in seeing his plays performed, and was fully aware of Jonson's own outspoken regard for Shakespeare. Between 1900 and 1910, when Yeats visited Stratford several times, his remarks indicate a growing interest in Jonson.[14] In 1900 Yeats refers to Shakespeare's conversation as reported by Jonson ("one bull is all that remains of Shakespeare's talk") and says that, from this bull, we might erroneously conclude that Shakespeare and his contemporaries did not take their art seriously and conversed about it flippantly. According to Yeats, however, this was simply a façade, for they did have a theory of art, a philosophy, and a critical approach. Here Yeats argues that one of the reasons why England has ceased to create great art is that the modern artist lacks a critical and philosophical rationale.[15] A year later, in "At Stratford-on-Avon,"

13   *Vis*, p. 153.

14   See *Letters*, pp. 450, 478–79, 664–65, 671; *Ex*, p. 181. For a detailed examination of Yeats's interest in Jonson, see T. McAlindon, "Yeats and the English Renaissance," *PMLA*, LXXXII (May, 1967), 164–69.

15   *E&I*, p. 153. Yeats is thinking of Jonson's famous swipe at Shakespeare: "Many times hee fell into those things, could not escape laughter: As when hee said in the person of Caesar, one speaking to him; *Caesar thou dost me wrong.* He re-

he stresses the necessity for every artist to commit himself to a dominant point of view, to subscribe to some particular myth, even as "Shakespeare's myth . . . describes a wise man who was blind from very wisdom, and an empty man who thrust him from his place."

But Yeats's familiarity with Jonson's comments on Shakespeare goes further than this. In 1901 he mentions Jonson's observations on the extravagance of Shakespeare's conversation; whereas Jonson reacted negatively, Yeats believed that this extravagance was a sure sign of true creative power, an ingredient shared by the Irish, whose conversation, like that of Shakespeare, was full of "reckless abandonment and naturalness."[16] Then in September, 1906, Yeats wrote to Bullen that he was "deep in Ben Jonson" and inquired if he felt that Jonson intended his portrait of Virgil in *Poetaster* to stand for Shakespeare, and not, as was generally believed by scholars, for Chapman. Yeats adds that he finds it difficult to believe that the dull plays written by Chapman "could have made Jonson say as he does that whatever event of life came upon one, one could find appropriate words for it in the writings of 'Virgil.' "[17] In Jonson's *Poetaster,* which centers on the conflict between poets and men of affairs, a subject dear to Yeats, Caesar's sympathies are entirely with the poets, and Virgil is appraised thus in Caesar's presence:

> That, which he hath writ,
> Is with such iudgement, labour'd, and distill'd
> Through all the needfull vses of our liues,
> That could a man remember but his lines,
> He should not touch at any serious point,
> But he might breathe his spirit out of him.
>
> [V, i, 118–23]

plyed: *Caesar did never wrong but with just cause* and such like: which were ridiculous" (*Ben Jonson,* ed. C. H. Herford and P. and E. Simpson [Oxford, 1925–52], VIII, 584).

16 *Ex,* p. 81.

17 *Letters,* p. 479. Sidney Lee, whose book Yeats may have read (see n. 5 above), argues that Jonson's tribute is to Shakespeare, not Chapman. Herford and Simpson, however, favor Chapman. Today, scholars are inclined to be skeptical of such speculation. When Poel produced *Poetaster* in London on April 26, 1916, Virgil appeared as Shakespeare: " 'The Stratford bard walked in alive,' reports an onlooker, 'among the courtiers of Augustus' " (*Ben Jonson,* I, 432–37). Yeats could well have seen this production.

Even though Yeats posed the issue of the identity of Virgil to Bullen in the form of a question, he was evidently already convinced that Jonson praised Shakespeare, not Chapman. This conviction remained with him, for ten years later he makes a further reference to the play in which he interprets Virgil to be Jonson's disguise for Shakespeare.

In "Discoveries" (1906) Yeats refers to the play by drawing attention to Caesar's noble lines on the poetic imagination that can illuminate a man's life and give added glory to his other achievements:

> To shew, your titles are not writ on posts,
> Or hollow statues which the best men are,
> Without Promethean stuffings reacht from heaven!
>
> [V, i, 13–16]

Yeats then gives examples of this Promethean fire, without which even the best of men is "but a hollow statue," and finds it ablaze in Shakespeare, Tintoretto, men whose "minds were never quiescent" but "always in exaltation."[18] The tremendous creative energy of a Shakespeare could suitably answer to Jonson's description of the condition of inspiration.

Some years later, in *Per Amica Silentia Lunae* (1917), Yeats again refers with approval to Jonson's Virgil in *Poetaster*, whose presence he felt was unmistakably intended as a veiled compliment to Shakespeare. "Surely of the passionate dead we can but cry in words Ben Jonson meant for none but Shakespeare: 'So rammed' are they 'with life they can but grow in life with being,' "[19] Yeats declares, seeing in Shakespeare's burgeoning creativity, as depicted by Jonson, an appropriate description of the continuing desire to create evinced by the still restless spirits of dead writers. The passage from Jonson that Yeats is thinking of derives from Horace's opinion of Virgil:

> His learning labours not the schoole-like glosse,
> That most consists in echoing wordes, and termes,
> And soonest wins a man an empty name:
> Nor any long, or far-fetcht circumstance,
> Wrapt in the curious generalties of artes:
> But a direct, and *analyticke* summe

18 *E&I*, pp. 278, 279.
19 *Myth*, p. 360; see also *Au*, p. 291.

Of all the worth and first effects of artes.
And for his *poesie,* 'tis so ramm'd with life,
That it shall gather strength of life, with being,
And liue hereafter, more admir'd, then now.

[V, i, 129–38]

The notion of Shakespeare as a self-begotten genius, not a pedantic scholar like the bald heads that edit and annotate the lines of young men, is repeatedly present in Yeats's attitude toward Shakespeare. Jonson's famous lines in his panegyric on Shakespeare prefixed to the First Folio—lines that Yeats nowhere mentions but that no doubt he knew very well—recognize Shakespeare's genius as having outdistanced erudition ("small Latine, and lesse Greeke") and established its own identity.

Toward the close of the panegyric, it will be recalled that Jonson regards Shakespeare's volume of plays as fit offspring of his genius, perhaps a consolatory gesture to the shade of Shakespeare for the death of his only son, Hamnet, in 1596:

Looke how the fathers face
Liues in his issue, euen so, the race
Of *Shakespeares* minde, and manners brightly shines
In his well torned, and true-filed lines.

The idea of a poet's verses substituting for a flesh-and-blood heir was a common Elizabethan one that Shakespeare too had made the theme of several sonnets. It is likely that Yeats had this conceit in mind when in "Pardon, Old Fathers" he rather defiantly tells his lusty ancestors that the only progeny he can boast of is his volume of verse:

Although I have come close on forty-nine,
I have no child, I have nothing but a book,
Nothing but that to prove your blood and mine.

Regardless of the rightness or wrongness of Yeats's assumption that Jonson had intended his Virgil to represent Shakespeare, Yeats's own attitude toward Shakespeare is unambiguous: Shakespeare exemplified the abundance and verve that Yeats, at this time in his career, felt was essential in order that artistic creativity should flourish. Later, it is true, he came to feel that even Shakespeare's abundance at times overstepped the limits of artistic decorum (as, for example, in the blinding of Gloucester) but even this was far preferable to an attenuated art, the art of his contemporaries. Fecundity could be controlled whereas paucity was irredeemable.

During the decade, however, of his most active involvement with the fortunes of the Abbey Theatre, even while advocating a "joyful, fantastic, extravagant, whimsical, beautiful, resonant, and altogether reckless" form of drama, Yeats did not repudiate the necessity to observe form and exercise control. He recommended "the severe discipline of French and Scandinavian drama" rather than "Shakespeare's luxuriance"; and even while insisting on extravagance in dialogue, holding up Falstaff as a magnificent example, he cautioned his fellow Irish dramatists by saying, "Let us learn construction from the masters."[20] Perhaps this dualistic posture of Yeats is best seen in his appraisal of Victor Hugo's book on Shakespeare, *William Shakespeare* (1864), which he read sometime before 1890. In his essay *A Scholar Poet* (1890), a review of William Watson's poems, Yeats exalts the poet's role as being prophetic, "extravagant, exuberant, mystical," and deprecates those who would like to see him a handmaid to society, meek and restrained. Yeats opens his essay with a striking quotation from Hugo's book in which poetic fervor is praised and sobriety sarcastically denounced: " 'He is sober, discreet, temperate. He can be trusted.' Is this the description of a domestic? No; of a poet."[21] Hugo is here ridiculing the critical attitude that would invest Shakespeare, of all poets, with sobriety and discretion.

Yeats's early enthusiasm for Hugo's frothy praise of Shakespeare gave place, however, to a more guarded approach. Ten years later, by 1901, Yeats had come to feel that the poet should not be like a meteor hurtling away on its own independent and unfettered career, but, on the other hand, constantly draw on an "unwritten tradition" even as a magician links himself to "a cult with ancient technicalities and mysteries." And, like the magician, the poet should be "fond of words and verses that keep half their secret to themselves." Yeats here recalls his early excessive enthusiasm for Hugo on Shakespeare by saying that it then seemed to him "that it did not matter what tune one wrote to, so

20   *Ex,* pp. 169, 80, 150, 166.
21   *New Island,* pp. 204–5.

long as that gusty energy came often enough and strongly enough. And I delighted in Victor Hugo's book upon Shakespeare, because he abused critics and coteries and thought that Shakespeare wrote without care or premeditation and to please everybody."[22] Shakespeare as an untamed genius warbling his native wood-notes wild was the generally cherished nineteenth-century concept that Milton and even Ben Jonson had helped to disseminate. But Yeats, though recognizing an occasional lapse of unity and compression in Shakespeare, would have nothing to do with this oversimplified and slightly patronizing approach. In 1921 Yeats could regard the fabric of Shakespeare's plays as consisting of the raw stuff of life, as well as book learning: the language of Shakespeare, "its warp fresh from field and market—if the woof were learned." Some years later, in a letter to Monk Gibbon, Yeats said he thought "that both Dante and Milton and perhaps Shakespeare toiled through libraries of works with the conscious purpose of learning to think poetically, which is much the same as believing in some scheme of the world."[23] For Yeats to reject the then fairly popular idea of Shakespeare as simply fancy's child, a natural genius, and to class him with Dante and Milton, both men of weighty classical learning, provides a remarkable insight into Yeats's impression of Shakespeare.

Still, Yeats's revision of an earlier attitude toward Hugo should not be taken to mean a total recantation of his previous concurrence with Hugo's views on Shakespeare. He continued to characterize Shakespeare's art as "abundant, extravagant, exuberant," and maintained all his life that this is what art had to be in order to be art. And it is even possible that in his short essay "The Emotion of Multitude" (1903), Yeats draws to some extent on his reading of Hugo on Shakespeare. In the essay Yeats shows how the Shakespearean subplot is often a shadow of the main plot: "Lear's shadow is in Gloucester, who also has ungrateful

22   *E&I*, pp. 6, 10, 5. During the period of his interest in the Noh drama of Japan, Yeats dismissed the "magniloquence of Hugo" as vulgar (*E&I*, p. 236). He also deplored the way in which he and his contemporaries were "deafened and blinded . . . by that art of Hugo that made the old simple writers seem but as brown bread and water" (*E&I*, p. 356).

23   *Au*, p. 87; Monk Gibbon, *The Masterpiece and the Man: Yeats as I Knew Him* (New York, 1959), p. 137.

children"; and in *Hamlet,* "the murder of Hamlet's father and the
sorrow of Hamlet are shadowed in the lives of Fortinbras and Ophelia
and Laertes, whose fathers, too, have been killed."[24] Hugo had also
drawn attention to this recurrence, citing as examples the same plays
that Yeats refers to, and claiming with evident self-satisfaction that he
was the first critic to notice this "peculiarity," "the most eminent commentators and critics" having failed to do so. Yeats also employs this
device in several of his plays, most notably in *On Baile's Strand,* where
Fool and Blind Man are lesser counterparts of Cuchulain and Conchubar, respectively.[25]

Again, Yeats must have approved of Hugo's stressing that Shakespeare's diversity, as contrasted with Greek unity, was a characteristic
feature of the Elizabethan Age, but that since each age expresses itself
uniquely, the modern theater ought to imitate neither Shakespeare nor
the Greeks.

Still, it is clear that Hugo's book on Shakespeare, in spite of these
interesting observations that must have held Yeats's attention, was not
for him a work that would have had lasting importance. It confirmed
some of his earlier views, but Hugo's torrential bombast, sweeping
generalizations, and lack of precise criticism could not have appealed
to Yeats. Secure in his own reputation, Hugo throws out opinions on
Shakespeare, Moses, Job, Aeschylus, and Michelangelo with breezy
abandon, a total contrast to Yeats's method, which is always one of carefully considered particularity. Rarely does Yeats refer to Shakespeare
without citing a specific example from his works to substantiate his point.

A book that upheld Yeats's belief in the continuity of art was Hein-
rich Heine's *Shakespeare's Maidens and Women* (1839). Opposed to
Hugo's concept of Shakespeare as a blazing meteor that suddenly flashed
across the firmament, Heine considers Shakespeare's art an integral
part of an old and great tradition. In his section on Lady Macbeth, he

24   *E&I*, pp. 105, 215–16.

25   Interestingly enough, as early as 1904 it had been noticed by the first
critic to write a book on Yeats that his "two rude clowns . . . must owe something
of their fantastic foolery and glimmerings of sense to Shakespearean creations of the
same kind" (Horatio Sheafe Krans, *William Butler Yeats and the Irish Literary
Revival* [New York, 1904], p. 145).

compares the ancient legends concerning Macbeth with the play as Shakespeare wrote it, paying particular attention to the witches, whom Shakespeare has transformed. He points out that in the old Norse legend "those wondrous women are plainly Valkyries, terrible divinities of the air," but that Shakespeare changed them into mischief-making witches who delude men with false promises and half-truths. Shorn of their dignity as personifications of the fates, Shakespeare's witches are for Heine petty, mean, spiteful; accordingly, Macbeth's ruin is "not a pre-determined necessity" as in the ancient fate, but is, in fact, his own choice. Man is not the victim of forces operating from without. He is responsible for his own ruination. To Heine, then, Shakespeare has translated the old heathen notion of fate into the Christian one of man's individual responsibility for his acts. Concluding his argument that all great art is deeply rooted in certain antecedents, Heine declares that Shakespeare, after all, could not entirely free himself from the old heathen view of man's being a puppet in the hands of malign forces, and so, despite certain despicable and mean traits that mark his witches, they remain on the whole "strikingly grand."

Yeats adverts with approval to Heine's placement of Shakespeare in the context of a continuing tradition, observing that "the old images, the old emotions, awakened again to overwhelming life, like the gods Heine tells of, by the belief and passion of some new soul, are the only masterpieces." After his brief infatuation with Hugo's book on Shakespeare, Yeats had increasingly come to feel that "works of art are always begotten by previous works of art," and that all art is "descended from savage ceremonies taught amid what perils and by what spirits to naked savages."[26]

There was much else in Heine's book on Shakespeare that must have appealed to Yeats. Like Yeats, Heine had exalted Merry England, which flourished in "gleaming color, masque merriment [and] transcendent-dreaming passion." Life was then still a gay tournament, Heine maintains, and Shakespeare appeared at a time when England was "lighted by the last rays of setting chivalry." So also Yeats, in *A Vision*,

26 *E&I*, pp. 352–53.

sees the Renaissance as "the breaking of the Christian synthesis," with
Shakespeare uneasily poised between the two worlds of medievalism and
modernity. Heine regarded the Renaissance as an age in which the loss
of faith was still incipient, for though Roman Catholicism was on its
way out as regarded doctrine, "it existed as yet with all its magic in
men's hearts." Again, like Yeats, who detested "the triumph of the
Puritan and the merchant" that came with the rise of Cromwell, Heine
repeatedly deprecates the "absolute Puritan dominion" which, long
after, had a cold, deadening influence and not only shattered the golden
age of Elizabethan literature, but reduced it to total oblivion.

Yeats's mistrust of the Renaissance, for being the age in which the
rationalistic mind displaced the imagination and poured contempt on
ancient myth, persisted with him all his life in spite of occasional fluctua-
tions. In later years he asseverated his hatred of materialism and at the
same time affirmed the existence of an immaterial world controlled,
dominated, and in fact created, by the spirit. The existence of such a
transcendent world was recognized effortlessly by primitive man, but
after the Renaissance that recognition faded, Yeats believed, and Newton, Hobbes, and Locke—"Locke sank into a swoon; / The Garden died"—
began to rule men's minds. Berkeley was for Yeats the great corrective
to this precipitate movement, and his Preface to J. M. Hone's and M. M.
Rossi's book, *Bishop Berkeley*, is a powerful statement of his own accord
with Berkeley's idealism.[27] In the Preface Yeats turns to Coleridge on
Shakespeare for a clarification of his own understanding of Berkeley's
philosophy, but before we consider Yeats's reading of Coleridge, it is
necessary to glance at what Yeats felt about Berkeley.

Yeats's Preface opens with an arresting statement: "Imagination,
whether in literature, painting, or sculpture, sank after the death of
Shakespeare; supreme intensity had passed to another faculty."[28] We
have noted earlier how repelled Yeats was by the realistic mode of
apprehending Shakespeare that Dowden, Beerbohm Tree, and others

27 For a thorough investigation of Yeats and Berkeley, see Torchiana, chapter 6.

28 *E&I*, p. 396.

had so effectively popularized; now Yeats begins his Preface, in which he earnestly vindicates the Berkeleyan stand against materialism, by declaring that with Shakespeare's death, imagination, or the world of ideas, was suppressed by the rising tide of intellect in its most destructive form. "The first great imaginative wave had sunk, the second had not yet risen." "Descartes, Locke, and Newton took away the world and gave us its excrement instead," Yeats elsewhere angrily charges, but then softening, adds, "Berkeley restored the world. . . . [He] has brought back to us the world that only exists because it shines and sounds. A child, smothering its laughter because the elders are standing round, has opened once more the great box of toys." While applauding Berkeley's rejection of empiricism and his insistence on man's being the creator of his own world, Yeats in his Preface goes beyond Berkeley: he points out that Berkeley, being a bishop, had to be wary and so "deliberately refused to define personality, and dared not say that Man in so far as he is himself, in so far as he is a personality, reflects the whole act of God; his God and Man seem cut off from one another."[29] Accordingly, Yeats's dominant personalities in "Long-legged Fly," Caesar, Helen, and Michelangelo, have minds that "move upon silence" as they give to history a new direction and, by so doing, share in some sense the divine essence that moved upon the face of the waters.

Thus, for Yeats, the artist's mind at the moment of creation is not far removed from that of God when the earth was created. Yeats discerns this thought in Berkeley, too, but explains that he could not state it explicitly: "Though he could not describe mystery—his age had no fitting language—his suave glittering sentences suggest it; we feel perhaps for the first time that eternity is always at our heels or hidden from our eyes by the thickness of a door." Yeats had been earlier moving toward the position of regarding the external world as a kind of mental construct created by the collective minds of men, as his above-mentioned letters to Sturge Moore concerning Ruskin's enigmatic black cat clearly reveal. There he had argued that "things are more or less 'real' according to the extent to which they are capable of being shared with

29 *E&I*, p. 399; *Ex*, p. 325; *E&I*, p. 408.

others."[30] Yeats concludes his Preface with the statement that Berkeley too had come round to thinking of perception as

> some always undefined apprehension of spirits and their relations. Looking for a clue, I think of Coleridge's contrast between Juliet's nurse and Hamlet, remember that Shakespeare drew the nurse from observation, from passive sense-impression, but Hamlet, the Court, the whole work of art, out of himself in a pure indivisible act.

Significantly, Yeats begins his Preface with the death of Shakespeare marking the end of an era; he concludes with the idea of Shakespeare as creator, bringing into being a phenomenological world which is an extension of his own mind, drawn "out of himself in a pure indivisible act." Yeats says that in his later writings, Berkeley too had thought of God as a pure, indivisible act which "creates passive 'ideas'—sensations—thrusts them as it were outside itself." That is, as God creates the world by projecting his thoughts and ideas outside of himself, we human beings also create our worlds from within our own minds. This mind, autonomous and gestatory, Yeats likens to the artistic imagination working at white heat, to Shakespeare when he drew Hamlet, but not to Shakespeare when he drew the nurse, because the nurse is merely the product of observation, of an empirical response to surrounding data.

Coleridge's insistence that the Shakespearean universe is an imaginative construct, not simply a duplication of nature, came close to the Berkeleyan belief that man is the author of his own world. That Yeats, in his Preface to Berkeley, should turn to Coleridge on Shakespeare is therefore not surprising. Coleridge in his *Lectures and Notes on Shakespeare and Other English Poets* says of the nurse that she "is the nearest of anything in Shakespeare to a direct borrowing from mere observation"; and of Hamlet he says: "Now one of Shakespeare's modes of creating character is, to conceive any one intellectual or moral faculty in morbid excess, and then to place himself, Shakespeare, thus mutilated or diseased, under given circumstances." Yeats, we should notice, considers Coleridge's remark on Hamlet an apt illustration not so much of

---

30 *E&I*, p. 403; *Yeats and TSM*, p. 64. See *Identity*, pp. 236–38, for Yeats's "Seven Propositions" concerning reality, and *Letters*, pp. 713–14, for his agreement with Whitehead's theory "that nothing exists but 'organisms,' or minds."

Berkeley's thought as of his own thought, which tended to outdistance Berkeley. To Yeats, Shakespeare's greatest plays are the product of a solipsism that does not owe its veracity to an external referent, but is a self-born mocker of man's enterprise. Far from being a trite reflection of life, his plays transcend it; and by asserting their individuality they become their own lawgiver as well as judge. Shakespeare, Yeats felt all along, created a separate reality that existed outside of mundane reality as we know it, and this was not to be regarded as simply an intensified form of human experience, but at moments could even provide us with a glimpse of reality beyond the grave. Consider, for example, his reference in *A Vision*, under Phase 20, to what Thomas Lake Harris, the now little-known nineteenth-century American prophet and visionary, wrote of Shakespeare: " 'Often the hair of his head stood up and all life became the echoing chambers of the tomb.' "[31]

Although Yeats's reference to Harris is only in passing, Harris' section on Shakespeare must have struck an echoing chord in Yeats, as his recollection of this excerpt attests. In a passage remarkable for its "now vague, now vulgar, now magnificent style," as Yeats well describes it, Harris speaks of Shakespeare as being one who "had seasons of profound gloom, when his spirituality would stir from its deeps: then the long arcades of history would seem as the echoing chambers of the tombs, till he would imagine specters and the hair of his flesh would arise for terror." For Harris, Shakespeare was fascinated by the unseen world: "he shared in the instinctive fear, that was then diffused throughout Christendom, of the terrors of the unseen world." That Yeats, as he says, remembered this passage after so long a time is not surprising, for Harris' comments on Shakespeare's personality and genius for looking beyond outward appearance into a more profound reality would not, one feels, go against the grain of Yeats's impressions of Shakespeare. To Harris the characters and situations of the Shakespearean universe are not simply representations of realistic data, but phantoms from a realm lurking behind the visible world.

31 *The Wisdom of the Adepts, Esoteric Science in Human History* (Fountain Grove, 1884), p. 442. One copy of this exceedingly scarce—and fascinating—work is in the Boston Public Library.

Harris sees Shakespeare as "the most profoundly secretive of men"; as one who regarded nature as the loam for his art, for "all were fishes for him that came into his net." Harris considers Shakespeare a detached spectator of life, an artist first and only after that a man, for though he "would game and drink, bandy jokes, argue, play a part, seeming to enact the fool with the rest of the jolly company," this was to him but a study. Yeats's Shakespeare too, as we shall see, is, as a man, elusive; his personality remains indecipherable from his plays. But Harris, despite such eloquent praise for Shakespeare, faults him for one deficiency: he lacks spirituality. "All this greatness was tarnished, all this splendor blurred and dimmed by his avoidance of his own deeper life," Harris laments. Thus for Harris, as for Emerson, Shakespeare fritters away his profound insights in the production of works of art, rather than employing them profitably in the exploration of spiritual realities. Instead of writing wasteful plays, Harris and Emerson would have Shakespeare leave for posterity a treatise on his spiritual discoveries—a view which Yeats would hardly have concurred in, although he did agree with Harris' view of Shakespeare as a visionary.

Coleridge too had emphasized the ideal nature of Shakespeare's characters and had insisted that we are too often deluded into regarding them as real, flesh-and-blood figures, whereas we should see them as timeless beings in whom "there is neither past nor future, but all is permanent in the very energy of nature." So also, Yeats reminds us in "Lapis Lazuli" that, regardless of the enormity of the tragedy confronting them, Hamlet, Lear, Ophelia, and Cordelia are not subject to the human proneness to weep:

> Yet they, should the last scene be there,
> The great stage curtain about to drop,
> If worthy their prominent part in the play,
> Do not break up their lines to weep.

Forever outside of human emotion, these incredible beings depict its agony with unruffled composure.

Yeats must have read Coleridge on Shakespeare some time before 1910, for in a letter to his father written in that year, he declares, "Juliet has personality, her Nurse has character," an observation that seems to derive from Coleridge's remarks on the nurse. Again, it is possible that Yeats's early attitude toward Hamlet was to some extent influenced by Coleridge's analysis of him as one to whom "the external world, and all its incidents and objects, were comparatively dim, and of no interest in themselves." In 1897 Yeats wrote of Hamlet that he saw the body's will and pleasure "perishing away, and sighed," and in 1901 he described Hamlet as one "who saw too great issues everywhere to play the trivial game of life."[32] But toward the end of his life, as we shall see in the following chapter, Yeats changed his position on Hamlet and came to regard him as a man of action rather than a dreamer, a position that Coleridge would undoubtedly have found unacceptable.

Another Shakespearean example that Yeats used, perhaps with Coleridge in mind, occurs in his consideration of the contrast between art and life, the former being a complete arc, the latter remaining incomplete. In Romeo "we see all his arc, for in literature we need completed things."[33] Coleridge too had analyzed Romeo as imperfect at the play's beginning, but groping his way toward the completion of his nature—first in his inadequate involvement with Rosaline, and finally in his successful union with Juliet.

Despite Yeats's careful reading of the critics, his Shakespeare does not seem to have been created by them; he himself observed, "For we do not seek truth in argument or in books but clarification of what we already believe."[34] In his reading he either found a confirmation of convictions already held and so did not hesitate to use the evidence they furnished to reinforce his own position, or he reacted against a particular approach and made this the starting point for a forceful presentation of his own views on Shakespeare. His attitude toward Shakespeare emerges from the encounter, and since he changed his ground while attempting to establish a settled relationship with Shakespeare, these changes provide at the same time an extraordinary picture of Yeats's own development as poet and thinker.

32 *Letters,* p. 548; *Myth,* p. 274; *E&I,* p. 107.
33 *Au,* p. 288.
34 *Ex,* p. 310.

3

Shakespeare in Yeats's History Book

Hamlet. What's his weapon?
Osric. Rapier and dagger.
Hamlet. That's two of his weapons: but, well.

. . . .

Horatio. You will lose this wager, my lord.
Hamlet. I do not think so. Since he went into
  France, I have been in continual practice. I
  shall win at the odds.

　　　　　　　　　　　　　　　　　　—Hamlet

Shakespeare himself foreshadowed a symbolic
change, that is, a change in the whole
temperament of the world, for though he
called his Hamlet "fat" and even "scant of
breath," he thrust between his fingers agile
rapier and dagger.

　　　　　　　　　　Yeats, *Autobiography*

ᖴOR YEATS, a pioneer in the revival of poetic drama, which had
suffered three hundred years of neglect, Shakespeare was at once
comrade and rival. Yeats's relationship with Shakespeare changed often
before about 1920. His posture was neither one of reverent homage like
Matthew Arnold's, nor one of brash defiance like Shaw's, but an index
of his own development as poet, dramatist, and critic. His changing
attitudes toward Shakespeare and the Renaissance reflect the stages

through which he passed from his early work to his *Last Poems, On the Boiler,* and *Purgatory.*

Throughout his life he viewed the world as consisting of opposites, but, whereas the early Yeats tended to see these opposites as distinct entities, the later Yeats pictured them burrowing into one another like interlocking gyres and effacing each other's identity in the conflict. Evidently, a struggle in which the combatants are almost indistinguishable because so fiercely engaged becomes far more stirring than a simple exchange of hostilities from a distance. An example of Yeats's approach to history as a simple polarization of forces may be seen in an early essay of his, "The Autumn of the Body" (1895), which also happens to be an extraordinary blueprint for *A Vision,* which appeared thirty years later. In the essay he traces the progressive fracturing of unity from the first poets of the *Kalevala* to "Homer's preoccupation with things"; next, to Virgil, who was yet more excited by external objects than was Homer; then to Dante, who further weakens unity with his "traffic among many things"; and so to Shakespeare, who "shattered the symmetry of verse and of drama that he might fill them with things and their accidental relations to one another." The impingement of the external world on the artist's private vision becomes progressively violent. Yeats next considers Wordsworth and Browning as inheritors of the destruction; they carry forward the fissiparous process that Shakespeare ratified so emphatically.[1]

Like Ruskin, Yeats here sees history as a steady declension, with the Renaissance marking a decisive stage in the process. After the Renaissance, the declivity becomes yet more steep. What the essay also implies is that the further back one goes, the better the art produced, so that history becomes a simple slide rule for measuring excellence. Shakespeare then is necessarily inferior to Dante, Virgil, and Homer. As a young poet and dramatist seeking to establish his identity, Yeats seems to have rightly sensed that his first and most formidable adversary was Shakespeare. Understandably, he was soon dissatisfied with this position and drastically revised it, though he never repudiated it altogether. A few

1 *E&I*, p. 192.

years later Yeats wrote to George Russell that "The Autumn of the Body" was an inadequate interpretation of literary history. His own powerful response to Shakespeare must have convinced him that the theory was too mechanical to be sound, that artistic greatness could not be reduced to a simple historical formula. Accordingly, in "The Celtic Element in Literature" (1897), he classified Shakespeare with "the old writers." Yeats evidently felt that any diagram of history which denied to Shakespeare an exalted position was suspect. Now, instead of being viewed as an iconoclast of an established and unified tradition, he has been given a place of honor within that tradition. But despite this back-pedaling, Yeats still has reservations. He also gives examples of Shakespeare's having "looked at nature without ecstasy . . . in the modern way."[2] Many years later, with a touch of irony, he was to tell of the schoolchildren he visited who were learning "to cut and sew, be neat in everything / In the best modern way."

At the time Yeats wrote the essay, he was anxious to infuse his work with Irish nationalism, though not to the exclusion of a wider appeal. In the essay Shakespeare is shown to possess the Celtic consciousness, the antithesis to the reductive modern mind inaugurated by the Renaissance. In addition, Yeats felt strongly that myths were essential if modern man were once again to comprehend the world in its fullness, free of the insularity that science conferred on every ancient concept. The "conviction that the world was now but a bundle of fragments possessed me without ceasing," Yeats declared, and therefore sought in myths for a common reservoir from which poet and artist could draw. Only by means of their restoration would it be possible to reunify an age in which music and verse, speech and music, painting and religion had parted company.[3]

Yeats's emphasis during this period is on Shakespeare's identification with the primitive imagination. Helen, Deirdre, Lear, Mab, Puck, and Tristan are all "images of the primitive imagination," for life in those remote times, shaped and conditioned by the loneliness of great forests and the imminent danger of parting and death, found itself

2 *Letters*, p. 402; *E&I*, pp. 177–78.
3 *Au*, pp. 116–17.

naturally in communion with tragedy, not comedy.[4] In this essay, as in "The Autumn of the Body," the steady descent of art from the past to the present is maintained, but Shakespeare has been transferred, despite his chronological position, to a place among the old writers.

Yeats's references to Shakespeare during this period (the 1890s) are fairly general. He is clearly going his own way but feels that he should have the decency to tip his hat to Shakespeare as one among several respectable figures not to be ignored. The keen insights into Shakespearean particularities that he develops later are as yet absent: he reverently classifies Shakespeare with Homer, Aeschylus, Sophocles, and Dante, maintaining that they were actually "folk-lorists with musical tongues"; he calls attention to their universality of appeal and the catholicity of their outlook, but the predatory extraction of Shakespeare's uniqueness that he begins to display after the turn of the century, the ability to throw into relief Shakespeare's vision—these seem to be skills that stemmed from his visit to Stratford in 1901. Thus, Shakespeare and Dante are seen to belong to a time when unity held sway, when "philosophy and belief" prevailed, an attitude that Yeats was later to revise considerably with reference to Shakespeare.[5]

In later years Yeats himself recognized his early preoccupation with the homogeneity of the past: in "Four Years: 1887–1891," published in 1921, he describes his yearning during those years for a past era when the arts were unified, so that "poet and artist confined themselves gladly to some inherited subject-matter known to the whole people," or what he called Unity of Being. He states that he "thought constantly of Homer and Dante" as exemplifying this unity. Greatly influenced by William Morris at this time, Yeats says of him that he "never seemed to care greatly for any poet later than Chaucer and though I preferred Shake-

---

4 *E&I*, p. 182. See also *E&I*, pp. 176, 185–86; "The Message of the Folklorist," *UP*, p. 284, in which Yeats points out that Ariel's imprisonment in a cloven pine goes back to a legend thousands of years old. See also Yeats's record of his meeting with Joyce where he argued that great art like that of Homer and Shakespeare sprang from the union of folk imagination and the artist's individualism (*Identity*, p. 88).

5 See *UP*, p. 284; *Literary Ideals in Ireland: A Controversy between John Eglinton and WBY in the Saturday Issues of the Daily Express* (Dublin, May, 1899), p. 17; *UP*, p. 266.

speare to Chaucer I begrudged my own preference." He then traces the fracturing of sensibilities that took place in Europe "a little before Shakespeare's birth." Chaucer's abandonment of the melodious octosyllabic line for the more versatile and descriptive decasyllabic, the parting of painting from religion, and the rigid class barriers that rapidly developed—all these were symptomatic of the disappearance of Unity of Being.[6] Yeats's belief that the Renaissance was an age of disunity ("It was at the Renaissance that the devil got loose, and I do not know who is going to put him back in the bottle again"[7]) remained with him in one form or another all his life, but, as will be seen later, he did not bring to it a fanatic's condemnation. His admitted preference for Shakespeare to Chaucer was in itself a triumph of the spirit over the letter, his refusal to become the victim of an orthodoxy.

In 1900, in "The Symbolism of Poetry," Yeats's continuing uneasiness about Shakespeare, whose presence in the Renaissance tended to upset the otherwise fairly justifiable theory of steady deterioration, may be seen in his regarding Shakespeare as among "the writers of ancient times," though he quickly adds that he was "on the edge of modern times."[8] Clearly Shakespeare was proving troublesome. If the Renaissance was to be condemned, then Shakespeare would have to share in that condemnation, but Yeats was too honest a writer to make a theory, however attractive, prevail over his personal beliefs. As noted, it was not until 1921 that he was to state plainly the conflict between his personal feelings for Shakespeare and the tyranny of a theory.

Meanwhile he continued to think of Shakespeare as one born out

---

6 *Au*, pp. 116–17. For a useful survey of Morris' influence on Yeats, see T. McAlindon, "The Idea of Byzantium in William Morris and W. B. Yeats," *Modern Philology*, LXXII (May, 1967), 307–19. Yeats's attitude toward Morris was, however, not as admiring and uncritical as Professor McAlindon would like us to believe (see below, pp. 68, 70–71). Nor was Yeats entirely admiring of Byzantium. Thomas R. Whitaker, *Swan and Shadow: Yeats's Dialogue with History* (Chapel Hill, 1964), pp. 88–89, notes perceptively that Yeats's description of Byzantium in *A Vision*, pp. 279–80, is shot through with irony. See also Peter Faulkner, *William Morris and W. B. Yeats* (Dublin, 1962), pp. 10, 16–20.

7 Donald T. Torchiana and Glenn O'Malley, "Some New Letters from W. B. Yeats to Lady Gregory," *A Review of English Literature*, IV (July, 1963), 12–13. Yeats made this colorful observation in 1913.

8 *E&I*, p. 153.

of due time who exemplified in his best work the attitudes of a past era. In "At Stratford-on-Avon," written a year later, Yeats again pictures the Renaissance as a portentous development in the history of Western culture. He laments that even Shakespeare is infected by the contagion of foreign influences, particularly Italian, which the Greeks were preserved from; they could achieve a "simplicity and unity" that elude Shakespeare. And so, "no man, even though he be Shakespeare, can write perfectly when his web is woven of threads that have been spun in many lands," Yeats reasons. Despite his stature, Shakespeare is a victim of his times and one of the few survivors in the surrounding decay who

> wrote at a time when solitary great men were gathering to themselves the fire that had once flowed hither and thither among all men, when individualism in work and thought and emotion was breaking up the old rhythms of life, when the common people, sustained no longer by the myths of Christianity and of still older faiths, were sinking into the earth.[9]

Shakespeare seems to be here pictured as one of "the last romantics [who] chose for theme / Traditional sanctity and loveliness," a description of himself that Yeats gives us in "Coole Park and Ballylee, 1931," and an attitude toward the past that he never discarded but at the same time never allowed to become one of sentimental nostalgia. He could summon up that past era with emotion, but to evoke the brutality and disintegration of the present was no less essential to the statement of his vision. He also came to view Shakespeare with a new respect: not simply as a leftover from the past, but, rather, as the very spirit and expression of his own age, divided and tormented, yet full of ebullience.

Envisioning an Irish Renaissance in twentieth-century Ireland, Yeats gradually developed a new tolerance and even fervor for the Renaissance in Europe and England. In 1904 he could admit, "England and France . . . have great works of literature which have taken their subjects from foreign lands," a sign of restlessness; but he could immediately add, "Shakespeare observed his Roman crowds in London, and saw, one doubts not, somewhere in his own Stratford, the old man

---

9 *E&I*, pp. 109, 110. For other examples of Yeats's having felt during these years that Shakespeare belonged to "the old nation" and that his imagination was essentially inward looking, see *E&I*, pp. 279, 365.

that gave Cleopatra the asp," a sign of basic unity. Earlier, Yeats exhorts the Irish author to freely imbibe foreign influences, but at the same time to "really make all that he has seen and felt and known a portion of his own intense nature." This unique combination of diversity and unity in a state of fusion Yeats sees Shakespeare accomplishing, so that "we say of the men of the Renaissance, 'What a nature,' 'How much abundant life.' " Yeats concludes his essay saying that he sees an Ireland "where the tide of life is rising," poised on the threshold of its own Renaissance, and he likens this triumphant upsurge to the art of Shakespeare: "When Timon makes his epitaph, we feel no sorrow, for life herself has made one of her eternal gestures, has called up into our hearts her energy that is eternal delight." The energy, the personality displayed by the men of the Renaissance as symbolized in Timon's grand defeat, were becoming for Yeats prototypes of a historical recurrence that he prognosticated would soon sweep over Ireland; and as the high-water mark of the Renaissance in Europe was its drama as embodied in Shakespeare, so "in Ireland, where the tide of life is rising, we turn . . . to the imagination of personality—to drama, gesture."[10]

This shift in Yeats's attitude toward both Shakespeare and the Renaissance, discernible around 1904, is further ratified a few years later when Yeats seems to make a deliberate attempt to place Shakespeare in his historical context and interpret him as a manifestation of his own times. "Discoveries" (1906) concludes with a wish for the recovery of an age when poets wrote for both peasant and prince, when Chaucer could place the drunken Miller's tale alongside that of the virtuous Knight: realism and idealism harmoniously conjoined. Yeats suggests that with Shakespeare this combination once again is featured. As exponents of idealism he cites Shelley, Landor, and Villiers de l'Isle-Adam; as exponents of realism, Dickens and Molière. "Molière being but the master of common sense lived ever in the common daylight, but Shakespeare could not," for Shakespeare was not the hard-boiled realist Molière was, Yeats implies. At the same time, he was no detached idealist either, for "Shakespeare seems to bring us to the very market-

10 *Ex*, pp. 158–63.

place, when we remember Shelley's dizzy and Landor's calm disdain of usual daily things," Yeats argues. Neither idealist nor realist, Shakespeare comes close to combining "a Shelley and a Dickens in the one body."[11] By balancing two opposites against each other and locating Shakespeare at the pivotal point of equilibrium, thus denoting tension in repose, Yeats could see Shakespeare in a historical perspective that was later to find its most eloquent exposition in *A Vision*.

But even Shakespeare fails. After having given the accolade to him, Yeats says that he lacks perfect equilibrium, though he almost achieves it: "I have come to think of even Shakespeare's journeys to Rome or to Verona as the outflowing of an unrest, a dissatisfaction with natural interests, an unstable equilibrium of the whole European mind."[12] The word "even" indicates how close Yeats felt Shakespeare had come to that trembling possibility, but without quite succeeding.

Yeats now seems to deal more realistically with the problem of fitting Shakespeare into an era that destroyed past equilibrium, yet, paradoxically, could produce such a genius of which no other age, however unified, could boast. It became evident to him that the very turbulence of the Renaissance was an important and indispensable ingredient in Shakespeare's work; and so carefully structured is Yeats's historical map that he situates Shakespeare immediately after the climax of the Renaissance has been reached, explaining this with reference to the exceptional qualities in Shakespeare's plays.

II

In 1907 Yeats visited Italy. Perhaps, as Hone believes, the impact of this trip was responsible for his change in attitude toward the Renaissance.[13] Actually, three years before this, Yeats had expressly stated that

---

11   *E&I*, pp. 295–96. Another interesting combination denoting the equilibrium of the Renaissance is "a Herrick and Dr. Johnson in the same body," which was "not so difficult before the Mermaid closed its door," but, Yeats adds, it "is no longer possible" (*Au*, p. 177). See also W. B. Yeats, *The Unicorn from the Stars* (New York, 1908), p. ix, for the same kind of suggestion.

12   *E&I*, pp. 296–97.

13   Hone, p. 219. See also *Au*, p. 332, where Yeats mentions his first contact with Castiglione's book; *Man and Poet*, pp. 156, 170.

Shakespeare and his age were inextricably entangled; that the intensity of Shakespeare's art, surpassing reality, derived from the variety and abundance of the Renaissance, so that

> Richard II, as Shakespeare made him, could never have been born before the Renaissance, before the Italian influence, or even one hour before the innumerable streams that flowed in upon Shakespeare's mind, the innumerable experiences we can never know, brought Shakespeare to the making of him.

Here Yeats recognizes, in the very discordance of the Renaissance, the ingredients Shakespeare used to write his play. Even though the artist creates a world that is "the image of [his] secret thoughts," exemplified by Edgar Allan Poe, whose characters are bizarre and unreal, he also needs an external framework in which to fit his vision, and "he must know enough of the life of his country, or of history, to create this illusion."[14] Yeats therefore acknowledges the outward-looking mind as a distinctive Renaissance feature, fostered by no earlier age, and proves it by citing Shakespeare's Richard. It becomes evident that any attempt to establish fixed landmarks in the development of Yeats's thought is difficult. Although his attitudes change, the change is anticipated by hints, and the new attitude never completely abrogates the old.

We have seen that till now Yeats's admiration for Shakespeare induced him either to classify him among the established writers of antiquity, or to see him as a product of his turbulent age. In his essay "J. M. Synge and the Ireland of His Time" (1910), however, Yeats seems to be drawing away from Shakespeare, complaining of the lack of unity that marks his work. A few years later he prefers to identify himself (and the Irish) with the Japanese Noh dramatists, rather than with the Greeks and Romans, judging the Noh dramatists to be "more like us even than are Shakespeare and Corneille." But such a movement away from the abounding variety of Shakespeare's art was not sudden. As early as 1903, after his first rapture on discovering Nietzsche, "that strong enchanter," Yeats wrote to George Russell: "I feel about me and in me an impulse to create form, to carry the realization of beauty as far as possible." He wrote John Quinn at the same time, "I have

14 *Ex*, pp. 144–45.

always felt that the soul has two movements primarily: one to transcend forms, and the other to create forms. Nietzsche, to whom you have been the first to introduce me, calls these the Dionysiac and the Apollonic, respectively. I think I have to some extent got weary of that wild God Dionysus, and I am hoping that the Far-Darter will come in his place."[15] Not excess but restraint: this seems to be Yeats's growing concern from 1903 on.

His essay on Synge contains perhaps the severest attitude that he was ever to adopt toward Shakespeare. Here he contrasts the unity and the restraint of Greek drama "with the troubled life of Shakespearian drama," pointing out that in Sophocles, even when "Oedipus speaks out of the most vehement passions, he is conscious of the presence of the Chorus, men before whom he must keep up appearances. . . . Nobody is hurried or breathless. . . . Nothing happens before our eyes," and because of a "continuous exclusion of the animation of common life . . . thought remains lofty and language rich." Lacking the formal control of a conventionalized drama, Shakespeare's plays are, on the other hand, often too lifelike: on his stage "everything may happen, even the blinding of Gloucester"; he "has no formal check except what is implied in the slow, elaborate structure of blank verse, [and] obtains time for reverie by an often encumbering euphuism, and by such a loosening of his plot as will give his characters the leisure to look at life from without."[16] The "encumbering euphuism" and "loosening of his

15 *E&I*, pp. 333, 233; *Letters*, pp. 379, 402, 403. Yeats had read Nietzsche the previous year. (For a detailed discussion of Yeats's reactions to Nietzsche, see *Identity*, pp. 91–98.) It is of course probable that Yeats did not confine himself to Thomas Common's collection of scattered reflections by Nietzsche (*Nietzsche as Critic, Philosopher, Poet, and Prophet*, ed. Thomas Common [London, 1901]), which John Quinn had lent him (see B. L. Reid, *The Man from New York* [New York, 1968], p. 217), but went on to read a more inclusive edition of Nietzsche. We do know that Yeats again read Nietzsche "at the end of the nineteen-thirties" (*Man and Poet*, p. 294). Yeats would have been in partial agreement with certain of Nietzsche's attitudes toward Shakespeare (e.g., Nietzsche's view of Shakespeare as a "great barbarian," rather than a finished artist), but he would not, of course, have used Nietzsche's terminology. (For a fuller treatment of Nietzsche's views on Shakespeare, see George A. Morgan, *What Nietzsche Means* [New York, 1941], p. 214, n. 34.)

16 *E&I*, pp. 333–34. T. S. Eliot too could not condone the blinding of Gloucester on stage. See his essay "Seneca in Elizabethan Translation" (1927). For a brief summary of Eliot's early distaste for much in Shakespeare, see Phillip L. Marcus, "T. S. Eliot and Shakespeare," *Criticism*, IX (Winter, 1967), 64.

plot" are the inartistic devices Shakespeare employs to achieve what is already inherent in the very structure of Greek drama. Yeats seems here to disapprove of the too obvious maneuvers that Shakespeare occasionally makes his characters perform in order that they might be allowed to deliver their soliloquies undisturbed. Perhaps Yeats observes this "time for reverie" obtained by an "often encumbering euphuism" in Hamlet's abrupt dismissal of Rosencrantz and Guildenstern, "Aye, so, God be wi' ye! / Now I am alone," followed by his soliloquy "Oh, what a rogue and peasant slave am I!" or in his instructions to his companions to "go a little before," immediately after which he delivers his soliloquy "How all occasions do inform against me." For Yeats, at this point in his relationship with Shakespeare, the slow unfolding of Shakespeare's plots, combined with the side eddies of soliloquies that bring the action to a temporary halt, was a breach of structural unity and cohesion. Hamlet in his mother's chamber and Kent's provocative conduct with Oswald are two examples of what Yeats calls a "loosening" of Shakespeare's plots. Clearly Yeats is not questioning Shakespeare's greatness, but he is questioning the informal design of Shakespeare's plots and technique. Coming too close to life, Shakespearean drama lacks the artistic detachment of Greek drama. No longer venerating Shakespeare as one who harked back to the unity of the past, Yeats now sees all the disunity of the Renaissance epitomized in him.

There is no evidence that Yeats read Dr. Johnson on Shakespeare, but it would be astonishing if he had not.[17] His criticism of Shakespeare in the above passage bears distinctly the Johnsonian stamp. The lack of unity in Shakespeare never ceased to disturb Yeats. A few years later he was to pay a handsome tribute to Shakespeare, only to immediately modify it by giving priority to Sophocles over Shakespeare. Writing to Lady Gregory in 1919, he recalled: "You and I and Synge, not understanding the clock, set out to bring again the theatre of Shake-

17 Yeats mentions Dr. Johnson at least five times in his works, and each reference suggests a close acquaintance with Johnson's views. See *Au*, p. 177; *The Arrow*, I (February 23, 1907), 3; *Ex*, pp. 359, 362; and *Vis*, p. 296. Dr. Johnson, like Yeats, had objected strongly to the "extrusion" of Gloucester's eyes on stage, "an act too horrid to be endured in dramatic exhibition" (*Dr. Johnson on Shakespeare*, ed. W. K. Wimsatt [Harmondsworth, Middlesex, 1969], p. 126).

speare or rather perhaps of Sophocles." If laxity in construction is a flaw for Yeats, it is heightened in Shakespeare, whose entire world is an intensification of our actual world. "Do we not feel an unrest like that of travel itself when we watch those personages, more living than ourselves, amid so much that is irrelevant and heterogeneous . . . when we are carried from Rome to Venice, from Egypt to Saxon England, or in the one play from Roman to Christian mythology?" Yeats asks in 1925. Clearly, the variety and range of Shakespeare's canvas is not altogether a qualification, in Yeats's eyes, at this time in his life. Yeats's vexation with Shakespeare's carrying his audience from Rome to Venice (a reference to the Roman plays and to *The Merchant of Venice* and *Othello*), from Egypt to Saxon England (*Antony and Cleopatra* and *Cymbeline*), or in the one play from Roman to Christian mythology (*King Lear*—though Lear's gods are Apollo and Jupiter, the play has unmistakable Christian elements) denotes an attempt to come to grips with Shakespeare's uneven achievement, rather than to offer him a mechanical homage. And so, after about 1920, Yeats became increasingly concerned with the necessity for order, form, the assertion of the artist's control over his material. "Self-knowledge and self-mastery" come to the fore in Phase 16 of *A Vision*, "for the being must brag of its triumph over its own incoherence," Yeats informs us. (Yeats locates himself at Phase 17, where the conscious exercise of artistic control is further realized.) At Phase 20 this domination is on the wane, and so Shakespeare, at this phase, fails to create entirely on his own; he borrows his plots and does little to remold them. Yeats's insistence during these years on the supremacy of the artist over his material appears in "Four Years: 1887–1891" where, writing of York Powell, his father's friend and an eminent historian, Yeats saw "a man of genius, [who] had not enough ambition to shape his thought, nor enough conviction to give rhythm to his style."[18] Like Ben Jonson, who wished that Shakespeare had blotted a thousand lines, Yeats too seems to favor a more organic and deliberate body of work.

As late as 1938, in *On the Boiler*, Yeats recalls that, as a young

18   *Ex*, p. 252; *Vis*, pp. 294, 138, 139; *Au*, p. 72.

man, he used to speak of "the difficult transition from topic to topic in Shakespearean dialogue."[19] He then compares "the Elizabethan plot broken up into farce and spectacle" with "the elaborate unity of Greek drama. . . . Civilisation rose to its high tide mark in Greece, fell, rose again in the Renaissance but not to the same level."[20] And Dorothy Wellesley reports that in a conversation with her at about the same time, Yeats observed: "The Greek drama alone achieved perfection; it may be thousands of years before we achieve that perfection again. Shakespeare is only a mass of magnificent fragments."[21] But perhaps Yeats's most powerful indictment of Shakespeare occurs in *A Vision,* where he recognizes him to be "the greatest of dramatists," but adds, "we might, had the total works of Sophocles survived . . . not think him greatest." Yeats stated in 1937 that all his life, in his own work, he had insisted on "construction" as being one of the great essentials in art.[22]

In Yeats's scheme, Shakespeare's tremendous creative genius springs from the loosening of the grip of Christendom, tradition, and collective

19 *Boiler,* p. 28. It is not easy to say what Yeats means by this. He always emphasized vivid and passionate speech in the theater (see, e.g., *Ex,* pp. 183, 210, 218), pointing to Falstaff as an example (*Ex,* pp. 108, 150, 166–67, 211–12). After about 1905 Yeats became increasingly concerned with using the "common idiom" in his plays (*Letters,* p. 462); later, in the 1920s, he insisted on "the syntax and vocabulary of common personal speech" in his verse (*Letters,* p. 710; see also p. 892), and, in his translation of *Oedipus at Colonus,* aimed at being "more idiomatic and modern" (*Letters,* p. 721).

20 *Boiler,* pp. 28–29. In 1906 Yeats had called English literature "the greatest of all literatures but that of Greece" (*Ex,* p. 206). According to Hegel, too, the two periods when art flourished unsubordinated to religion were those that produced the Greek tragedians and Shakespeare (*Hegel on Tragedy,* ed. Anne and Henry Paolucci [New York, 1962], p. xvi. See also Anne Paolucci, "Bradley and Hegel on Shakespeare," *CL,* XVI (1964), 211–25; A. C. Bradley, "Hegel's Theory of Tragedy" in *Oxford Lectures on Poetry* [London, 1950] [first pub. 1909], pp. 69–95). That Yeats read Hegel with keen interest is evident from his many references to the philosopher (See *Letters,* pp. 725, 813; *Yeats and TSM,* p. 121; *Vis,* pp. 202–3, 301; *Boiler,* p. 22; *E&I,* pp. 396, 466).

21 *Letters to DW,* p. 194. According to Yeats's historical pattern, this perfection would be reached in about A.D. 3,500. Phase 15 of the next millennium (A.D. 2,500) would, like Byzantium, create an impersonal art, because "each age unwinds the thread another age had wound" (*Vis,* p. 270), and "an age is the reversal of an age" ("Parnell's Funeral"). But A.D. 3,500 would, like the Age of Pericles, be doubly antithetical and therefore capable of repeating that achievement.

22 *Vis,* p. 294; *Letters,* p. 892.

belief—the forces of cohesion—as secularism begins to take control. With the crumbling of these long-established values, individual personality finds itself liberated and Shakespeare exults in this emancipation through the variety and the profundity of his characters and plots, "those personages more living than ourselves," as Yeats describes them. But Yeats's reservations must always be weighed against the flexibility of his attitude toward Shakespeare. No stereotyped response could displace his sensitivity to Shakespeare. As his Naoise and Deirdre display "the dignity of Greek drama" in full measure by playing chess while conscious of the imminence of death, so Yeats could also hail the presence of this dignity in Shakespeare: "no actress has ever sobbed when she played Cleopatra," he declared in 1937.[23]

Ambivalence is the word that perhaps best describes Yeats's relationship with Shakespeare, which, far from being languid, was informed by stress and strain. Although uncompromising in his denigration of the blinding of Gloucester, only three years later, in 1913, he could unblushingly hold up *King Lear* and the *Divine Comedy* as superb examples of unified art, calling them "vast worlds, moulded by their weight like drops of water," while dismissing contemptuously "the pedantic composure of Wordsworth, the rhetoric of Swinburne, the passionless sentiment of Tennyson."[24]

Yeats's open letter to Lady Gregory entitled "A People's Theatre" (1919) marks the transition from his early position on Shakespeare to the position he consistently maintained thereafter, which was fully stated six years later in *A Vision*. That several important statements in the letter find a place in "Dove or Swan" of *A Vision*[25] is of course not surprising, since by the end of November, 1917, the first part of *A Vision* had been outlined,[26] and though much remained to be organized, the division of human nature into twenty-eight phases based on the ratio of subjectivity to objectivity had been completed. Later he preferred the symbolic terms *antithetical* and *primary* for subjective and objective,

23   *Vis,* p. 294; *E&I,* p. 523.
24   *E&I,* pp. 354, 351–52.
25   See *Ex,* p. 250; *Vis,* p. 289.
26   For a thorough analysis of these and other related matters, see *Man and Masks,* pp. 223–39. See also *Letters,* p. 716.

respectively, though he continued to use the older terminology as well.

Section 4 of the letter to Lady Gregory traces the rise of objectivity and the obfuscation of subjectivity from Dante to modern times, with Shakespeare somewhere in between the extremes:

> The objective nature and the subjective are mixed in different proportion as are the shadowed and the bright parts in the lunar phases. In Dante there was little shadow, in Shakespeare a larger portion, while you and Synge, it may be, resemble the moon when it has just passed its third quarter.[27]

In place of the rather uncertain attitude toward Shakespeare that Yeats evinced heretofore, a new precision seems to have appeared, which could, without dogmatism, give to different personalities a secure position on "the wagonwheel," as Yeats humorously calls it in his poem, "The Phases of the Moon." Furthermore, it allowed Yeats to trace fascinating correspondences between the phases of epochs widely separated in time, yet bound by the macrocosmic unity of the Great Wheel. The letter to Lady Gregory is, then, a precursor to *A Vision,* in the nature of a trial run: Dante and Shakespeare, in historical sequence, are considered exponents of preponderant subjectivity and increasing objectivity, respectively.

Dante, living at a time when individual personality was yet inchoate, describes his poverty and his exile. Yeats calls this "the first passage of poignant autobiography in literary history"; but Yeats believes that Dante considered this self-revelation "his chief misfortune," for "he has had to show himself to all Italy and so publish his human frailties that men who honoured him unknown honour him no more." Absorbed in the contemplation of an inner world, a world untainted by realism, he created his work out of himself, shunned publicity, and had communion with "but few and intimate friends." So complete was subjectivity in him that even if he had written plays, Yeats postulates that he would have been indifferent to the idiom of his time (quite unlike Synge, as Yeats points out elsewhere), "writing from his own thought and passion" and "observing little." Dante, then, denotes a condition of maximum subjectivity and unity.[28]

27 *Ex,* p. 253.
28 *Ex,* p. 250.

Shakespeare, several centuries after Dante, reveals the splintering of that unity, but increasing objectivity in him has not yet succeeded in obliterating past subjectivity, as later happens with Dryden, Pope, and the other Augustans:

> Shakespeare, more objective than Dante—for, alas, the world must move—was still predominantly subjective, and he wrote during the latest crisis of history that made possible a theatre of his kind. There were still among the common people many traditional songs and stories, while Court and University, which were much more important to him, had an interest Chaucer never shared in great dramatic persons, in those men and women of Plutarch, who made their death a ritual of passion.[29]

A few years later Yeats was to move Shakespeare still further from subjectivity, suggesting this in imagery connotative of a sudden explosion; and in the letter to Lady Gregory it is possible to see him feeling his way toward this less ambiguous rationale.

Here, though still considering Shakespeare "predominantly subjective," he places him at a point where contrary forces are briefly locked in equal combat, and calls this moment "the latest crisis of history that made possible a theatre of his kind." Clearly this is an acknowledgment that Shakespeare was integral to his age, that his genius was inseparable from the divisive forces, however deplorable, that characterized the Renaissance. Shakespeare's involvement with the Court and his interest in Plutarch's "great dramatic persons" (Yeats has here in mind *Julius Caesar, Antony and Cleopatra, Coriolanus,* and *Timon of Athens,* plays whose plots Shakespeare found in Plutarch) bespeak the loss of unity with the appearance of class barriers, for Chaucer had been able to write for both peasant and nobleman. Yet the implication in his statement is unmistakable: total subjectivity and unity were, to Yeats, attractive, but he also felt that these by themselves were incapable of bringing to birth great drama. Dante, Yeats noted, would hardly have been equipped to write plays. A few years earlier, his criticism of William Morris was that he was too subjective, "too continuously lyrical";[30] had Morris learned from Chaucer how to explore the outside world, his art would have been more robust, more masculine, Yeats argues.

Yeats seems to regard Shakespeare as endowed with qualities that,

29 *Ex,* pp. 251–52.
30 *Ex,* p. 220.

having come to him from the combination of his genius and his age, were conducive to the engendering of great drama. Lacking the subjectivity of a Dante, Shakespeare, on the other hand, possesses the necessary objectivity to interest himself in the world without, "in great dramatic persons," an interest that Yeats, whose own plays often portray such persons, would applaud.

III

During the period 1919–25 Yeats's grasp on history tightened, and he began to formulate, with growing confidence, a pattern in human development and artistic creativity that rose and fell with astonishing regularity.[31] He now began to feel that the subjective mind of ancient man was by itself inadequate, for history necessarily implied change, a feature most pronounced in Western man's evolution. Asiatic quiescence lacked the dynamism of Europe (one has only to read "Meru" to see how vigorously he posits both aspects), so that a combination of the two would lead to greater variety and productivity than an insistence on only one. The clash of opposites and the mingling of contraries, represented by the interlocking gyres, came with the Renaissance and gave to the age its distinctive character.

In "Four Years: 1887–1891" (1921), "The Tragic Generation" (1922), and *A Vision* (1925), Yeats's attitude toward Shakespeare is stated with unprecedented firmness. Whether he could convincingly locate Shakespeare on the chart or not seems to have become for Yeats the test for the validity of his interpretation of history. He accepted the challenge. This is indicated not only by the fact that in *A Vision* no other person is discussed with the thoroughness that Yeats brings to his examination of Shakespeare, but also, more significantly, by the curious fact that Shakespeare is the only figure invoked at considerable length twice: first, in "The Phases of the Moon" (pp. 151–54, as an example of the human Phase 20), and then in "Dove or Swan" (p. 294, as an example of the historical Phase 16). It is certainly more than a coin-

31 For Yeats's reading of historians during this period (e.g., Spengler, Vico, Adams, Petrie, Frobenius, Marx, Sorel, Gerald Heard, etc.), see Whitaker, *Swan and Shadow*, pp. 76–84. See also T. L. Dume, "William Butler Yeats: A Survey of His Reading" (Ph.D. diss., Temple University, 1950); and *Ex*, pp. 313–14.

cidence that of about fifty names in each of the two sections, each name being illustrative of some phase or historical development, Shakespeare's is the only name that receives detailed attention in each section. Of the other one hundred or so names, only those of Napoleon and Aretino occur in both sections: the former is discussed in one section (p. 153) and mentioned briefly in the other (p. 296); the latter is mentioned briefly in both sections (pp. 138, 294). From this time onward Yeats's relationship with Shakespeare remains constant. Perhaps this settled attitude serves to partly explain why Shakespeare's characters step directly into three of his last poems: "Lapis Lazuli," "An Acre of Grass," and "The Statues."

In "Four Years" (1921) Yeats pointedly insists on regarding Hamlet as an active and efficient controller of events and not a mere dreamer. The comment occurs in a passage identifying William Morris' portrait (which hung over Yeats's mantelpiece) with the Middle Ages and with Buddha's "motionless meditation." In spite of Yeats's regard for Morris, he now confesses that his serene contentment is cloying: "To-day I do not set his poetry very high. . . . The dream world of Morris was as much the antithesis of daily life as with other men of genius, but he was never conscious of the antithesis and so knew nothing of intellectual suffering." But contrasted with Morris and Buddha as types of Asiatic inwardness is Hamlet. Morris and Buddha have "no trait in common with the wavering, lean image of hungry speculation, that cannot but because of certain famous Hamlets of our stage fill the mind's eye. Shakespeare himself foreshadowed a symbolic change, that is a change in the whole temperament of the world, for though he called his Hamlet 'fat' and even 'scant of breath,' he thrust between his fingers agile rapier and dagger." The agility that Hamlet displays spearheads the direction of the Renaissance and leads to greater objectivity and world awareness, comparable to the Roman statues, "with their world-considering eyes," which succeeded the antithetical civilization of the Greeks.[32]

---

32 *Au*, pp. 86–87; *Vis*, p. 277. As early as 1904, Yeats had adumbrated the alternation of subjective and objective in a historical context: after having "drunk the cold cup of the moon's intoxication, we thirst for something beyond ourselves . . . the hot cup of the sun" (*Ex*, p. 26).

Hamlet as "the wavering, lean image of hungry speculation" contains an echo from Caesar's description of Cassius ("Yond Cassius has a lean and hungry look: / He thinks too much" [*Caesar*, I, ii, 194–95]) that Yeats perhaps intends the reader to recognize, for Morris, he maintains, was incapable of thought: intellectual suffering, speculation, and casuistry were beyond him. Even his language, Yeats goes on to say, was "exhausted from abstraction," quite unlike "the language of Chaucer and Shakespeare, its warp fresh from field and market." And Yeats's reservations about Morris appear elsewhere too, when he observes that his "poetry often wearies us as the unbroken green of July wearies us." The symbolic change in the whole temperament of the world that Hamlet signaled was, to Yeats, an instance of the prophetic role that the artist fills, his art an adumbration of impending changes in the complexion of the age, and he felt that Shakespeare too had consciously counted himself among the prophets with his lines: "the prophetic soul / Of the wide world dreaming on things to come" (Sonnet 107), a quotation that Yeats employs more than once in advocating his theory.[33] Hamlet, therefore, represents for Yeats the Renaissance and, though such an oversimplification may fail to do full justice to Yeats's new attitude, it is easy to see that he has a respect for this period, absent or but lightly hinted at in his earlier writings.

Yeats considered Hamlet a type of near-perfect man, who combined the opposite ingredients of action and contemplation. He detected the presence of such ingredients in Robert Gregory, whom he identified with Renaissance man, that is, with Hamlet. This may be detected in the thrice repeated refrain, "Soldier, scholar, horseman, he," that rings through "In Memory of Major Robert Gregory" (1918) and is almost a verbatim echo of Ophelia's lament over what she thinks is the loss of Hamlet's sanity: "O, what a noble mind is here o'erthrown! / The courtier's, soldier's, scholar's, eye, tongue, sword" (III, i, 146–47). But interestingly, Yeats selects only two qualities from Ophelia's list, the soldier and the scholar, opposites that coexist in Hamlet, the first standing for action, the second for contemplation. In Hamlet, as in Gregory, the former quality is given a slight edge over the latter: Robert Gregory

33   *Au*, p. 87; *E&I*, pp. 61, 191; *Au*, p. 199.

died a soldier's death, and though Hamlet does not die on the battle-field, Fortinbras' epitaph for him, we recall, is "Let four captains / Bear Hamlet, like a soldier, to the stage" (V, ii, 375–76).[34] In his Introduction to *The Oxford Book of Modern Verse* (1936), Yeats remembers that his father had called the poets of the Rhymers' Club (Ernest Dowson, Victor Plarr, Richard Le Gallienne, Aubrey Beardsley, John Davidson, Lionel Johnson, Arthur Symons, Ernest Rhys) "the Hamlets of our age." "Scholar, connoisseur, drunkard, poet, pervert, most charming of men" is how Yeats, not without affection, describes the combination of op-posites in one such individual and adds, "Some of these Hamlets went mad, some drank . . . all had courage, all suffered opprobrium—gen-erally for their virtues or for sins they did not commit—all had good manners." Yeats's admiration and compassion for these Hamlets is evident here and in "The Tragic Generation" of his *Autobiography*.

But perhaps the most dramatic example of Yeats's shift from his early position on Shakespeare and the Renaissance to the final one may be seen in the sudden and quite unexpected appearance of Hamlet "thin from eating flies," a feline touch, in stanza 3 of "The Statues" (1938).[35] It is well known to cat owners that a propensity in a cat for flies and insects is the most likely cause for leanness.[36] Interestingly

---

34   The fighter plane Major Gregory was piloting crashed over Europe after he had brought down nineteen German planes (see Yeats's poems "Reprisals" and "An Irish Airman Foresees His Death"). In Castiglione's *The Book of the Courtier*—a book that Yeats knew very well (see *Au*, p. 332)—an important discussion, book I, par. 45, centers on whether the courtier should be more of a scholar or more of a soldier: the final decision is "in favour of arms." See also Corinna Salvadori, *Yeats and Castiglione: Poet and Courtier* (Dublin, 1965); Arnold Stein, "Yeats: A Study in Recklessness," *Sewanee Review*, LVII (1949), 603–26.

35   Perhaps Yeats has Hamlet's caustic retort to Claudius in mind: "Ex-cellent, i' faith; of the chameleon's dish. I eat the air promise-crammed. You can-not feed capons so" (III, ii, 84–86). It is also worth noting that when Yeats wrote "The Statues," he was thinking of Irving's intellectual pride (as Hamlet), which he greatly admired (see, e.g., *Au*, p. 77; *Ex*, p. 256). Sixty-four years after having seen Irving's *Hamlet*, Yeats celebrated him in a couplet: "What brushes fly and moth aside? / Irving and his plume of pride" ("A Nativity"). Perhaps this recalls the scene in which Hamlet, after trifling with Osric, the king's foppish messenger, contemptuously calls him a "water-fly" (V, ii, 82).

36   See *Cats Magazine*, XXV (May, 1968), 14. See also A. Norman Jeffares, *A Commentary on the Collected Poems of W. B. Yeats* (Stanford, 1968), p. 495: "it is a common supposition that cats grow thin through eating flies."

enough, the hero of Yeats's early novel, *John Sherman* (1891), at one point wishes that he were a cat, for then he would be able "to leap about in the moonlight and sleep in the sunlight, and catch flies."[37] Furthermore, that Yeats saw Hamlet cast in a feline role by Shakespeare is perhaps hinted at by the presence of Grimalkin in the last line of the stanza, where she is certainly intended to remind us of the Graymalkin in the witches' sabbaths in *Macbeth*.[38]

What justification Yeats had for attributing certain feline characteristics to Hamlet must be determined by looking at Shakespeare's play. Energetic and given to intense speculation, Hamlet is throughout the play a searcher: he defines his resolve to obey the ghost's summons in terms of "the Nemean lion's nerve" (I, iv, 83) and, catlike in his craft, stalks the king, reduces him to the condition of a terrified mouse with the staging of his play, and finally when he does spring, leaves the king no chance to escape. The play that he stages is "The Murder of Gonzago" (II, ii, 510), but when the king, after his suspicions have been aroused, nervously asks what the play is called, Hamlet coins a new name on the spur of the moment, "The Mousetrap" (III, ii, 221), a title replete with meaning. With this jab he aggravates his antagonist's already unconcealed distress. *Hamlet,* we should remember, begins, ironically enough, with "not a mouse stirring" (I, i, 10), but this outward calm is of course deceptive for it is exceedingly short-lived. Although Hamlet seems to have called his play "The Mousetrap" without deliberate forethought, it is clear from his lines,

> The play's the thing
> Wherein I'll catch the conscience of the King,
> [II, ii, 578–79]

that he had earlier visualized the king as a rat caught in a trap. And it is not by accident that Shakespeare makes Hamlet begin his favorite speech, while in the company of the players visiting Elsinore, with a line that he instantly realizes is not quite correct: "The rugged Pyrrhus,

37 W. B. Yeats, *Collected Works* (Stratford-on-Avon, 1908), VII, 221.
38 Yeats's familiarity with the witch scenes in the play is evident from *E&I*, pp. 488, 518.

like th' Hyrcanian beast" is how Hamlet first remembers the line, but then corrects himself a moment later (II, ii, 472). Nevertheless, his error, a Freudian slip if ever there was one, is significant. If, as all the commentators are agreed, Hamlet feels that his case is comparable to that of Pyrrhus,[39] it is not difficult to see why he associates him with "th' Hyrcanian beast," which was the tiger of Hyrcania, a tract of land southeast of the Caspian Sea.[40] As "with eyes like carbuncles, the hellish Pyrrhus / Old grandsire Priam seeks" (II, ii, 439–40), so would Hamlet like to seek out Claudius and with tigerish ferocity spring upon him. We should also note that when Hamlet stabs Polonius behind the arras, he pictures him as a rat (III, iv, 23).

That Shakespeare saw his Hamlet as possessing certain feline traits seems undeniable, but more pertinent is the question whether Yeats regarded Hamlet in this light outside of his poem "The Statues." The evidence suggests that he did. Of Hamlet, Yeats writes: "I wished to become self-possessed, to be able to play with hostile minds as Hamlet played." The unusual use of the word "play" in such a context carries overtones of the metaphor, "as a cat plays with a mouse." In expressing his desire to be like Hamlet, it is noteworthy that Yeats visualizes him, not as having "resisted," "attacked," or "opposed" hostile minds, words that would ordinarily be more appropriate, but as having "played" with them. Clearly Yeats does not intend the word to have the harmless connotation of a child at play, but to depict something sinister and cruel, an enforcement of conscious superiority which can only be the "play" that a cat engages in before finishing off its hapless victim. Perhaps Yeats's admiration for—and identification with—the kind of ruthless mind that Hamlet possessed is corroborated by his observation, in 1922, in a letter to Olivia Shakespear, on Joyce's *Ulysses*.

> I am reading the new Joyce—I hate it when I dip here and there but when I read it in the right order I am much impressed. . . . It has our Irish cruelty and also our kind of strength and the Martello Tower pages are full of beauty. A cruel playful mind like a great soft tiger cat.[41]

39 See, e.g., Arthur Wormhoudt, *Hamlet's Mouse Trap* (New York, 1956), pp. 124–25; Eleanor Prosser, *Hamlet and Revenge* (Stanford, 1967), p. 153; Wendy Coppedge Sanford, *Theatre as Metaphor in Hamlet* (Cambridge, Mass., 1967), p. 15.

40 Cf. Macbeth's "th' Hyrcan tiger" (III, iv, 101).

41 *Au*, p. 57; *Letters*, p. 679.

The energetic unsentimentality of the Irish mind seems to have been for Yeats a qualification that Renaissance man also could rightly claim, and his striking lines from "The Tower" (1928), "I have prepared my peace / With learned Italian things," suggest his final reconciliation with the Renaissance after his early mistrust of its waxing intellectualism.

In stanza 3 of "The Statues," the convergence of Grimalkin and Buddha (or of West and East) in the last line perhaps signifies the impingement of Western man's energetic philosophy on Eastern man's passivity, even as in stanza 2 the Greek sculptors "put down / All Asiatic vague immensities." In the poem, then, Hamlet stands as a symbol of Western man, full of an insatiable curiosity and appetite for objective particles of knowledge, intellectual ideas that Yeats represents metaphorically as flies. As the last stanza indicates, the poet is sympathetic to this active reaching out that Hamlet denotes, and critical of Asiatic sluggishness embodied in Buddha. Hamlet, or Renaissance man, exhibits the spirit of his age and, by implication, that of Yeats's Ireland, which he saw, in "Under Ben Bulben," on the threshold of its own Renaissance to be created by "the indomitable Irishry": "But we may, if we choose, not now or soon but at the next turn of the wheel, push ourselves up, being ourselves the tide, beyond that first mark. But no, these things are fated; we may be pushed up." Yeats regretted that contemporary Europe was turning back to the formless void of Asia repudiated by the Renaissance, and he insisted that Ireland remain aloof from this "dip into ebbing Asia."[42] By isolating Hamlet's felinity in a single extraordinary line, and by employing a Shakespearean character as a kind of eloquent shorthand, Yeats has arrived at a compression of meaning characteristic of several of his last poems.

Even in his last prose work, *On the Boiler* (1939), Yeats subtly

42 *Boiler*, p. 29; *Vis*, p. 270. Yeats did, of course, read Spengler (see *Letters*, p. 716). Whitaker, *Swan and Shadow*, p. 241, points out that Spengler (Oswald Spengler, *The Decline of the West*, trans. Charles F. Atkinson [London, 1926–28], I, 347) too had differentiated between Greek and Indian on the one hand, and modern Faustian man on the other. The Faustian mind, for Spengler, was a type of Western consciousness "whose ethic is manifested in the Shakespearean tragedy of dynamic evolution and catastrophe." Whitaker further points out (p. 324, n. 54) that Yeats would also have read this passage quoted by Wyndham Lewis in his *Time and Western Man* (London, 1927), p. 288. That Yeats read this book with avid interest is apparent from *Letters*, pp. 733–34, and *Yeats and TSM*, p. 122.

reasons that Hamlet may appear to be a dreamer, but only because his "hesitations are hesitations of thought, and are concerned with certain persons on whom his attention is fixed; outside that he is a mediæval man of action." In support of his being essentially a "man of action," Yeats cites the swift efficiency with which he "changes the letters" and slays "the father of Fortinbras in single combat." Hamlet's hesitations, then, are deceptive, for they lead us to conclude that he is by nature a procrastinator—and Yeats castigates imperceptive English producers for perpetuating this fabrication. As a further example of the dichotomy between appearance and reality, Yeats tells of the woman who thought herself "completely serious," yet was accurately painted by Sargent as "completely frivolous."[43] (The fascination that the conflict between opposites exercised on Yeats comes to the fore in his own personality too. He reports that his portrait, as painted by Augustus John, showed him as "an unshaven, drunken bar-tender," a depiction of his intrinsic self, even though on the surface he was "always particular about [his] clothes, never dissipated, never unshaven.")[44] Refusing to see Hamlet

---

43 *Boiler*, pp. 33–34. It is clear from his remarks here that Yeats was aware of Shakespearean criticism that called Hamlet a procrastinator. His statement suggests that he disagreed with such writers as Bradley, Dowden, Coleridge, and Goethe, who attributed Hamlet's delay to melancholy, "brooding thought," irresolution, and an excessively fine temperament, respectively. T. S. Eliot's chief objections are that Hamlet's feelings "obstruct action," that there is "delay in revenge," that the play is an "artistic failure," "puzzling and disquieting" ("Hamlet and His Problems," 1919, in *Selected Essays: 1917–1932* [London, 1932]; see also his *The Use of Poetry and the Use of Criticism* [London, 1933], p. 44, in which he slightly modifies his position on *Hamlet*). G. Wilson Knight, perhaps Hamlet's harshest critic, sees Hamlet as being death's representative, "the poison of negation, nothingness" (*The Wheel of Fire* [London, 1930, 5th ed. rev., New York, 1957], p. 41). Even J. Dover Wilson, perhaps one of Hamlet's kindest critics, admits that he is guilty of "procrastination," but only after the play within the play confirms the ghost's disclosure (*What Happens in Hamlet* [Cambridge, 1935], p. 202). E. E. Stoll seems to come closest to Yeats's position: he does not deny that Hamlet delays, but he does deny that this indicates incapacity (*Hamlet the Man*, The English Assn., Pamphlet No. 91 [1935], p. 10). Yeats may or may not have read these critics, but he certainly knew that his own reflections on Hamlet would be judged by most of his readers in the context of current critical attitudes toward the play. In passing we may note that Yeats's reference to Hamlet's slaying "the father of Fortinbras" is, of course, an error. It was Hamlet's father who "did slay this Fortinbras" (I, i, 84–86; also 59–64), but Yeats's oversight in no way impairs his point.

44 *Ex*, p. 308.

as a dreamer, Yeats insists on recognizing him to be intrinsically energetic and thus equates him with Ireland's intellectual Renaissance.

In Yeats's historical scheme described in "Dove or Swan" of *A Vision* there are peak periods when all that is most creative in man appears. These periods occur at Phase 15 of each one-thousand-year cycle (at 1500 B.C., 500 B.C., A.D. 500, and A.D. 1500), an antithetical, or subjective, cycle alternating with a primary, or objective, one. Two such cycles form a two-thousand-year span, Leda and the Swan inaugurating the first (2000 B.C.), and Mary and the Dove the second (A.D. 1). Yeats is careful to point out that these dates are "approximately correct"; that they "mark somewhat vaguely a period that begins in one country earlier and in another later"; that the figures are not to be taken "too literally." Since a peak alternates with a trough, when either one is reached a converse movement immediately begins. Around 1000 B.C. the Greeks have "grown barbaric and Asiatic," but with the appearance of Homer "civil order" becomes apparent. Then around the sixth century B.C., personality begins to assert itself, and the gyre is on its way toward the consummation of Phase 15, when Unity of Being becomes possible. J. B. Yeats had compared the condition "to a musical instrument so strung that if we touch a string all the strings murmur faintly."[45] Yeats developed the concept into an elaborate theory of equilibrium that could apply with equal force to an individual, a culture, or a nation.

In *A Vision* Yeats sees Unity of Being within a person's life if his four faculties (Will, Mask, Creative Mind, and Body of Fate) are in harmony with one another. In other words, Unity of Being prevails if the individual's urge (his Will) to realize his ideal (Mask) is carried out rationally (Creative Mind) and in keeping with his environment (Body of Fate). Any one of the four faculties, if out of tune, can cause discord. With cultures and nations the details may differ, though the principle remains the same (pp. 71–83). In describing Unity of Being, however, at the crest of each millennium, Yeats considerately simplifies the whole notion by demonstrating an equilibrium between two forces and not four. Thus, in the Elizabethan Age, these two forces are "in-

45 *Vis*, pp. 279, 291; *Letters*, p. 666; *Au*, p. 117.

tellect and emotion," "the reconciliation of Paganism and Christianity," *"primary* curiosity and the *antithetical* dream" (pp. 291–93). And at Phase 15 of the Age of Pericles, "Ionic and Doric influence unite" (p. 270); at Phase 15 of the Age of Justinian, Christianity and aestheticism unite (p. 279). Being opposites, Paganism and Christianity, during the Elizabethan Age, counteract each other and attain a point of equal thrust which, by its very nature, is full of stress and necessarily momentary; when an imbalance sets in, the resultant explosion of energy is like a tensioned spring suddenly uncoiling. Unity of Being having reached its acme, the inevitable sequel is its disruption, even as Old Tom, the lunatic, in "Old Tom Again" cheerfully sings:

> Things out of perfection sail,
> And all their swelling canvas wear.

"Imperious impulse held all together" for a while, "then the scattering came, the seeding of the poppy, bursting of pea-pod, and for a time personality seemed but the stronger for it. Shakespeare's people make all things serve their passion, and that passion is for the moment the whole energy of their being."[46] Shakespeare's situation has been precisely delineated. The Age of Shakespeare, explosive and full of restlessness, fractures the harmony of the Renaissance, very much as Yeats described Shakespeare's impingement in "The Autumn of the Body" (1895): "Shakespeare shattered the symmetry of verse and of drama that he might fill them with things and their accidental relations to one another." Has Yeats then, twenty-five years after writing this, come around again to regarding Shakespeare as a disruptive force? Evidently he has, but now his attitude has undergone a radical change. What was once censurable is now full of energy, passion, and personality.

In *A Vision* the imagery that Yeats employs is yet more tumultuous; the heterogeneity of the post-Renaissance scene is depicted in terms of artistic forms beginning "to jostle and fall into confusion," of "a sudden rush and storm" taking place. "In the mind of the artist, a desire for power succeeds to that of knowledge," and Yeats associates Shakespeare

---

46 *Au*, p. 174. Cf. *Vis*, p. 141, where the image of "a bursting pod" occurs under Phase 17.

"with the mythopoeic and ungovernable beginning of the eighth gyre." He goes on to say, "I see in Shakespeare a man in whom human personality, hitherto restrained by its dependence upon Christendom or by its own need for self-control, burst like a shell."[47] After the shattering of unity, depicted in the imagery of a seeding poppy, bursting pea-pod, and exploding shell, and the display of personality in Shakespeare (a subject to be considered in the next chapter), calcification sets in. Yeats traces the process from Shakespeare, Titian, Strozzi, and Van Dyck to Cromwell: whereas Shakespeare was full of an almost superhuman energy, the later figures "grow more reasonable, more orderly, less turbulent," until we reach "Cromwell's warty opinionated head." Objectivity has now prevailed, and Cromwell is its most repulsive expression. "Objective natures," Yeats informs us elsewhere, "are declared to be always ugly, hence the disagreeable appearance of politicians, reformers, philanthropists, and men of science."[48] Even at its most somber, Yeats's thought always conceals some unexpected revelation that brings delight.

After Cromwell, history becomes increasingly drab, except for Phase 22, when there is once again an efflorescence of human personality expressed in "all that is most beautiful in modern English poetry from Blake to Arnold." But though "the soul awakes" during this period, it is a spasmodic development that must give place before an all-encompassing movement toward intellect and objectivity as revealed in the scientific mind. Yeats sees Shakespeare as one situated on the crest of a

---

47 *Vis*, pp. 293–94. Knowledge and power are the attributes of the god in the poem "Leda and the Swan"; the artist now sees himself as creator, godlike in his fecundity. Although, according to Yeats's scheme, the Ages of Pericles and Elizabeth have a close affinity, they are also separated by a profound disparity: the Greek era is predominantly antithetical, but the Christian era is predominantly primary. Thus the Age of Pericles will find its perfect counterpart during the coming period, A.D. 3000–A.D. 4000. The complication arises because of the alternation of primary and antithetical within each two-thousand-year cycle: the first millennium of each era—whether predominantly antithetical or predominantly primary—is essentially primary, and the second is essentially antithetical. By this patterning, the Age of Pericles is doubly antithetical, whereas the Age of Elizabeth, though antithetical (being the second millennium of the two-thousand-year era), belongs to a predominantly primary era and must therefore take on that quality to the detriment of the other.

48 *Au*, p. 175; W. B. Yeats, *Four Plays for Dancers* (London, 1921), pp. 105–6.

stupendous movement: "Imagination, whether in literature, painting, or sculpture, sank after the death of Shakespeare; supreme intensity had passed to another faculty."[49] In Shakespeare were combined emotion and intellect; after him intellect triumphed, and though it had become for Yeats a commendable faculty, he also felt that its domineering presence destroyed the felicitous Shakespearean balance.

In Yeats's scheme, however, no absolute pronouncements are valid. It would be easy to conclude that he regretted the departure of subjectivity after the Age of Dante and Chaucer, and there is partial truth in this, but this regret was equivocal. Accompanying it was the welcome he extended to objectivity, which enabled the writer to get out of himself and produce great drama: Shakespeare's unique achievement. Although Yeats has a preference for certain periods, he brings to each, in his descriptions, a vigor that betokens a positive acceptance of every change on the wheel. The spectator in "The Gyres" is by no means unmoved at the passing away of a lofty era, yet his sorrow is swallowed up by an all-conquering joy at the unfolding historical pattern:

> Hector is dead and there's a light in Troy;
> We that look on but laugh in tragic joy.

Evidence of Yeats's refusal to allow himself to be trapped into making simplistic and dogmatic value judgments on the different phases may be noticed throughout his work. Perhaps the most outspoken clarification of the duality in each phase, especially in the Renaissance, appears in the sharp crystallization of two diametrically opposed points of view, seemingly irreconcilable, yet, in the Yeatsian canon, coexistent: "I detest the Renaissance because it made the human mind inorganic; I adore the Renaissance because it clarified form and created freedom."[50] The bold juxtaposition of contraries in *On the Boiler* is an indication of the perception toward which Yeats moved. His statement is a refusal to deny the one and affirm the other; it is an affirmation of both.

If the Elizabethan Age heralded the break-up of unity, at the same time it also introduced an increased awareness of form, line, control,

49 *Vis*, pp. 297–98; *E&I*, p. 396.
50 *Boiler*, p. 27. See also *Vis*, p. 206.

all un-Asiatic qualities that Yeats came later to consciously admire. For Yeats, the exercise of control that came with the Renaissance, along with an upsurge of the emotions and the free play of the imagination, could alone produce great art. The ambivalence of his attitude toward the Renaissance is reflected in his approach to Shakespeare, whose passion was free of the deadening realism that Yeats saw had taken possession of his own age in art and politics. Individual personality being now regarded as an "impurity," man seeks how best to "embody the common aim," for "solitude is difficult, and creation except among avowedly archaistic and unpopular groups will grow impossible." The negation of the writer's personality is seen in the work of Flaubert, who has "neither belief nor preference," and in painting, "where some accomplished brush paints with an equal pleasure, or with a bored impartiality, the human form or an old bottle, dirty weather and clean sunshine."[51] This steady ebbing out of the gyre is tersely summed up in "Three Movements" (1932):

> Shakespearean fish swam the sea, far away from land;
> Romantic fish swam in nets coming to the hand;
> What are all those fish that lie gasping on the strand?[52]

With history viewed as a linear movement in *A Vision*, it became possible for Yeats to chart periods with greater precision than before, to compare and contrast civilizations and representative figures. Thus, though he felt that Shakespeare and the Renaissance spelled the beginnings of modern disunity, at the same time he could also think of Shakespeare as one closely associated with his age, able to encompass it with a breadth of vision that the moderns, with their insularity, lacked, for "Shakespeare leaned, as it were, even as craftsman, upon the general fate of men and nations, [and] had about him the excitement of the playhouse," but Browning with "his psychological curiosity," Tennyson, Shelley, and Wordsworth with their "moral values that were

51 *Vis* (1925), pp. 212–13; *Vis*, p. 300.
52 "In his diary on January 20, 1932, Yeats noted, 'The Passion in Shakespeare was a great fish in the sea, but from Goethe to the end of the Romantic movement the fish was in the net. It will soon be dead upon the shore' " (*Identity*, p. 267).

not aesthetic values," are the helpless fish that lie gasping on the strand.[53] The oscillations in Yeats's relationship with Shakespeare finally come to rest with his Shakespeare occupying a position free of narrow interests, giving to "the excitement of the playhouse" all his creative energies, unsolicitous of values other than aesthetic ones.

53 *Au,* p. 188; see also p. 102.

4

Shakespeare in "The Phases of the Moon"

Alas, 'tis true I have gone here and there,
And made myself a motley to the view,
Gored mine own thoughts, sold cheap what is most dear,
Made old offences of affections new.

—Sonnet 110

ACCORDING to Yeats's system, the individual in a normal life cycle passes through twenty-eight phases from birth to death, comparable to Jaques' seven ages from "the infant / Mewling and puking in the nurse's arms" to "second childishness and mere oblivion, / Sans teeth, sans eyes, sans taste, sans everything." Yeats alludes to this passage briefly in a letter, while making the interesting observation that each person lives "differently through Shakespeare's seven ages," depending on the kind of person he is.[1] Thus, each person, in some sense, creates his own world independently of the experiences of others. Certain pronounced traits displayed by the individual serve to reveal his predominant nature, that is, the particular phase to which he belongs. But regardless of this larger designation, he passes through all twenty-eight phases, as Robartes chants them to Aherne in the poem "The Phases of the Moon."

On the larger wheel, as we have seen, each person may be assigned

1 *Letters*, p. 784.

to a particular phase, but Yeats never hesitated to make adjustments if fresh evidence called for a reappraisal. Thus, he transferred Ezra Pound from the highly subjective Phase 12 to a much later, objective phase, after seeing him feed the starving cats at Rapallo.[2] Such an act hinted at the humanitarian's and the reformer's zeal and was cause enough to exile Pound to a phase remote from the flowering of the self that the earlier phase denoted. Yeats also changed L. A. G. Strong's position when some unexpected character trait came to light.[3] Yeats saw civilizations, like the individual, passing through twenty-eight phases in a single millennium, but at the same time he felt that civilizations displayed certain distinctive features that enabled him to assign them to particular phases. Thus, a person's phase may or may not coincide with that of his period.

When harmony between a person's phase and that of his period exists, there is no stress, and great art, for Yeats, is not possible without stress. So Shaw, Yeats tells us, had no true quarrel with his period, for its phase and his personal phase coincided.[4] What justification Yeats felt he had for assigning Shakespeare to a particular phase, and how he viewed Shakespeare in relation to the phase of his period will be the subject of inquiry in this chapter.

In "The Tragic Generation" (1922), after a brief explanation of the layout of the phases, Yeats locates the mid-Renaissance at about Phase 15: "The mid-renaissance could but approximate to the full moon." He then goes on to say, "but we may attribute to the next three nights of the moon the men of Shakespeare, of Titian, of Strozzi, and of Van Dyck."[5] Here Yeats is not explicit about whether Phases 16 to 18 ("the next three nights of the moon") represent the late Renaissance, or whether these are the personal phases of the four artists mentioned. The rest of the section, however, seems to bear out the latter meaning: Wilde as a man is said to belong to Phase 19, and in *A Vision* too this

2 *Man and Masks*, p. 237. See also *Vis*, pp. 5–6, and *Letters*, p. 739.
3 L. A. G. Strong, "William Butler Yeats," in *Scattering Branches*, ed. Stephen Gwynn (New York, 1940), p. 215.
4 *Au*, p. 176.
5 *Au*, p. 175.

is his personal phase (p. 148).[6] If, as seems intended, Yeats put Shakespeare at Phase 16, then evidently, in *A Vision* three years later, Yeats found it necessary to move him to Phase 20, a phase farther from Unity of Being, for he describes it as "a phase of the breaking-up and subdivision of the being" (p. 151). Whereas Yeats could ascertain Pound's and Strong's phases on the basis of personal contact, he had to determine Shakespeare's by artistic considerations, by his own response to Shakespeare as dramatist. The possible reasons for this important—and perhaps uncomplimentary—adjustment merit our investigation. But before doing so, we must glance at Yeats's doctrine of the Mask, because its application to Shakespeare will help unravel what Hic in "Ego Dominus Tuus" found so baffling, yet enthralling.

In his many observations on Shakespeare, Yeats avoids making generalizations about Shakespeare the man, an attitude that stands out from a widespread desire on the part of Shakespearean critics of the time to treat the plays and poems (particularly the sonnets) as a biographical treasure hunt.[7] Yeats, on the other hand, permits himself to make very few observations on Shakespeare's personal feelings, and in "At Stratford-on-Avon," as we have noted, even these remarks are elicited from him less as voluntary speculation and more in the way of replies to Dowden's assertion that Shakespeare's having admired Henry and despised Richard was a temperamental and patriotic response. Meeting his opponents on their own ground, Yeats in this essay seeks

6 Page numbers of references from *A Vision* will be incorporated in the text, except where there might be ambiguity.

7 The titles of the following works are evidence of this trend: David Masson, *Shakespeare Personally* (1865; rpt. London, 1914); Edward Dowden, *Shakspere: A Critical Study of His Mind and Art* (London, 1875); H. S. Bowden, *The Religion of Shakespeare* (London, 1899); Frank Harris, *The Man Shakespeare and His Tragic Life-Story* (New York, 1909). F. J. Furnivall, in his Introduction to *The Leopold Shakspere* (London, 1877) maintains that Shakespeare the man is present in the plays and can be deduced from them, and that the sonnets are purely autobiographical. Sidney Lee, *A Life of William Shakespeare* (London, 1898) recommends caution: though he does not deny an autobiographical element in both plays and poems, he argues that Shakespeare the artist transcends his personal life, that his art is impersonal. Georg Brandes, *William Shakespeare* (London, 1899), follows Furnivall and Dowden in regarding Shakespeare's work as the mirror of his life, but Leslie Stephen, "Shakespeare as a Man," in *Studies of A Biographer* (London, 1902), IV, makes an effective rebuttal.

to demonstrate the danger that the critic runs of remolding Shakespeare to fit his own ideal; for whereas Dowden and others see Shakespeare as an imperialist, Yeats demonstrates that he can be more plausibly imagined as having a secret sympathy for the underdog trampled on by the conqueror. The essay concludes with the reminder that Shakespeare was not of an assertive and self-aggrandizing temperament, that the ambition and imperialism personified in Henry could not possibly be a representation of Shakespeare's private feelings, since he preferred anonymity to autobiography.

> The people of Stratford-on-Avon have remembered little about him, and invented no legend to his glory. They have remembered a drinking-bout of his, and invented some bad verses for him, and that is about all. Had he been some hard-drinking, hard-living, hard-riding, loud-blaspheming squire they would have enlarged his fame by a legend of his dealings with the Devil.[8]

But even before this, as early as 1896 in his essay "The Return of Ulysses," Yeats had pointed out that "the poet who writes best in the Shakespearian manner" is one "who delights to speak with strange voices and to see his mind in the mirror of nature."[9] Shakespeare, for Yeats, does not reveal his identity in his art; he conceals it by assuming a part, by putting on a mask. Continuing to develop a point of view which placed little premium on Shakespeare the man, Yeats insisted that Shakespeare's work was the embodiment of his personality, not of his life, which was, to all appearances, unexceptional.

Yeats had not yet perfected the theory of the Mask, though he had been experimenting with it even before 1900. The Mask was, for Yeats, the ideal toward which the individual strove, the antithesis to his actual self; and his whole life, if purposeful, could be viewed as a process of becoming that ideal. A timid and nervous person (as Yeats considered

---

8 *E&I*, p. 110. Yeats is doubtless thinking here of John Ward's, perhaps apocryphal, report of Shakespeare's fondness for the bottle ("Shakespear, Drayton, and Ben Jhonson, had a merry meeting, and itt seems drank too hard, for Shakespear died of a feavour there contracted": *The Shakspere Allusion Book*, ed. John Munro [London, 1909], II, 111); and of the well-known doggerel on Shakespeare's grave at Stratford ("Good friend, for Jesus' sake forbear / To dig the dust enclosed here. / Blest be the man that spares these stones / And curst be he that moves my bones").

9 *E&I*, pp. 200–201.

himself to have been in his youth) would then don a mask of brash self-confidence, but if he happened to be an artist, he might well create through his art assertive characters and be content to remain in his own life timid and nervous. Thus, Yeats tells us elsewhere that Balzac, a bull-necked man and a glutton, probed esotericism, and, in "Ego Domi-nus Tuus," that Keats, "the coarse-bred son of a livery-stable keeper," made "luxuriant song."[10]

During the first two decades of the century, Yeats's interest in the alchemy of the Mask became an absorbing passion, reflected in the nature of his references to Shakespeare during the period. As Yeats's own thought developed, he constantly found in Shakespeare confirma-tion for each new position that he took. In about 1908 Yeats began to insist on the featuring of the artist's personality in his work, since "it is the presence of a personal element alone that can give it nationality in a fine sense, the nationality of its maker." Yet he also maintained that such art was not to be a mere confession, but inspired by an idea or an image. He said of himself in this connection: "Somebody has said that all sound philosophy is but biography, and what I myself did, getting into an original relation to Irish life, creating in myself a new character, a new pose." At about this time, in 1908, he started *The Player Queen,* a play in which the heroine steps outside herself in actually becoming the image that she has projected and in the process leaves her old self behind. "Man is nothing till he is united to an image," Septimus categorically declares, and in a letter to his father in 1909, Yeats quotes certain lines from the play that sum up its theme:

> Queens that have laughed to set the world at ease,
> Kings that have cried "I am great Alexander
> Or Caesar come again" but stir our wonder
> That they may stir their own and grow at length
> Almost alike to that unlikely strength.

These lines were not included in the play when it appeared in 1922, but their echo is heard in Yeats's description of Napoleon, Shakespeare's

---

10 *Au,* p. 57 (see also Yeats's description of himself in "Coole Park, 1929": "There one that ruffled in a manly pose / For all his timid heart" [quoted in *Au,* p. 277]); *E&I,* p. 443; *Au,* p. 166.

copartner in Phase 20,[11] who "sees himself as Alexander moving to the conquest of the East."

Yeats almost invariably felt that any change in the stand that he took had also been adopted by Shakespeare. The notion of the artist creating an image outside of and distinct from himself grew upon Yeats, and in "The Tragic Theatre" (1910), he saw Titian and Shakespeare as supreme examples of this objectivity; the "new images to the dreams of youth" that they hold up are the opposite of what is encountered in life. Shakespeare "shows us Hamlet broken away from life by the passionate hesitations of his reverie," for the greatest art does not reproduce "our daily mood," but, rather, "the moment of exaltation, of excitement, of dreaming," and the artist in his creation seeks to "express personal emotion through ideal form, a symbolism handled by the generations, a mask from whose eyes the disembodied looks." The Mask does not undergo change, but remains a constant image in the eyes of, say, a Napoleon who, seeing himself as Alexander, moves toward an identification with this chosen ideal. Yeats himself, when a boy, had made Hamlet "an image of heroic self-possession for the poses of youth and childhood to copy."[12] The artist's creation has the power to infuse life with new images. Yeats continued to develop this doctrine with growing excitement.

In *Per Amica Silentia Lunae* (1917), in many ways a forerunner of *A Vision,* the notion of the work of art being distinct from and in fact the opposite of the artist's personality is presented in a systematized form. All great artistic creation is viewed as the opposite of what the artist was in real life, his art the expresssion, not of his self, but of his anti-self. Dante, a lecherous man, "celebrated the most pure lady poet ever sung and the Divine Justice." The artist, seeking an image, becomes momentarily that image in his work, but when the act of creation is completed, he relapses to his former state: "when it is all over Dante can return to his chambering and Shakespeare to his 'pottle-pot.' They sought no impossible perfection but when they handled paper or parchment."[13] Yeats implies that, for Dante and Shakespeare, the greatness

11 *Ex,* pp. 233, 235; *Variorum Plays,* p. 749; *Letters,* p. 534; *Vis,* p. 153.
12 *E&I,* pp. 242–43; *Au,* p. 29.
13 *Myth,* pp. 329–30, 333.

of their art is in direct proportion to the extremity of opposites that separates their lives from their art. On the other hand, the saint and hero strive to actually become the ideal they have chosen. Unlike the artist who vicariously becomes his opposite in his characters, they seek fulfillment in their own lives: the saint through practicing self-abnegation, the hero through braving danger. But Yeats's preference is for the artist. The last stanza of "Among School Children" (1926) exalts the momentary ecstasy of artistic creation over the saint's penance. In that transcendent moment, the artist fuses with his work, and dancer and dance are indistinguishable from one another.

But a few years before this, in "Hodos Chameliontos" (1922), Yeats was already envisioning in his theory of the separation of life and art a possible merger of the two in certain cases. In this essay Yeats feels that the writer himself can be recreated through his art (even as six years earlier, in "Easter 1916," "MacDonagh and MacBride / And Connolly and Pearse" had suddenly found and been united with their heroic images in the Easter uprising), and as examples of this transformation he cites Dante, Villon, Juliet, and Cleopatra. Without including Shakespeare among those who thus recreate themselves, Yeats nevertheless boldly classifies two of his heroines along with Dante and Villon, an extraordinary refusal to regard imaginative beings as any less real than historical persons. Some years later, in "An Acre of Grass," he was again to juxtapose Shakespeare's heroes with historical figures, regarding them as the Mask that he wished to become:

> Grant me an old man's frenzy,
> Myself must I remake
> Till I am Timon and Lear
> Or that William Blake.

In *A Vision* Yeats regards Lear and Oedipus as prophetic souls, instruments of the Fates, so that the daughter who served Oedipus "as did Cordelia Lear—he too a man of Homer's kind—seemed less attendant upon an old railing rambler than upon genius itself" (p. 28). (Yeats seems to use the word *genius* in its original sense, that is: "The tutelary god or attendant spirit allotted to every person at his birth, to govern his fortunes and determine his character, and finally to conduct him out of the world"—*O.E.D.*) Lear, like Oedipus, develops a dimension that transcends his human predicament. So Yeats, identifying himself in his old age with Timon, Lear, and Blake, sees his own life as a ceaseless process of "becoming," a work of art in the making. Of himself Yeats could say that "the life of a man of genius, because of his greater sincerity, is often an experiment that needs analysis and record." Rather than allowing his life to go its own haphazard way, Yeats felt that it had to be organized and regulated. But Shakespeare's life, as Yeats sees it, eludes analysis and record. His is the supreme example of the artist whose achievement is concentrated in his art, not in his life. Disagreeing with Dowden's sentimental picture of Shakespeare as a "quiet country gentleman" spending his last "idle years" at Stratford, Yeats insists on imagining him seeking "for wisdom in itself at last, and not in its passionate shadows."[14] Shakespeare the man has attained the state of being that his art depicted.

Therefore, when Yeats turns to Shakespeare, seeking examples of individuals striving to achieve perfection, he chooses such examples not from Shakespeare's life but from his art. He sees Juliet and Cleopatra under compulsion to become their Masks, to unite with the image of themselves, guided by certain "personifying spirits." These spirits, "through their dramatic power," "bring our souls to crisis, to Mask and Image, caring not a straw whether we be Juliet going to her wedding, or Cleopatra to her death; for in their eyes nothing has weight but passion." (Perhaps, as examples, Yeats preferred Shakespeare's heroines to his heroes because of the complete transformation that they undergo from what they are at the beginning—Juliet inordinately young, and Cleopatra a "gipsy" and "strumpet." Juliet chooses to marry Romeo, though she knows that "it is too rash, too unadvised, too sudden" [II, i, 160], and Cleopatra, in death, is "Bravest at the last / . . . and being royal / Took her own way" [V, ii, 328–30].) Villon and Dante, like these two women, "become conjoint to their buried selves, turn all to Mask and Image," and "we gaze at such men in awe, because we gaze not at a work of art, but at the re-creation of the man through that art, the birth of a new species of man, and it may even seem that the hairs of our

14 *Au*, pp. 164–65, 68, 318.

head stand up."[15] In *A Vision* Yeats maintains the attitude in *Per Amica Silentia Lunae* that Shakespeare the man remains unchanged despite his artistic ventures into regions far removed from his nondescript self.

II

In "The Tragic Generation," when Yeats hinted that Shakespeare was a Phase 16 man, he was exploring in relatively unfamiliar territory; in *A Vision*, three years later, when he firmly assigns Shakespeare to Phase 20, he is more confident, more bold in drawing conclusions from the elaborate structure he erects, more familiar with its intricate mechanism.

When Helen Vendler upbraids Yeats for scattering artists (in "The Phases of the Moon" of *A Vision*) from "Shakespeare to Synge, from Goethe to Dostoevsky," "in no reasonable order," when she calls the collection of names "a gross menagerie" and compares it unfavorably with Alice's Wonderland, it is evident that, unless a careful attempt is made to analyze Yeats's reasons for assigning personalities to particular phases, such charges can be expected.[16] Certainly his categorization is personal, and in one sense, unscientific, though Yeats preferred to describe it as "exceedingly technical," and "a form of science for the study of human nature, as we see it in others." That he anticipated the kind of criticism Mrs. Vendler made is clear from his having called his system "arbitrary," "harsh," and "difficult," its "geometry an incomplete interpretation"; nevertheless, within the limits that Yeats himself prescribes, it is both systematic and consistent. As noted earlier, he was never rigid in his schematizing but was always ready to make adjustments. He warns the reader against concluding that he intended the scheme of human classification to be "exhaustive"; rather, he calls the descriptions simply "suggestions" to differentiate one type of person from another.[17]

Apparently alluding to his earlier erroneous classification of Shake-

15 *Au*, pp. 164, 165.
16 *Yeats's "Vision" and the Later Plays* (Cambridge, Mass., 1963), pp. 41–42.
17 *Letters*, p. 709; *Vis*, p. 23; *E&I*, p. 518; *Vis*, p. 87.

speare, Yeats informs us in *A Vision* that were Shakespeare "not himself
of a later phase, were he of the 16th Phase like his age and so drunk
with his own wine, he [would] not [have] written plays at all" (p. 294).
Phase 16 is described as one of "extreme subjectivity," a "self-absorbing
dream"; the individual of this phase "finds the soul's most radiant
expression and surrounds itself with some fairyland, some mythology of
wisdom or laughter" (pp. 137–38). To this phase—and Yeats chooses
his examples well—belongs Blake, among others. Shakespeare, at this
highly subjective phase, would clearly not have been a dramatist, but
perhaps a visionary, or prophet. Besides, as we have seen earlier, when
the individual's phase coincides with that of his period there is no
conflict and great art cannot ensue. Such was Shaw's unhappy plight.

The Will at Phase 20 is called "The Concrete Man," and evidence
of this in Shakespeare is found in his "projecting a dramatisation or
many dramatisations. He can create, just in that degree in which he
can see these dramatisations as separate from himself, and yet as an
epitome of his whole nature" (p. 151). Contrasted with this detachment,
the men of Phase 17 (Yeats's phase) are "never dramatic but always
lyrical and personal" (pp. 141–42).[18] Whereas the men of Phases 16 and
17 are full of personality in their lives, being "partisans, propagandists
and gregarious" (p. 143), Shakespeare is noted for his lack of personality, but his art is "the most passionate art that exists": Shakespeare's
"actual personality seemed faint and passionless," for, "unlike Ben
Jonson he fought no duels; he kept out of quarrels in a quarrelsome
age" (p. 153). Shakespeare's case is, for Yeats, unique. His genius is
all in his work, not in his life. Every artist would like to believe this
of himself, but as Yeats points out, this is not always so. Artists in
other phases display their personalities in their lives as well: Blake
could be full of hate and even madness (p. 138); Dante in politics was
such a partisan "that if a child, or a woman, spoke against his party he
would pelt this child or woman with stones" (p. 143); but Shakespeare
alone submerges his entire personality in his plays.

18 See *Man and Masks*, pp. 236–37; Morton Irving Seiden, *William Butler
Yeats: The Poet as a Mythmaker 1865–1939* (East Lansing, Michigan, 1962), pp.
79, 269; Gerald Levin, "The Yeats of the Autobiographies: A Man of Phase 17,"
Texas Studies in Literature and Language, VI (Autumn, 1964), 398–405.

Yeats further explains why the man of Phase 20 is called "The Concrete Man." "There is a delight in concrete images . . . unlike the impassioned images of Phase 17," but these images have to be derived from history: "he seeks some field of action, some mirror not of his own creation" (p. 152). Yeats is here thinking of Shakespeare's having borrowed his plots from Holinshed, Ariosto, Boccaccio, Plutarch, Chaucer, and others. He adds that "he fails in situations wholly created by himself, or in works of art where character or story has gained nothing from history." Perhaps Yeats here has in mind *The Tempest* and *Love's Labour's Lost,* the only two plays of Shakespeare whose plots modern scholarship has been unable to trace to any single external source.

Had Shakespeare belonged to an earlier phase, Yeats explains, his images (or characters) would have been "impassioned" (Phases 17 and 18) or "declamatory" (Phase 19: Wilde's images were "violent, arbitrary and insolent" [p. 150]; perhaps Yeats has *Salome* in mind here), but at Phase 20 Shakespeare's images "reveal through complex suffering the general destiny of man" (p. 152). The sufferings of his heroes and heroines are not depicted in a bizarre context, but they touch humanity at all points, a reflection that Yeats makes elsewhere too, calling Shakespeare "a great many-sided man." Dante, at an earlier phase than Shakespeare's, "attained, as poet, to Unity of Being, as poet saw all things set in order" (p. 144), but Yeats never ascribes this to Shakespeare. He sees Shakespeare's art as full of variety and, as such, not an aspirant for unity.[19] Only now Yeats does not regret the absence of unity as he would have previously, and it becomes clear why he cited Dante and Villon as examples of artists who recreate themselves through their art, but not Shakespeare, whose self-effacement in a noisy and combative age permitted him to create personalities that lead lives of their own, undominated by their creator.

Since Yeats's system in *A Vision* is based on the tension that arises between opposites, both *Will* and *Mask* call for attention, and, at the same time, *Creative Mind* and *Body of Fate* are nearly as important. The Mask of Phase 20 is derived from Phase 6, where Walt Whitman is situated, and so Shakespeare's desire would be to create persons re-

19 *Ex,* p. 276.

sembling Whitman.[20] To Whitman, according to Yeats's analysis, "experience is all-absorbing, subordinating observed fact, drowning even truth itself. . . . Impulse or instinct begins to be all in all" (p. 114), and we have only to think of Othello, Lear, and Antony to be persuaded that this seems an appropriate description of an important facet of Shakespeare's tragic heroes. Even though Yeats tells us, however, that the Mask of Phase 20 "is derived from Phase 6, where man first becomes a generalized form, according to the *primary tincture,* as in the poetry of Walt Whitman," he goes on to say, "but this *Mask* he must by dramatisation rescue from a *Body of Fate* derived from Phase 24, where moral domination dies out before that of the exterior world conceived as a whole" (pp. 151–52). That is, Shakespeare is not content to simply portray his heroes as subjective individuals absorbed in their own impulse and instinct, but he dramatizes and objectifies them as well, without subjugating them to a personal moral scheme, for at Phases 19, 20, and 21, there is "logical deduction from an observed fact" (p. 114). This insight of Yeats is exemplified in Shakespeare's heroes, whose behavior follows logically from the situations that they face. Thus Yeats saw in Macbeth nobility struggling with reality, Macbeth's overpowering sense of sin—his nobility—pitted against his wife's ambition and the instigation of the witches, or reality.[21] The interaction between the hero's own volition and the circumstances that surround him produces great drama. In Shakespeare, Yeats always sees more than one force operating.

Yeats emphasizes the subordination of Shakespeare's own personality to that of his great heroes. Shakespeare makes them *antithetical* (or subjective) men, and, because he is located in a near *primary* phase (nearing objectivity), he is able to grant them an independence that less objective writers (Shelley, Landor, Dante) would not have been able to concede. Shakespeare imposes neither his own ethic nor the

20 So also the men of Phase 17, who are "almost always partisans, propagandists and gregarious" (p. 143) are attracted by the Mask of Phase 3, which is their opposite; in this phase "simplicity and intensity are united" and Yeats mentions Landor's shepherd, Morris' *Water of the Wondrous Isles,* Shelley's "wandering lovers and sages" (p. 109), and no doubt Yeats has in mind his own Michael Robartes and Cuchulain, lonely men who have little traffic with the world.

21 *Man and Poet,* p. 318.

ethic of his age on his characters, but true to the largeness of his vision, he sees them as inhabitants "of the exterior world conceived as a whole" (p. 152), timeless in their universality.

In an earlier phase, as noted above, Shakespeare would not have been a dramatist; and one phase later, rigidity has set in, for the artist has developed a pushing personality that he imposes on his art: he flaunts "a manner peculiar to himself and impossible to others. We say at once, 'How individual he is' " (p. 155). Yeats's observation is pejorative. Shakespeare, "faint and passionless" as a man, would no longer be Shakespeare at this phase. In his examination of Phase 21, Yeats goes on to stress the "domination over all circumstances," the "dominating constructive will" (pp. 155–56) that marks out men of this phase. Seeing it as one of the most despicable of all the phases, Yeats takes the opportunity of making the persons of Phase 21 those contemporaries of his whose realism and socialistic zeal he hated: Lamarck, Shaw, Wells, and Moore (p. 154). Resenting their officiousness and cocky self-assurance, he declares that the will of such men is so "intellectually dominating" that it "imposes itself upon the multiplicity of living images, or events, upon all in Shakespeare, in Napoleon even, that delighted in its independent life"; for they are tyrants and must kill their adversaries (pp. 156, 157). Perhaps Yeats is here thinking of Shaw's splenetic antagonism toward Shakespeare, an attitude that piqued Yeats.[22] If the man of Phase 21 is a novelist, "his characters must go his road, and not theirs" (p. 157), unlike those of Shakespeare, whose art is neither a doctrine to be propounded nor a sermon to be delivered.

Poised between Unity of Being (or the antithetical) and increasing objectivity (or the primary), Shakespeare is ideally situated to be the surpassing playwright that he is: "for the *primary* is not yet strong

22 In 1919 Yeats scornfully dismissed Shaw's condemnation of "Shakespeare's 'ghosts and murders' " as being evidence of a "Garden City mind," incapable of comprehending any reality other than what could be perceived by the five senses (*Ex*, p. 276). Perhaps Yeats is referring to Shaw's Preface to *Man and Superman* (1903) in which Shaw castigates Shakespeare for his lack of ideas, for his exploitation of popular religion for professional purposes ("for example Sydney Carton and the ghost in Hamlet"), and for "factitious melodramatic murders and revenges and the like" (*Shaw on Shakespeare: An Anthology of Bernard Shaw's Writings . . . on Shakespeare*, ed. Edwin Wilson [New York, 1961], pp. 223–26). See also *E&I*, p. 283, where Yeats defends Shakespeare's "murders, and ghosts."

enough to substitute for the lost Unity of Being that of the external world perceived as fact" (p. 152). That is, subjectivity still holds sway, but incipient objectivity provides the necessary corrective to excessive subjectivity. Phase 21, as noticed, brings with it the objectivists who perceive the external world as fact; and an antithetical phase close to Unity of Being (Phase 15) would have made Shakespeare's art, as was Dante's, too subjective to be great drama. It is evident that Yeats's choice of Phase 20 for Shakespeare, poised between the subjective and the objective, is not a whimsical impulse, as Helen Vendler would have us believe, but is dictated by the overall coherence and consistency of his system.

III

Not only does Yeats in *A Vision* furnish sound reasons for locating Shakespeare at Phase 20, but he also displays a remarkable insight into certain aspects of Shakespeare's art: his success as a dramatist; his urge to personify rather than to characterize, to create "always from *Mask* and *Creative Mind,* never from situation alone, never from *Body of Fate* alone" (p. 153); his ability to use the False Mask imaginatively; and above all, the increasingly realistic nature of his world as distinct from the pervasive symbolism of earlier phases—these are some of the important features that Yeats touches on in his brief but concentrated treatment of Shakespeare.

The success that came to Shakespeare as dramatist was alien to his unambitious temperament, for though Yeats calls Phase 20 a phase of ambition, he adds that this ambition asserts itself in Napoleon's own person, but with Shakespeare, through the persons of his art (p. 154). Shakespeare's success "came to him . . . as something hostile and unforeseen" (p. 153), and quoting from Sonnet 110,

> Alas, 'tis true I have gone here and there,
> And made myself a motley to the view (p. 152),

Yeats describes Shakespeare's success as one "that rolls out and smooths away, that dissolves through creation, that seems to delight in all outward flowing, that drenches all with grease and oil; that turns dramatisa-

tion into desecration" (p. 152). Belonging to a phase that seeks fulfillment in self-dramatization, Shakespeare feels compelled to express himself
through the medium of the dramatist's art, though conscious that the
desecration of his own identity will inevitably ensue. Thus Yeats cites
Shakespeare as one who achieved public recognition without reveling in
it, perhaps hinting at the contrast between Shakespeare on the one hand,
and Shaw and Wilde on the other, who exulted in what Yeats may have
felt were their instant triumphs on the London stage. There seems to
be a suggestion of identification with Shakespeare on Yeats's part, for to
Yeats also success came as something hostile and unforeseen. Yeats speaks
of Shaw, "the formidable man," and Wilde as playwrights who "would
have long divided the stage between them," and ironically tells of his
own bewilderment at *Arms and the Man*, a bewilderment mingled
with "admiration and hatred," while implying that his own meditative
and nostalgic play, *The Land of Heart's Desire*, first presented as a
curtain-raiser for *Arms and the Man*, was eclipsed by Shaw's "athletic
wit."[23]

In Yeats's analysis of Phase 20, he notes that a conspicuous feature
of Shakespeare's art is that he always creates from Mask and Creative
Mind, and therefore his characters are diverse.[24] The men of Phase 17,
however, are obsessed by their Mask. Yeats says of Dante that he "had an
intellect that served the *Mask* alone" (p. 144). The Will in Phase 17
is called "The *Daimonic* Man" (p. 140), which indicates its intense
desire to be unified with its daimon, or Mask. In other words, since
Shakespeare creates from both Mask and Creative Mind, the persons
of his art are not repetitions of the same image which would be the
case if Mask alone was in operation. The heroes of Shelley have a same-
ness about them that inevitably results from his total commitment to

23 *Au*, pp. 168–70.
24 Yeats's own equivalents for these mystifying forces considerably clarify
them: "When I wish for some general idea which will describe the Great Wheel as
an individual life I go to the *Commedia dell 'Arte* or improvised drama of Italy. The
stage-manager, or *Daimon*, offers his actor an inherited scenario, the *Body of Fate*,
and a *Mask* or rôle as unlike as possible to his natural ego or *Will*, and leaves him
to improvise through his *Creative Mind* the dialogue and details of the plot" (*Vis*,
pp. 83–84).

his Mask. Yeats seems to suggest this when he says of Phase 17 that the Will finds "a *Mask* of simplicity that is also intensity" (p. 141). Shakespeare's heroes are far from simple: they are diverse because formed by the joint endeavors of Mask and Creative Mind; also, they are dramatic, whereas the images of Phase 17, it will be recalled, have "an intensity which is never dramatic but always lyrical and personal" (pp. 141–42).

At the same time, Shakespeare does not create "from situation alone, never from *Body of Fate* alone" (p. 153), as the naturalists of Phase 21 and thereafter tend to do. Shaw, a socialist, and Ibsen, a realist, see all life conditioned by situation alone, or as Yeats says elsewhere, "when the *primary* phases begin man is moulded more and more from without" (p. 84). Man, for them, is the product of his environment, but Yeats's Shakespeare, more existentialist than sociologist, "must personify rather than characterise, create not observe that multitude" of characters that he brings into being (p. 152); for, according to Yeats, great art does not result from mere observation no matter how faithful that observation is. By positioning Shakespeare at Phase 20, Yeats sees him as one happily endowed with qualities that draw their strength from both the antithetical and the primary; he thus occupies a balanced position in which his dramatic genius can best display itself .

"Both Shakespeare and Balzac used the False *Mask* imaginatively, explored it to impose the True" (p. 153), the False *Mask* being Superstition, the True *Mask*, Fatalism (p. 151). Yeats's designation of Shakespeare's Mask as Fatalism is significant and deserves careful scrutiny. What precisely does he mean by this, and why is it contrasted with Superstition? In an age riddled with superstition, and Yeats does not use the word pejoratively, Shakespeare looks beyond the popular beliefs of his time and sees his tragic heroes move toward their destinies with the joy of acceptance. Their fatalism is seen in their recognition of the existence of a cosmic pattern to which they willingly conform, without making an attempt to resist their destinies. Long before, Yeats had seen in Shakespeare, as in Dante, Bunyan, and Thomas a Kempis, a deep moral and spiritual preoccupation, a communing with God and with angels through the language of allegory and symbolism, and he points to "Hamlet's objection to the bare bodkin" as an instance of this.[25]

25 *E&I*, pp. 368–69.

Hamlet rejects the bare bodkin because at that point in his life death would be premature, and Yeats would perhaps see in this an acceptance of one's destiny, not in despair but in acquiescence. In "He Wishes His Beloved Were Dead" the lover's desire is that his beloved might learn this truth:

> But know your hair was bound and wound
> About the stars and moon and sun.

For Yeats, nothing in Shakespeare's tragedies happens by accident, and though to the more simple-minded Elizabethan in Shakespeare's audience the ghostly and magical ingredients in *Hamlet* and *Macbeth* might have seemed a demonstration of his own superstitions and beliefs, to the better informed they represented external forces that controlled the lives of the heroes and propelled them toward a predetermined destiny.

Yeats's examination of Phase 20 concludes with his depiction of Shakespeare as more realist than symbolist. This surprising reversal of his general attitude toward Shakespeare must lead us to conclude that here, perhaps unfortunately, he has allowed the logic of his system to prevail over personal conviction. Although in "The Symbolism of Poetry"—an early essay, written in 1900—Yeats considered Shakespeare one who used the external world to supply "emotional symbols" in order to represent inner states of existence,[26] twenty-five years later when he wrote *A Vision*, the system called for a steady movement away from the symbolical preoccupation of the antithetical stages toward the realism of the primary stages. It appears that Yeats, feeling compelled to present Shakespeare as deferring to this trend, overstated the case, to the detriment of Shakespeare the symbolist:

> At Phase 19 we create through the externalised *Mask* an imaginary world, in whose real existence we believe, while remaining separate from it; at Phase 20 we enter that world and become a portion of it; we study it, we amass historical evidence, and that we may dominate it the more, drive out myth and symbol, and compel it to seem the real world where our lives are lived. [P. 154]

Still, there is, perhaps, a suggestion in this passage that to Yeats it is really we, the readers of Shakespeare, who are defaulters and not Shakespeare. Yeats is here attacking the tireless Shakespearean research that we are so surfeited with. Shakespeare at Phase 20 is on the borderline

26 *E&I*, p.162.

of out-and-out realism, and so the temptation for his admirers to compel his world "to seem the real world where our lives are lived" proves irresistible. Having located Shakespeare at this late phase, Yeats, alas, has to make him conform to the features of such a classification, and in the process he subordinates Shakespeare to the exigencies of the system. But one would like to believe that Yeats attaches the blame for Shakespeare's increasing realism, not to Shakespeare, but to his too literal and undiscriminating readers.

Yeats had noted the increasingly dramatic nature of thought among those he placed at Phase 19 (including Wilde and Byron): "His thought is immensely effective and dramatic" (p. 148), and later, "but there is less symbol, more fact" (p. 149). Shakespeare necessarily carries the process further, for myth and symbol are driven out at Phase 20. This denial of Shakespeare's being essentially a symbolist is startling when it is recalled that just three years earlier Yeats had located him at Phase 16, a phase of extreme subjectivity. There Yeats had pointed out that "Shakespeare's people make all things serve their passion, and that passion is for the moment the whole energy of their being—birds, beasts, men, women, landscape, society, are but symbols and metaphors, nothing is studied in itself, the mind is a dark well, no surface, depth only." Yeats gives no examples here, but a scene that could have occurred to him as being illustrative of his description—considering how frequently he mentions it elsewhere—would be "Lear's rage under the lightning," where the storm is a symbol of Lear's own inner perturbation.[27]

Sense experience, the storm in *King Lear,* powerfully reflects the mental anguish that Lear experiences. Elsewhere, Yeats considers the "correspondence . . . between . . . sight, hearing, taste, and smell, and certain mental qualities," and asserts that "when Shakespeare compares the mind of the mad Lear to the 'vexed sea,' we are told at once something more laden with meaning than many pages of psychology." As Yeats observed in 1915, external nature can become "a landscape that is symbolical of some spiritual condition." He developed this idea in a later essay, showing how the sudden transmutation of sense experience

---

27 *Au,* p. 174; *Boiler,* p. 35. See also *E&I,* p. 301, and *Letters,* p. 441, where Yeats adverts to Lear on the heath.

into the depiction of a mental or a spiritual condition could be likened to "the sudden 'blacking out' of the lights of the stage."[28] The thought occurs in "Lapis Lazuli" but is now lifted onto an apocalyptic plane of reality: the last scene of *Hamlet* and of *King Lear* is suddenly transformed into the spectacle of the entire world breaking up, a cataclysmic finale to the very drama of human existence on the stage of the world:

> Black out; Heaven blazing into the head:
> Tragedy wrought to its uttermost.
> Though Hamlet rambles and Lear rages.

Thus, even after formally denying to Shakespeare (in *A Vision*) the symbolistic intensity of the earlier phases, Yeats actually continued to regard him as a fellow symbolist. Nor should his observation on Shakespeare's heightened realism be interpreted as being a total castigation, for Yeats's own later plays develop a note of realism absent in his early plays. *Purgatory,* though having nothing in common with the realism of a Shaw or a Galsworthy play, does possess a brutal realism of its own that compels the audience to accept it as representing the real world. It is possible for us to "enter that world and become a portion of it" (p. 154) in a way that was not possible with early plays such as *The Shadowy Waters, The Wanderings of Oisin,* and *The Countess Cathleen.* Even the powerful symbolism with which *Purgatory* is charged appears at times with blatant directness. The Old Man tells his son: "The shadow of a cloud upon the house, / And that's symbolical." Symbolism now is not being covertly slipped in, but overtly brandished.

Having, since 1901, emphasized impersonality in Shakespeare, Yeats, toward the end of his own career, became increasingly insistent on its being one of the fundamental requirements for poetry to achieve a measure of greatness and permanence. Concerning *The King of the Great Clock Tower,* written in 1934, he says, "I made up the play that I might write lyrics out of dramatic experience, all my personal experience having in some strange way come to an end." Perhaps one can legitimately wonder whether, if he had revised *A Vision* once again, he would have placed himself in Phase 20 in the company of Shakespeare, whose

---

28 *The Works of William Blake,* ed. E. J. Ellis and W. B. Yeats (London, 1893), I, 238; *Au,* pp. 45, 196.

impersonality he had so consistently insisted on. In *Pages from a Diary Written in Nineteen Hundred and Thirty,* Yeats wrote that his character was so little himself that all his life it had thwarted him. "It has affected my poems, my true self," he declared, "no more than the character of a dancer affects the movements of the dance." Writing to Olivia Shakespear in 1926, he speculated that "to grow old is to grow impersonal, to need nothing and to seek nothing for oneself."[29] Perhaps near the end of his life, Yeats, with his striving toward the impersonal and the universal in his work, came to believe that his position on the wheel could be correspondingly moved up from Phase 17, from subjectivity toward greater objectivity.

In his Introduction to *The Oxford Book of Modern Verse* Yeats does not deny the artist personal experience, but requires that it be universalized in his art: the Dark Lady has "private reality," but it is only "among the women Shakespeare had imagined" that she becomes universal. Here the reference to "the women" suggests clearly that Yeats is thinking of the plays, not of the sonnets. Nearly thirty years before this, in "Poetry and Tradition" (1907), Yeats had seen the personal affairs of the poet's life—"his enemy or his love or his cause"—metamorphosed into art, or, as Yeats puts it, "the phoenix can but open her young wings in a flaming nest." The same thought appears in "Sailing to Byzantium," where the poet, invoking the sages standing in God's holy fire, desires that his heart be consumed away and he be gathered into the artifice of eternity. In "Poetry and Tradition," interestingly enough, Yeats suggests that if the poet's mistress can recognize herself in the poet's verses—a possible oblique reference to Shakespeare and his sonnets—then such verse is not a complete artistic success. But immediately after this failure, Yeats sees in the creation of Timon and Cleopatra perfect artistic accomplishment: "Timon of Athens contemplates his own end, and orders his tomb by the beached verge of the salt flood, and Cleopatra sets the asp to her bosom, and their words move us because their sorrow is not their own at tomb or asp, but for all men's fate."[30]

29   *Letters,* p. 819; *Ex,* p. 308; *Letters,* p. 715.
30   *E&I,* p. 255.

Again, "A General Introduction for My Work" (1937) opens with Shakespeare as an example of a poet who displays impersonality. After a dutiful salute to Dante, Milton, Raleigh, Shelley, and Byron, Yeats elaborates the point with reference to Shakespeare's dramatic persons: Lear, Romeo, Rosalind, and Cleopatra, and he contrasts them with the Dark Lady whom, according to Yeats, Shakespeare did not view with the detachment he could bring to the others, and therefore she was less of an artistic achievement. In language reminiscent of the lines in "Byzantium," "Before me floats an image, man or shade, / Shade more than man, more image than a shade," Yeats affirms that the poet, as poet, is no longer a man of the everyday world, but, rather, "he is more type than man, more passion than type. He is Lear, Romeo, Oedipus, Tiresias; he has stepped out of a play, and even the woman he loves is Rosalind, Cleopatra, never The Dark Lady."[31] Yeats would perhaps agree with Wordsworth that in his sonnets "Shakespeare unlocked his heart," and not with Browning's retort, "If so, the less Shakespeare he!"

Yeats's statement above, "he has stepped out of a play," with reference to the dramatist, is arresting. Has Shakespeare then himself been metamorphosed into a character like his creations? And does not the statement imply that the dramatist does not make the character his mouthpiece, but that the converse holds true? Rather than say that Shakespeare is Hamlet—a usual Romantic approach to the play—Yeats would say that Hamlet is Shakespeare; that Hamlet controlled Shakespeare, not Shakespeare Hamlet. This, in fact, was Yeats's assertion in a letter to Sean O'Casey in 1928. The transformation of the artist into an artifact (the theme of "Sailing to Byzantium"), which Yeats had granted to Dante and to Villon in 1922, but without mentioning Shakespeare, now seems to be a process that he sees Shakespeare too undergoing, and he thus accords to him the highest achievement of the artist. The mysterious relationship between the artist and his creation was a subject that always fascinated Yeats; it was in Shakespeare's art that he saw the autonomy of both the dramatist and his characters, along with their interaction.

31 E&I, p. 509.

5

Shakespeare's Fabric of This Vision

Prospero. . . . These our actors,
As I foretold you, were all spirits, and
Are melted into air, into thin air:
And, like the baseless fabric of this vision,
The cloud-capped towers, the gorgeous palaces,
The solemn temples, the great globe itself,
Yea, all which it inherit, shall dissolve,
And, like this insubstantial pageant faded,
Leave not a rack behind. We are such stuff
As dreams are made on.

—The Tempest

An Cathaoirleach. Do you not think we might leave
the dead alone?
Dr. Yeats. I am passing on. I would hate to leave
the dead alone.

—Yeats, "Debate on Divorce"

ENERALLY regarded as the outstanding feature of the modern
stage, the disappearance of the hero in the realist drama of the
late nineteenth and early twentieth centuries was the trend set by Ibsen,
Strindberg, and Shaw. The quasi-hero, a prey to his circumstances,
could no longer act, but simply react. Yeats, repelled by realism, which
he regarded as a tame recording of observation, swung to the other
extreme and strongly advocated a rejection of what is merely seen and

heard. In a letter to the *Daily Express* (1895), he deplored the naturalistic direction in which Irish novelists were going, asserting that "they have, perhaps, bowed to the fallacy of our time which says that the fountain of art is observation, whereas it is almost wholly experience." With characteristic emphasis, he then adds, "The creations of a great writer are little more than the moods and passions of his own heart, given surnames and Christian names and sent to walk the earth."[1] This statement accords to the writer supreme authority; his characters are merely an excuse for his self-assertion. But, as might be expected, Yeats did not allow this point of view to monopolize his attitude indefinitely.

During the nineties he strove to tether his verse more firmly than before to Ireland, so that it might be informed by the spirit of nationalism. But he was, at the same time, constantly seeking to widen the range of appeal that his work would have by carrying it beyond a purely local basis into an area of general acceptance. So also, his early play, *The Shadowy Waters,* with its perplexing symbolism that indicates his desire for subjectivism as opposed to drab realism, was repeatedly revised in order that its mysteries might become less inscrutable to his readers. Yeats knew that the danger attendant on a too firm upholding of subjectivism was that his own position could become as vulnerable as that of the realists he was so vehemently attacking, for it exposed him to the charge of a solipsism that deprived the work of dramatic validity.

It was therefore necessary to counteract this upholding of subjectivism with a position that transcended both extremes, yet remained capable of drawing on either, if necessary. A compromise would be a feeble solution, because a negative attitude was always unattractive to Yeats: he found Ibsen's attempts to combine "the utmost sincerity [with] the most unbroken logic" an "imperfect pleasure." Thus Yeats's early novel *John Sherman,* though a subjective work in that it portrayed opposing forces within Yeats's own personality, was at the same time an attempt to dramatize the entire conflict and place it in a framework outside himself. His own misgivings about its excessive symbolism, as

---

1 *Letters,* p. 249. For a detailed study of Yeats's concept of the hero, see Alex Zwerdling, *Yeats and the Heroic Ideal* (New York, 1965), chapter 1.

seen in his amusing remark on the difficulty of keeping "the characters from turning into eastern symbolic monsters," indicates his awareness of what needed to be eschewed. Another autobiographical work that proved troublesome was his unpublished novel, *The Speckled Bird,* written between about 1896 and 1900.[2] Yeats's visit to Stratford-on-Avon in 1901 is important, because it seems to have confirmed his feeling that his work needed liberation from an overloaded symbolism; besides, the experience of seeing Shakespeare's plays provided a hint about the direction that his own art could profitably take.

In April, 1901, Yeats was at Stratford and saw the entire English historical cycle of Shakespeare's plays performed. The opening sentence of "At Stratford-on-Avon," "I have been hearing Shakespeare as the traveller in *News from Nowhere* might have heard him, had he not been hurried back into our noisy time," establishes the tone of the essay. Morris' traveler finds himself in a strange and incredible world; he feels like "a being from another planet." Yeats, deeply stirred by the spectacle of Shakespeare on the stage, wrote to Lady Gregory from Stratford: "I feel that I am getting deeper into Shakespeare's mystery than ever before." With their tremendous vitality, abounding in vivid personalities, the plays seemed to provide him with an answer to the question that had not till then been satisfactorily dealt with. Was the greatest art born of detachment, or was it but a thinly disguised manifestation of the author's personal beliefs? Shakespeare's plays had their roots in a historical past, but they far surpassed the factual content that this comprised and could certainly not be regarded as specimens of the realistic drama that Ibsen and others were busy popularizing. Also, equally important, they were by no means the outpourings of Shakespeare's personal thoughts and ideas, nor did the characters answer to the description of "puppets," which Yeats had six years earlier said the old Greek and English dramatists created.[3] Although Yeats would never have denied the dramatist his vital role in the shaping of the play, it is also true that, after his Strat-

---

2 *Ex,* p. 166; *Letters,* p. 92; see Curtis Bradford, "The Speckled Bird: A Novel by W. B. Yeats," *Irish Writing,* XXXI (Summer, 1955), 9.

3 *E&I,* p. 96; William Morris, *News From Nowhere* (London, 1899), p. 60; *Letters,* pp. 349, 255.

ford visit, he never sees the hero of a great play as a passive mouthpiece for his creator, least of all the hero of a Shakespeare play.

Shakespeare's historical plays, he declared, displayed "something extravagant and superhuman, something almost mythological." The domain of art seemed suddenly to consist of territory carved out neither from the author's personality nor from his environment, but to be both autonomous and strangely exciting. Surpassing in intensity the people who inhabit the earth, the personages of the poet's imagination possess an almost palpable existence of their own. Yeats confesses that "the theatre has moved me as it has never done before," and he describes the Shakespearean world as being "to me almost too visible, too audible, too full of an unearthly energy." Undoubtedly this is, for Yeats, a world peopled by beings who owe their existence, not only to the mortal mind of the dramatist, but to some creative power beyond the frontiers of human capability. Incredible as this may appear, Yeats is not being simply figurative here, but, as as we shall see later, intends that such preternatural intervention be consciously recognized. Appropriately, he defines this world in terms of Prospero's magical prowess: watching the plays acted, he felt "as if the world might suddenly vanish and leave nothing behind, not even a little dust under one's feet." Although he does not undertake to state explicitly the character of this artistic creation, as he does twenty years later, there are hints and suggestions that make his conviction implicit: he goes on to say, "The people my mind's eye has seen have too much of the extravagance of dreams . . . to seem more than a dream, and yet all else has grown dim before them."[4] Limiting their existence to the dream world and, at the same time, granting them an individuality exceeding that of mortal men—"Mortal men our abstracts are" is what the severed head in *The King of the Great Clock Tower* sings—Yeats, through a deliberate contradiction, asserts their defiant ambiguity.

Furthermore, by employing flashes of Shakespeare's imagery, he emphasizes the dream quality of the Shakespearean world that partakes of life, yet transcends it as well. Confronted by these all-powerful per-

4 *E&I*, pp. 109, 97.

sonalities, even the figures of history seem weak and spineless. Elsewhere Yeats quotes approvingly Goethe's statement: "We do the people of history the honour of naming after them the creations of our own minds," and, in his appraisal of Shakespeare's Richard II, affirms that "the historical Richard has passed away for ever and the Richard of the play lives more intensely, it seems, than did ever living man." The greatest writers, Yeats declares, possess "a power, little affected by external things, being self-contained, self-created, self-sufficing"; not being subservient to history, they "think the world is but their palette," and use it to portray a personal vision. "Through ideas [we] discover ourselves," Yeats believed. In 1902, Yeats said that he loved "symbolism, which is often the only fitting speech for some mystery of disembodied life," and recalled that he had once seen a production of *Hamlet* during which, while the actors came walking in, the thought occurred to him that these were unreal people, "ghostly kings and queens setting out upon their unearthly business."[5]

Transcending reality, art, Yeats believes, formulates its own laws. The exaltation of art above life had of course been variously proposed by Pater, Wilde, and other symbolists, but Yeats reveals himself here as a far more definite precursor of Pirandello than any of the others. To call him a precursor is perhaps unjust, because Yeats's own later plays explore the relationship between art and life, but Yeats was quick to acknowledge Pirandello's obsession with the subject: to Wyndham Lewis he wrote that "Pirandello . . . alone of living dramatists has unexhausted, important material."[6] In his *Six Characters in Search of an Author* (1921), Pirandello shows how, given certain suitable conditions, a work of art is evoked; it assumes a tangible form; bodiless figments of the poet's imagination become corporeal, and a living person mysteriously impinges on the scene.

In 1900, in the essay "The Symbolism of Poetry," Yeats had already adumbrated this doctrine that Pirandello made the theme of a play twenty-one years later. The visible aspects of the material world, Yeats explained, when suitably conjoined, "call down among us certain disem-

5 *Ex*, pp. 144, 145, 236, 237; *E&I*, pp. 382–83.
6 *Letters*, p. 776.

bodied powers"; likewise, the poet seeks to establish a harmonious pattern, which becomes an invitation for "the god it calls among us." Yeats, at the turn of the century, was aware of the need to be wary; in his essay "The Celtic Element in Literature" (1897), where the same doctrine is delicately hinted at, he confesses in a footnote appended in 1924: "I should have added as an alternative that the supernatural may at any moment create new myths, but I was timid."[7] The growing belief that a work of art was not merely an offspring of the author's mind but also owed its origin to a power outside and beyond him began to find justification in Yeats's own experience as a dramatist.

But this was no sudden discovery. As early as 1897, Yeats's Michael Robartes had informed his eager listener that by having surrounded himself with great art—paintings, the works of Shakespeare, Dante, and Milton—he had begun to establish contact with the "gods," who are images, and he mentions Roland, Hamlet, and Faust as examples of these images "who have taken upon themselves spiritual bodies in the minds of the modern poets and romance-writers, and under the power of the old divinities." These images are self-begotten, and the poet's mind is simply employed as a womb for their growth and sustenance. The incantatory lines, "Come from the holy fire, perne in a gyre, / And be the singing-masters of my soul" in "Sailing to Byzantium," a much later poem, are evidently a continuation and an intensification of this doctrine. Robartes also points to King Lear, whose head is "still wet with the thunderstorm," and mysteriously tells his host that "he laughs because you thought yourself an existence who are but a shadow, and him a shadow who is an eternal god."[8] Yeats would perhaps at this point want us to remember Theseus' observation: "The best in this kind are but shadows: and the worst are no worse, if imagination amend them" (*Dream,* V, i, 208–9). Seeing in Shakespeare these ideas demonstrated at their highest intensity, Yeats turned to his work for examples to effectively illustrate his argument.

In July, 1901, a few months after his return from Stratford, Yeats began writing his play, *On Baile's Strand.* Nearly three years later,

---

7   *E&I,* pp. 157, 185.
8   *Myth,* pp. 274, 275.

when the play was being rehearsed for production in Dublin while Yeats was in New York, he gave to Frank Fay a description of Cuchulain's appearance and character. He was diffident, however, about this analysis and added: "I write of him with difficulty, for when one creates a character one does it out of instinct. . . . It is as though the character embodied itself. The less one reasons the more living the character." The same year he wrote to Olivia Shakespear commending a novel she had written, particularly her depiction of the heroine, who has "depths of feeling in her," and adds, "it is always bad when a writer makes you feel that he knows all that is in any of his people." The keen sense of the independence of a work of art, both from its historical and social milieu and from its creator's ideas and opinions, finds expression in a letter to Fiona Macleod dated November, 1901. Here, he gently undermines Macleod's retelling of certain Irish folktales for being "subjective, an inner way of looking at things assumed by a single mind. They have little independent life." He also praises certain of his correspondent's narratives as being "objective . . . and independent," though adding that this commendable quality disappears when "the more mortal part of you begins to speak, the mere person, not the god."[9] Without specifying who "the god" is, Yeats nevertheless lifts the creative act onto a superhuman plane.

Thus, having moved from an early detestation of realism to an insistence on subjectivism as its corrective, Yeats then radically changed his position after discovering in Shakespeare's plays an art that was neither the one extreme nor the other. Equally significant to him was the fact that this art was not a colorless hybrid of the two but, rather, outdistanced both and created for itself totally new standards by which alone it could be understood. Far removed from his early appraisal that characters in a work of art are docile puppets is Yeats's new idea that they are invested with demoniacal authority. The puppets dominate their master, who finds himself in the grip of an unearthly power he is helpless to resist. (In "The Dolls," the doll maker is abashed by the loudmouthed impudence of his puppets.) Before 1904, Yeats's unorthodox opinion that a cleavage existed between dramatist and hero had found

9 *Letters,* pp. 425, 439, 357-58.

utterance only in letters to friends, but in this year he openly stated that an ancient writer "saw his hero, if it was a play of character, or some dominant passion . . . moving before him, living with a life he did not endeavour to control."[10] Although Yeats implies that there is some control outside that of the author, he does not yet commit himself, being perhaps restrained by the unpreparedness of his readers for a theory that gave to transcendent powers a collaborative role with the dramatist.

Around 1912, while dabbling in automatic writing, Yeats "was first accosted by a spirit named Leo Africanus, the Italian geographer and traveler, who showed great astonishment when Yeats said he did not know him. Leo Africanus professed to be his attendant spirit or guide."[11] This discovery not only confirmed, but also superseded, Yeats's theory of the Mask—for the Mask, after all, was still but one aspect of the individual—and established the existence of a transcendent power outside the individual, guiding and even controlling him. Although Leo Africanus' attention to Yeats must have been welcome, in that it opened up new and illimitable possibilities, Yeats does not seem to have remained enamored of his obscure guide for long. There are indications in his later writings that Shakespeare took Africanus' place, and that Yeats came to regard him as his daimon.

II

The theory of the daimon may be simplified to bring only those aspects relevant to Yeats's concept under scrutiny. An individual at any particular moment in his life is but a fraction of his ultimate being, which is "the Daimon or ultimate self of that man," and is made up of all the incarnations he has passed through and is yet to pass through. The daimon is analogous to the total individual, including his childhood, youth, middle age, and old age. Yeats's theory, however, like Plato's, goes beyond the barriers of birth and death; for Yeats, the daimon comprises his incarnate existence as well. It is the sum of all

10 *Ex*, p. 164.

11 *Man and Masks*, p. 195. See also *Ex*, p. 59, where Yeats refers to Plutarch's description of how daimons "return to be the schoolmasters of the living, whom they influence unseen."

that the individual has been, is, and will be, not only in this life, but in past, present, and future existences as well. A human being is obviously only a partial manifestation of this comprehensive being, and if wise, will allow himself to be guided by his highly experienced daimon. It will be recalled that Proust in *Remembrance of Things Past* depicts his characters in the time-dimension, showing us not only what they are at that moment, but also what they have been in the past: seen thus they appear as "monstrous creatures . . . occupying in time a place far more considerable than the so restricted one allotted them in space."[12] But Proust's gamut embraces only a single life on earth; Yeats's encompasses the whole, for the daimon is the total identity of the individual.

Yeats feels that the daimon is anxious to guide and instruct the earthly or human aspect of itself in the same manner in which a stage manager offers his actor a mask or a role and encourages him to do his best in the playing of a part that may well be the direct opposite of what he is in himself.[13] The daimons of different individuals, being extensions of their human counterparts and existing on a higher plane, are not subject to barriers of time and distance and may therefore communicate with each other. On earth these same individuals, separated by insuperable barriers, are restricted to communicating with none but their contemporaries. When communication between daimons takes place, certain remarkable phenomena ensue on earth. Yeats recounts the simultaneous appearance to him and to several others of a woman shooting an arrow at a star. He then discreetly asks, "Had some great event taken place in some world where myth is reality and had we seen some portion of it? One of my fellow-students quoted a Greek saying, 'Myths are the activities of the Daimons.' "[14] From this it follows that people's acts may be influenced by daimons of men still living, but more important,

12 *Vis*, p. 183; Marcel Proust, *Remembrance of Things Past*, II, *The Past Recaptured* (New York, 1932), 1124. Yeats calls the daimon "my own buried self" (*Au*, p. 223); this definition, though including the Unconscious, does not stop short at the Freudian limits of the word but embraces the metaphysical too. Yeats knew Freud's theories very well: see *Au*, p. 139; *Myth*, p. 341; *Ex*, p. 378; *Vis*, p. 235.

13 *Vis*, pp. 83–84.

14 *Au*, p. 224. See also Virginia Moore, *The Unicorn: William Butler Yeats's Search for Reality* (New York, 1954), pp. 387–89.

even of men long dead, and unconsciously these persons may perform great deeds or create works of art at the behest of daimons.

"Such things come from beyond the will," Yeats asserts, and he argues that, if the person is an artist, a daimon of some previous artist may "use" him for its own purpose: "Because only the living create, [a daimon] may seek the assistance of those living men into whose 'unconsciousness' or incarnate *Daimon,* some affinity of aim . . . permits it to enter." What is meant by this is that mortal men may suddenly find themselves, like pieces on a chessboard, controlled by the daimons of fellow mortals who perhaps lived centuries before but are nevertheless still deeply interested in human life. Their passions have not been fully expended: "Helen may still open her chamber door to Paris or watch him from the wall," for in life, all her energies were consummated in her passion for her lover, so that even after death that emotional momentum persists. But in addition to those who lived passionately, such as Helen and Paris, there are artists whose passionate creative energies are unallayed by death, and their daimons pursue their unachieved artistic goals through living writers with whom they find "some affinity of aim." Being "out of nature," as in "Sailing to Byzantium," and therefore unable to express themselves, they seek out some living artist whose genius conforms to their own and compel him to utter what they dictate. Yeats sees Shakespeare's daimon as still possessing such an undiminished, or rather a burgeoning, urge to create: "Surely of the passionate dead we can but cry in words Ben Jonson meant for none but Shakespeare: 'So rammed' are they 'with life they can but grow in life with being.'"[15] Although dead, Shakespeare, or rather his daimon, continues to impose itself vicariously on the world through the art of a living poet.

Yeats indicates at least twice in his writings that he considers the daimon of Shakespeare to have "some affinity of aim" with his own poetic genius. In an unpublished section of *Pages from a Diary* he states that he "communicate[s] with the living mind of Shakespeare" when reading

---

15 *Letters,* p. 830; *Vis,* pp. 233–34; *Myth,* p. 360. (Yeats's essay *Per Amica Silentia Lunae* is a detailed statement of his theory of the daimon: *Myth,* pp. 319–69.)

"of Coriolanus among the servants of Aufidius." An underlying sympathy with certain ancient writers has often been claimed by the moderns; for example, Southey, surrounded by books in his library, speaks of beholding "the mighty minds of old," but when Yeats speaks of communicating with the living mind of Shakespeare, he is making a very special kind of claim. He has in mind the part played by the daimon of Shakespeare, as will become clear from a passage in the published section of *Pages from a Diary* (1930). Here, he reverts to the subject of Shakespeare's influence, but he understandably makes it impersonal and does not specify that he writes about himself in relation to Shakespeare. He also brings his definitions more in line with the terminology employed in *A Vision:* "I should have said not that the living mind of Keats or Shakespeare but their daimon is present. . . . The daimon of Shakespeare or Keats has, however, entered into a sleepless universality."[16] He prefers to use the term daimon rather than the living mind because the latter could very easily be understood to mean that Shakespeare still lives in his plays. But this is a commonplace tribute to Shakespeare—Yeats has in mind something more intrinsic and far reaching.

The "sleepless universality" of Shakespeare's daimon suggests a range of influence that is not confined to the plays, but becomes direct and independent of their media, and at the same time embraces them. We shall shortly see that the implication here is that Yeats's own rapport with Shakespeare's daimon places him under its control, and so his art bears the impress of Shakespeare's genius.[17] This communion between poet and daimon is what Yeats refers to in a letter to Sean O'Casey about Shakespeare: "The ancient philosophers thought a poet or dramatist Daimon-possessed." Yeats gave O'Casey several reasons why the Abbey Theatre rejected his play *The Silver Tassie*. After pointing out that the play was too full of the author's own opinions to be effective drama, Yeats adds, "There is no dominating character, no dominating

16 Quoted in Torchiana, p. 136; *Ex*, p. 332.
17 Cf. Wyndham Lewis, *Time and Western Man* (London, 1927), p. 198: "Shakespeare, writing his *King Lear*, was evidently in some sort of a trance. . . . To create *King Lear*, or to believe that you have held communion with some historic personage—those are much the same thing." Yeats must have read this passage (see above p. 75, n. 42).

action." So imperious should the dramatic personages become that "the whole history of the world must be reduced to wallpaper in front of which the characters must pose and speak." (It was over two decades earlier that Yeats had said that the historical Richard has passed away for ever, but Shakespeare's Richard still lives, more intensely than did any living man.) Asserting their authority over history, these presumptuous characters even dominate their creator: Yeats avers that "Hamlet and Lear educated Shakespeare," and through them he "found out that he was an altogether different man to what he thought himself, and had altogether different beliefs." Hamlet and Lear, full of charismatic energy, become Shakespeare's mentors and exist outside him. Still the terrain is not totally unfamiliar, and we can yet recover our bearings by looking for the landmark of the Mask, the artist's opposite, through which Yeats's declaration falls into a recognizable pattern. Hamlet and Lear are the opposite of what Yeats believed Shakespeare to be in real life: faint and passionless. Shakespeare's Mask is his dramatic work. With the next statement that Yeats makes in his letter, however, it is clear that he goes beyond the theory of the Mask by lifting the entire concept into the realm of the daimon. When he asserts that "a dramatist can help his characters to educate him by thinking and studying everything that gives them the language they are groping for through his hands and eyes, but the control must be theirs, and that is why the ancient philosophers thought a poet or dramatist Daimon-possessed,"[18] he no longer regards Hamlet and Lear as ultimate products of Shakespeare's liminal or subliminal mind, but as the agents of a power that simply uses him as dramatist to forward its own ends. And carrying the theory to its utmost limit, Yeats elsewhere shows how, instead of mortal dominating image, the process can be reversed under exceptional circumstances: a man who died playing Hamlet "would be Hamlet in eternity."[19] Here, the man, by coming dangerously close to the essence of the image and identifying himself with it at the moment of death,

18 *Letters*, p. 741. In his own work Yeats found that Crazy Jane's language was becoming unendurable: "he wrote to his wife that he wanted to exorcise that slut" (*Man and Poet*, p. 272).

19 *Myth*, p. 355.

finds himself unable to escape it. Man is now subordinate to art, as it were, and the image compels him to yield up his individuality to it.

Yeats concludes his remarkable essay, *Per Amica Silentia Lunae*, with a disclosure of his awareness that his mind is being guided by some daimon beyond his own consciousness. "Once, twenty years ago," Yeats reports, "I seemed to awake from sleep to find my body rigid, and to hear a strange voice speaking these words through my lips as through lips of stone: 'We make an image of him who sleeps, and it is not he who sleeps, and we call it Emmanuel.'" Emmanuel, or God with us, takes control, and the artist feels impelled to create in accordance with the wishes of a force outside himself. Life becomes a play in which human beings are actors, the daimons dramatists and producers. About the time he was stating these realizations, in 1916, Yeats also asserted that "if our modern poetical drama has failed, it is mainly because, always dominated by the example of Shakespeare, it would restore an irrevocable past."[20] Always conscious of Shakespeare's domination, Yeats, even in acknowledged defeat, chooses to go down triumphant with Shakespeare as ally.

A daimon may collaborate with a human artist, as did Shakespeare with Yeats, in the preparation of a work of art; this concept of art may partially explain Yeats's insistence on its having the ability to shape and mold life, quite unlike Auden's refusal to entertain such a notion, which to him seemed presumptuous. At the same time, for Yeats, life itself being a vast drama, the boundary between art and life is an exceedingly tenuous one. In "Two Songs from a Play" God's death is "but a play," and, echoing Jaques's idea that the world is a stage, Yeats sees all human life as, in a sense, something unreal, even as Polonius is not really dead "when Hamlet seems to kill him," for, *Hamlet* being a play, Polonius' death is but an illusion created by the dramatists. Art and life, the preternatural and the natural, divine and human, are all telescoped in Yeats's patterning of things. Daimons shape history in the form of wars, megalomaniacs, religions, and schools of philosophy, and Yeats likens this rather frightening form of remote control to the witches as they dance around their cauldron and shape the destinies of

20 *Myth*, p. 366; W. B. Yeats, *Four Plays for Dancers* (London, 1921), p. 88.

men.[21] Clearly, he intends the reader to be reminded of Macbeth's terrible end, prepared for him by the witches, whom he calls "these juggling fiends. . . . / That palter with us in a double sense" (V, viii, 19–20).

Yeats's most explicit acknowledgment of Shakespeare as a prevailing influence on himself is contained in a statement made in 1938. After giving several instances of artists who found fulfillment in some presence outside themselves—Horne who "became the foremost authority upon Botticelli," Ricketts who "made pictures that suggest Delacroix," and Synge who "fled to the Aran Islands" and "found among forgotten people a mirror for his bitterness"—Yeats then claims for himself Shakespeare as his presiding genius:

> I gave certain years to writing plays in Shakespearean blank verse about Irish kings for whom nobody cared a farthing. After all, Asiatic conquerors before battle invoked their ancestors, and a few years ago a Japanese admiral thanked his for guiding the torpedoes.

By combining the seeming irrationality of an Oriental belief in the potency of ancestral guidance with Shakespeare's hand in his own plays, Yeats clearly states what had hitherto been covert: Shakespeare was his unseen mentor. Some years before this he had broached a similar assumption in the form of a question, judiciously leaving the onus of decision with his reader: "When a man writes any work of genius, or invents some creative action, is it not because some knowledge or power has come into his mind from beyond his mind?"[22] The characters created by a great artist are a transmutation of his personality into an intensified and transcendent form; they partake of his nature, yet surpass it, for "breathless mouths," as in "Byzantium," have also played a role in imparting to them a perfection that human life lacks. The works of Shakespeare are much greater than the man.

The dramatic heroes of Shakespeare's plays are embodiments of his yearning to identify himself with his Mask, or his opposite. Under

---

21 *Vis* (1925), p. 172. See also *E&I*, pp. 488, 518, where historical and political changes are dictated by "the brindled cat" (*Macb.*, IV, i, 1), and where each age creates anew its own concept of perfection—"eye of newt and toe of frog" (*Macb.*, IV, i, 14), respectively.

22 *Boiler*, p. 15; *Au*, p. 164.

the instigation of his daimon, who, it will be recalled, has been compared by Yeats to a stage manager encouraging an actor to assume a role alien to his temperament, Shakespeare creates personages that are patterns of this ideal coalescence between himself and his Mask. But such a coalescence can only be achieved through death. Since death plays so vital a role in Shakespearean tragedy, it is not unexpected that Yeats found, in Shakespeare's dramatic encounter with death, a form of experience that tallied with his own persuasion.

III

Yeats's repeated emphasis on esctasy at the instant of death, particularly as experienced by Shakespeare's tragic characters, illuminates his own concept of death. His reaction to the stoical calm with which Synge accepted death and to the gay insouciance of Mabel Beardsley as her death approached, celebrated in "Upon a Dying Lady," suggests his admiration for those who could assert man's superiority over death, a superiority that man has to create and then exercise in order not to be overwhelmed by the experience. The poem "Death" ends with an assertion even more dauntless than that in Donne's sonnet "Death Be Not Proud": "Man has created death." Many years later Yeats was to make his Cuchulain affirm, when death was near, "I make the truth!" Synge's death in 1909 profoundly affected Yeats, as "The Death of Synge" shows. Pathos and sentimentality appealed neither to Yeats nor to Synge. Yeats often spoke with respect of Synge's taciturnity, and his distaste for the Ophelia scenes (in a production of *Hamlet* which he saw a few months after Synge's death) confirms this attitude: "their pathos, as they are played, has always left me cold."[23] The speaker in "Human Dignity" knows that the noisy utterance of his "heart's agony" would well afford emotional relief (cf. Tennyson's "Home They Brought Her Warrior Dead"), but then, human dignity would be compromised, and so he chooses silence instead:

> I could recover if I shrieked
> My heart's agony
> To passing bird, but I am dumb
> From human dignity.

23 *Au*, p. 318.

In 1901 Yeats had said that Shakespeare's characters "with their indifference to death and their immense energy seem at times no nearer the common stature of men than do the gods and the heroes of Greek plays." Disdaining death, they approach the condition of superhuman beings. Yeats had explicated Blake's works in the early nineties and had found much that he could agree with. He could also agree in many ways with Nietzsche, whom he read with delight, and "whose thought flows always, though with an even more violent current, in the bed Blake's thought has worn."[24] Nietzsche's emphasis on the superman who could rise above the conditioning forces of environment and history, refusing to remain subservient to these restraints and laughing in joy at death and destruction, was a posture that Yeats could applaud. Like Blake and Nietzsche, who advocated man's ability to create his own world, repudiating the world of convention and tradition, Shakespeare too seems to have been, for Yeats, a great emancipator. In terms of Yeats's philosophy, death meant the unification of man with his daimon, in short, the achievement of completeness.

In his later works, "sex and the dead" loom large. Yeats equates the two in a statement made in 1938: "The arts are all the bridal chambers of joy. No tragedy is legitimate unless it leads some great character to his final joy." Yeats goes on to mention the last speeches of Hamlet, Cleopatra, Lear, and Oedipus as indicative of the "pure, aimless joy" that the spirit attains to after death. Cleopatra, it will be recalled, while dying, thinks of death in terms of sexual imagery: "The stroke of death is as a lover's pinch, / Which hurts, and is desired" (V, ii, 290–91). In 1934, in a letter to Olivia Shakespear, Yeats wrote of "the old association of love and death," with particular reference to Shakespeare's tragedies. And in "Lapis Lazuli," it is likely that when Yeats visualizes Hamlet and Lear as being gay, gaiety transfiguring all that dread, his basis for this understanding is in Lear's statement toward the close of the play: "I will die bravely / Like a smug bridegroom. What! I will be jovial" (IV, vi, 191–92). A few years earlier, Yeats had spoken of our "amazed attention" being fixed "on Oedipus when his death approaches," because

24   *E&I*, pp. 109, 130.

he is on the point of achieving "a oneness with some spiritual being or beings." Again, that remarkable poem "Chosen" depicts sexual ecstasy in the same imagery used elsewhere to represent the freedom from human bondage that death signals. The poem concludes with the zodiac being changed into a sphere, or the imperfect becoming perfect: the twelve cones denote the inadequacy of human life, but they give place to the *Thirteenth Cone*, "the phaseless sphere," which symbolizes, among other things, God, completeness, and eternity. Man on earth is incomplete because he is at best but a fraction of his total being. Axiomatically, his daimon too is incomplete; hence both man and daimon "feed the hunger in one another's hearts" and yearn to achieve completion through unification.[25]

"Parting" (1926), a short poem strongly reminiscent of the balcony scene in *Romeo and Juliet* and written immediately after "Chosen," continues the interplay between the passion of love and the ever-present possibility of death. "The murderous stealth of day" advances on night's passion in Yeats's poem, where, as in *Romeo and Juliet* (III, v), the lovers intrepidly defy the death that stalks them and find their ecstasy in "love's play." At the same time, love and death are identified, and this, as Stallworthy points out, follows the well-established Elizabethan practice.[26]

In *A Full Moon in March* (1935) Yeats has perhaps employed the Shakespearean motif of love and death converging in a supreme moment of spiritual and emotional fulfillment. The Queen's desire for love is matched by her virgin cruelty, and in the end both desire and refusal are present: her suitor is beheaded, and she kisses the lips of the decapitated head. The tone of the play is set by the Second Attendant's line in the opening song: "Thank the Lord, all men are fools" (27), which Yeats very likely intends as an echo of Puck's ejaculation, "Lord, what fools these mortals be!" (*Dream*, III, ii, 115). Puck's prophecy "Jack shall have Jill; / Nought shall go ill" (III, ii, 461–62) is ultimately fulfilled, but the differences between the lovers, caused by the fickleness

25 *Letters*, p. 730; *Boiler*, p. 35; *Letters*, p. 828; *Ex*, p. 299; *Vis*, pp. 210–11; *Myth*, p. 335.
26 Stallworthy, pp. 143, 147. See also Hone, p. 433.

of the men, is disturbingly suggestive of the precarious nature of the marriage bond. And though the play ends on a note of happy marital union, does not Theseus' solemn line at the end, "The iron tongue of midnight hath told twelve" (V, i, 346), carry a hint at time's inescapable presence, which even love cannot escape? Yeats's play *The King of the Great Clock Tower* (1935), a variation on the theme of *A Full Moon in March,* ends on a similar note: "A moment more and it tolls midnight" (137), and "A slow low note and an iron bell" (174). As in Shakespeare, "Youth's a stuff will not endure" (*Twel.,* II, iii, 46), so in Yeats, "The innocent and the beautiful / Have no enemy but time" ("In Memory of Eva Gore-Booth and Con Markiewicz"). In Shakespearean comedy, superficially at least, every lover has his lass, but *Love's Labour's Lost* is of course a notable exception. There Biron philosophically observes at the play's end,

> Our wooing doth not end like an old play:
> Jack hath not Jill: these ladies' courtesy
> Might well have made our sport a comedy.
>   [V, ii, 857–59]

In Yeats's play, the tragic strand inherent in love has been intensified with devastating effect; it is as if the Shakespearean undercurrent of melancholy present in all his comedies has been transformed into an overwhelming torrent in Yeats. The Second Attendant, in *A Full Moon in March,* singing for the decapitated lover's head, says:

> I sing a song of Jack and Jill
> Jill had murdered Jack.
>   [166–67]

Perhaps the song is a deliberate variation on Biron's significant lines.

The songs in Shakespeare's comedies are sad. Feste, in *Twelfth Night,* sings of being slain by a fair cruel maid (II, iv, 52), and of the ephemeral nature of youth and love (II, iii, 42–46); Rosalind, in *As You Like It,* insists on pricking the bubble of romance—but at the same time rejoicing in its beauty—by telling Orlando that "men are April when they woo, December when they wed. Maids are May when they are maids, but the sky changes when they are wives" (IV, i, 129–31). *Love's Labour's Lost* is not the only comedy of Shakespeare's in which the seeds of estrangement between Jack and Jill show faint signs of germination. In some of his later plays they sprout and assume monstrous proportions: Othello strangles Desdemona; Antony accuses Cleopatra of fickleness; and Leontes charges Hermione with infidelity. The dual theme of love and hate that culminates in death is both Shakespearean and Yeatsian. In *A Full Moon in March,* we are shown the theme distilled, as it were, and by means of subtle touches Yeats makes us aware of the links that bind his work to that of Shakespeare's.

In spite of the joy or ecstasy experienced by man and daimon at their unification after death, throughout life they remain at odds with each other, the daimon goading man to become what he is not by imposing on him tasks beyond his capacity: "When I think of life as a struggle with the Daimon who would ever set us to the hardest work among those not impossible, I understand why there is a deep enmity between a man and his destiny, and why a man loves nothing but his destiny. In an Anglo-Saxon poem a certain man is called, as though to call him something that summed up all heroism, 'Doom eager.'" The immortality of the soul is an essential part of Yeats's philosophy, and the gaiety that he repeatedly attributes to Shakespeare's tragic hero about to die springs from the hero's envisioning the unification with his daimon that awaits him after death. Perhaps Yeats's most striking statement of ecstasy and death coinciding is contained in "A General Introduction for My Work" (1937), where Macbeth, Antony, Hamlet, and Cleopatra, at the moment when they face death, are held up as paradigms of tragic ecstasy. Death means for them "the sudden enlargement of their vision," for the inadequacy, or, rather, the incompleteness of the human condition now gives place to a largeness of vision hitherto impossible, so that Yeats could say elsewhere, "It is even possible that being is only possessed completely by the dead."[27]

27 *Myth,* p. 336; *E&I,* pp. 522–23, 226. Yeats's curious account of the presence of the supernatural at the end of Shakespeare's tragedies, of cold winds blowing and the thermometer falling (*E&I,* p. 523), may be related to Louis Lambert's "conflict between his desire of eternity and his sexual desire." On his wedding day he goes into a trance, and Yeats says, "Balzac, could he have known our modern psychical research, would have noticed that the medium passing into trance is cold, that the thermometer may register a chill in the air," the reason for this being that "its heat had come not from itself but from the now absent soul" (*E&I,* p. 441).

Strangely enough, Yeats mentions neither Othello's nor Lear's final speeches as examples of the sudden enlargement of vision at the moment of death. T. S. Eliot's criticism of Othello for his cheering himself up at the end is well known. Since the "pathos" of the Ophelia scenes left Yeats "cold," as he himself said, it is likely that *Othello* affected him in much the same way.[28] The death of Cordelia too may have seemed unnecessary to him, unmitigated pathos devoid of the grand indifference to death that Yeats valued. Dr. Johnson, we remember, could not bear to reread *King Lear* for many years because he was so shaken by the death of Cordelia. But Yeats's mentioning of Macbeth's speech, "She should have died hereafter," as an example of "ecstasy at the approach of death" is significant, because this is the only context in which he brackets it with the speeches of Hamlet, Antony, and Cleopatra. As an illustration of the point Yeats is making here, Macbeth's famous lines are exceedingly apposite; Macbeth, it will be recalled, on hearing of Lady Macbeth's death, furiously inveighs against the transience of human existence. (Macbeth's lines are quoted here in full so that they may be read alongside the song that Yeats wrote for the Second Musician.) :

> She should have died hereafter:
> There would have been a time for such a word.
> To-morrow, and to-morrow, and to-morrow,
> Creeps in this petty pace from day to day,
> To the last syllable of recorded time;
> And all our yesterdays have lighted fools
> The way to dusty death. Out, out, brief candle!
> Life's but a walking shadow, a poor player
> That struts and frets his hour upon the stage
> And then is heard no more. It is a tale
> Told by an idiot, full of sound and fury,
> Signifying nothing.
>
> [V, v, 17–28]

Macbeth's account of life, though an expression of personal disillusionment, is also an expression of mankind's despair before the insoluble mystery of life and mortality. In a stanza written in 1933, which Yeats intended for his play *The King of the Great Clock Tower* but did not

28 *Au*, p. 318.

include when the play was published, may be seen how Macbeth's rage against "being" itself becomes the nucleus of the Second Musician's song with which the play was intended to open.

> All love is shackled to mortality,
> Love's image is a man-at-arms in steel;
> Love's image is a woman made of stone;
> It dreams of the unborn; all else is nought;
> To-morrow and to-morrow fills its thought;
> All tenderness reserves for that alone.[29]

In Yeats's lines the speaker's painful awareness of the ephemeral nature of things human ("To-morrow and to-morrow fills its thought") brings him close to Macbeth's realization and makes him long for images of permanence (" a man-at-arms in steel" and "a woman made of stone") , or what Yeats calls "the artifice of eternity." With Macbeth, however, flux is ubiquitous. Overcome by the futility and stupidity of existence, Macbeth rails at life, seeing it as an artifice, "a poor player." The difference between Shakespeare's lines and Yeats's, one line of which clearly echoes Shakespeare's, needs emphasis because it is all too tempting to trace correspondences and lose sight of the fact that even when Yeats does take from Shakespeare, he marks what he takes with his own insignia and thus makes it recognizably his own. "Shackled to mortality" as man is, it is not surprising that Yeats's preoccupation with death as an integral part of the human condition becomes yet more pronounced toward the end of his life.

Yeats also came to feel that death could be viewed as a transition from one realm to another, like "passing from one room into another," as the mad old ship's carpenter stoutly maintains. True, in book 3 of *A Vision* and in *Purgatory,* the experience of the afterlife, sometimes horrible and ugly "if death has been violent or tragic," is shown to vary from individual to individual, but what Yeats calls "true death" may be the happy fate of some. For such persons, the different experiences of

---

29 *Letters,* p. 817. That *Macbeth* must have been insistently present in Yeats's mind while he wrote these lines is suggested by his mentioning, in the same context, the apparition of "a child's hand and arm and head" that he saw for the seventh time. "Does it promise me five months or five years?" he asks. The apparitions of "a bloody Child" and "a Child crowned" give to Macbeth a guarantee of the future that later proves to be hollow (IV, i, 75–103).

life are a progressive initiation into the mystery of death, and Yeats calls
these experiences *"Initiationary Moments."* When regarded as a kind
of sacerdotal ceremony to which the aspirant has to be initiated, death
becomes for him not an end, but a consummation. The true initiate
analyzes the changes that take place in himself (generally imperceptible
to others because they are so slight and gradual) from experience to
experience in his own life, for "the sensuous image is changed from time
to time at predestined moments," and when death comes it is not unexpected but is in fact his culminating experience that he welcomes
("At *The Critical Moment* [the sensuous images] are dissolved by analysis. . . . When all the sensuous images are dissolved we meet true
death"[30]). Yeats's thought here is complicated but far from forbidding.
He mentions with approval Rilke's reference to Hamlet as an example
of one who experienced "true death," and dismisses the hero of Ethel
Mannin's novel for not analyzing his experiences and thus failing to
meet true death.[31] For him, death was merely an accident. ("An Irish
Airman Foresees His Death" portrays a condition in which the hero
goes to meet true death, and, as noted, Yeats had identified him with
Hamlet even then.) Yeats could approve of Rilke's choice of Hamlet,
because it agreed with his own attitude toward Hamlet. This is evident
from an observation that he made as early as 1909 after seeing the play:

> I came back for Hamlet at the graveside: there my delight always begins
> anew. I feel in Hamlet, as so often in Shakespeare, that I am in the
> presence of a soul lingering on the storm-beaten threshold of sanctity.
> Has not that threshold always been terrible, even crime-haunted?[32]

Hamlet is here seen in the garb of what Yeats, many years later, was to
consider that of an initiate about to partake of some extraordinary mys-

---

30 *Boiler*, p. 32; *Vis*, p. 225; *Letters*, p. 917.

31 In *Rainer Maria Rilke: 4 December 1875–29 December 1926*, ed. William Rose and G. Craig Houston (London, 1938), pp. 41–84. For Yeats's reaction to
this essay, see *Letters*, p. 913, and William Rose, "A Letter from W. B. Yeats on
Rilke," *German Life and Letters*, XV (October, 1961), 68–70.

32 *Au*, p. 318. Yeats perhaps had Shakespeare's Sonnet 34 in mind when he
created the striking imagery here: " 'Tis not enough that through the cloud thou
break / To dry the rain on my storm-beaten face." When Martin in *The Unicorn
from the Stars* is dying after being shot, Father John exclaims, "O who has dared
meddle with a soul that was in the tumults on the threshold of sanctity" (476).

tical experience; this suggests a consistency of attitude that provides evidence of the unity of Yeats's views and is also an excellent illustration of his line in "The Coming of Wisdom with Time": "Though leaves are many, the root is one."

The juxtaposition of crime and sanctity in Hamlet's situation is striking. Yeats was to say in *A Vision*, over ten years later, that "before the self passes from Phase 22 it is said to attain what is called the 'Emotion of Sanctity,' and this emotion is described as a contact with life beyond death. It comes at the instant when synthesis is abandoned, when fate is accepted." Perhaps Yeats saw Hamlet lingering on the storm-beaten threshold of sanctity because of his changed aspect in the last act of the play. Hamlet's abrupt confrontation with death in the graveside scene, and his acceptance of its prevailing presence when Horatio suggests that the duel be called off, lead to his magnificent words at the end, "the readiness is all." Yeats's renewal of delight in the graveside scene, quoted above, indicates his recognition of Hamlet's striving toward authenticity through the acknowledgment that death is not something outside him to be evaded as long as possible, but a part of himself, his own possession. Yeats's agreement with Rilke's analysis of the play as the dramatic progression of Hamlet from one Initiationary Moment to another before his final encounter and union with true death reveals a remarkable similarity to the existentialist's condition as stated by Kierkegaard and Heidegger. Yeats's "critical moment," when true death is met, is similar to Heidegger's regarding death not as something outside of the individual, but as the ever-present possibility that he nurses within himself.[33]

Hamlet's readiness for death, and his detection of a special providence in the fall of a sparrow, would win Yeats's praise, even as the

---

33 *Vis*, p. 181. Since the English translations of both Kierkegaard's and Heidegger's works appeared after Yeats's death—Kierkegaard's important works between 1941 and 1959, and Heidegger's *Sein und Zeit* in 1949—it is unlikely that Yeats knew them firsthand; however, he did know Husserl's *Ideas* (see *Boiler*, p. 26). Here, in fact, is an example of the way in which the writers of a particular period create its own Zeitgeist—one thinks of Johnson's *Rasselas* and Voltaire's *Candide*, of Yeats's *A Vision* and Spengler's *Decline of the West* (see Johnson's remark in Boswell's *Life*, ed. R. W. Chapman, [London, 1970], p. 241, and Yeats's letter to Olivia Shakespear in *Letters*, p. 716).

centenarian of "In Tara's Halls" is the man the poet declares he would praise. This extraordinary man can summon, not only the generations of his house, but death as well:

> He bade, his hundred and first year at end,
> Diggers and carpenters make grave and coffin;
> Saw that the grave was deep, the coffin sound,
> Summoned the generations of his house,
> Lay in the coffin, stopped his breath and died.

Death is, to Yeats, a positive step that the hero takes in the completion of his life. His death, his destiny, is integral to his life; it is not an undesirable eventuality. In Shakespeare's tragedies he found this truth exemplified.

Yeats's poem "The Man and the Echo" (1938) is an examination of his own past (consisting of Initiationary Moments) preparatory to the moment when "all's arranged in one clear view" (or the Critical Moment) and true death can be experienced. The poet tries to understand some of the crucial moments in his life: the questions raised revolve around his early play *Cathleen Ni Houlihan,* which inspired certain Irishmen to revolt and die; Margot Ruddock, who went mad as a result of his having criticized her poetry; and Coole Park, whose destruction he might have been able to prevent.[34] Tormented by these anxieties, "all seems evil until I / Sleepless would lie down and die," but when Echo reiterates his death-wish,[35] he rouses himself and rejects so easy a solution: "There is no release / In a bodkin or disease," he sternly reminds himself in lines that are certainly intended to recall Hamlet's rejection of the bare bodkin.[36] Hamlet's self-questioning and Yeats's reappraisal of his past coalesce with the use of the single magnificent word *bodkin,* evidence of the kind of Shakespearean shorthand that mastery of his craft enabled him to use with telling effect.

A similar abbreviated Shakespearean touch occurs in "Vacillation," where the poet exhorts the reader to

---

34 See *Man and Poet,* p. 138; *Au,* pp. 220–21; *Letters,* p. 856; John Unterecker, *A Reader's Guide to William Butler Yeats* (New York, 1959), p. 290.

35 Yeats mentions with appreciation Webster's powerful echo scene in *The Duchess of Malfi* (see W. B. Yeats, *Collected Works,* III, 211).

36 Yeats alludes to Hamlet's rejection of the bare bodkin elsewhere too: see *E&I,* p. 369; *Myth,* p. 355.

> Begin the preparation for your death
> And from the fortieth winter by that thought
> Test every work of intellect or faith,
> And everything that your own hands have wrought.

Like Shakespeare, who could confidently predict that his patron would heed at last the poet's earnest exhortation to marry and leave behind an heir to posterity, but only "when forty winters" had besieged his brow,[37] so Yeats makes forty a significant year in human life after which the individual should take cognizance of his Initiationary Moments and analyze them. Having done this, he would then be able to

> call those works extravagance of breath
> That are not suited for such men as come
> Proud, open-eyed and laughing to the tomb.

Yeats had made his Cuchulain, too, "about forty" and evidently attached some importance to the question of his age.[38] His last play, *The Death of Cuchulain* (1939) is, in some ways, a demonstration of the process whereby the hero, having reached the Critical Moment after experiencing a series of Initiationary Moments, undergoes a perceptible change in attitude and behavior. The change in Cuchulain's "visible image" is abrupt, like the changes in Odysseus, Don Quixote, Hamlet, Lear, and Faust. In real life "our visible image changes slowly," but in art, where time is necessarily speeded up, the change is swift and pronounced, Yeats tells us.[39] Hence Eithne Inguba, Cuchulain's mistress, remarks on the change that has come over him:

> You're not the man I loved,
> That violent man forgave no treachery.
> If, thinking what you think, you can forgive,
> It is because you are about to die.
>
> [59–62]

Unlike the once aggressive Cuchulain of *On Baile's Strand* and *At the Hawk's Well*, he is here passive and yielding. Earlier, he and Aoife recall the Initiationary Moments that punctuated his life: when he met

---

37 Sonnet 2. That Yeats knew this sonnet well is evident from his reference to "some forty winters" (*E&I*, p. 278).

38 See *Letters*, p. 425.

39 *Boiler*, p. 33.

her "at the Hawk's Well under the withered trees"; fought with her and "it seemed that we should kill each other"; then "threw [her] on the ground and left [her] there"; later, slept with her and "begot a son that night between / Two black thorn-trees"; but "killed him upon Baile's Strand," and, finally, "went mad" and "fought against the sea" (106–7, 95, 140, 142–46, 108, 137–38).

The temerity with which Cuchulain faces death at the conclusion of *The Green Helmet* (1910) is an arresting example of how a Shakespearean awareness permeated Yeats's mind and then reappeared in his own work transformed into something quite different from Shakespeare, but with its roots embedded in his early contacts with *Hamlet*. Cuchulain, not only prepared, but eager, to pay the debt of his head to the mysterious and ghostly Red Man, is, like Hamlet, determined to follow the ghost despite the restraining hands of Horatio and Marcellus. Hamlet, we remember, impatiently shakes them off, crying out,

> Hold off your hands.
> *Horatio.* Be ruled: you shall not go.
> *Hamlet.*   My fate cries out,
> And makes each petty artery in this body
> As hardy as the Nemean lion's nerve.
> Still am I called! unhand me, gentlemen!
> By heaven, I'll make a ghost of him that lets me.
> I say, away!—Go on: I'll follow thee.
>   [I, iv, 80–86]

Cuchulain is only slightly less unceremonious with his wife Emer when she tries to hold him back from obeying the summons of the Red Man:

> *Emer (putting her arms about him).* It is you,
>   not your fame that I love.
> *Cuchulain (tries to put her from him).* You are young, you
>   are wise, you can call
>   Some kinder and comelier man that will sit at home in
>   the house.
> *Emer.* Live and be faithless still.
> *Cuchulain (throwing her from him).* Would you stay the great
>   barnacle-goose
>   When its eyes are turned to the sea and its beak to the
>   salt of the air?
>   [268–71]

A few lines later Cuchulain, still disdainful of death, jocosely tells the Red Man to hurry up and strike off his head:

> (*He kneels before Red Man. There is a pause.*)
> Quick to your work, old Radish, you will fade when the cocks
>   have crowed,
>
> [274]

a line that seems to recall Hamlet's badinage with the ghost when the latter enjoins the others to swear: "Well said, old mole! Canst work i' th' earth so fast?" (I, v, 162). And as Marcellus observed of the ghost that "It faded on the crowing of the cock" (I, i, 157), so Yeats's ghost, like Shakespeare's, "will fade when the cocks have crowed."

An oft-recurring theme in Yeats's plays and poems is indifference to death, such as he had particularly noticed in the heroes of Shakespeare a few years earlier. When Cuchulain presents himself before the Red Man unafraid of death, the Red Man, instead of beheading him, says:

> And I choose the laughing lip
> That shall not turn from laughing, whatever rise or fall;
> The heart that grows no bitterer although betrayed by all;
> The hand that loves to scatter; the life like a gambler's throw.
>
> [278–81]

Cuchulain belongs to the company of Shakespeare's tragic heroes who face death joyously, but he is not the only one: Mabel Beardsley, who "laughed into the face of death," Robert Gregory, who knew that he would "meet [his] fate / Somewhere among the clouds above," and Lady Gregory, who informed her would-be assassin that from "six to seven [she] sat at this table, / The blinds drawn up," also belong to this distinguished gathering.[40]

Toward the end of his life, Yeats seems to have deliberately sought out "a oneness with some spiritual being or beings," with Shakespeare's tragic figures whose ostensible defeat by the world insures their personal victory. "No tragedy is legitimate unless it leads some great character to its final joy," he affirms. Recognizing them to be misfits in their context, heroes amidst plebeians, Yeats seems to draw Shakespeare's tragic

---

40 *E&I*, p. 109; "Upon a Dying Lady"; "An Irish Airman Foresees His Death"; "Beautiful Lofty Things."

characters, through empathic participation, into his orbit by similarly assailing his own degenerate historical phase: "Yet we who have hated the age are joyous and happy."[41] We have seen how Richard was for him a symbol of aesthetic exaltation in a debased world; Shakespeare's other tragic heroes also share Yeats's heroic gaiety when confronted by the prospect of apocalyptic devastation. The hero, standing alone in a world of crumbling values, becomes an "image of despair," ineluctably conjoined with "a form of joy," because the soul's immortality is assured in the face of death. "Hamlet's 'Absent thee from felicity awhile' and all of Shakespeare's last words and closing scenes" establish the soul's supremacy in the cosmic drama that the true hero recognizes to be not tragedy, but some kind of dynamic and universal comedy. "Blessed be heroic death (Shakespeare's tragedies)," Yeats wrote in a letter to Ethel Mannin in 1935.[42] In *The Death of Cuchulain,* Cuchulain, about to be decapitated by a blind beggar who hopes to earn twelve pennies for the deed, calmly anticipates the ecstasy of death and says of his soul, "I say it is about to sing" (183).

Yeats found in Shakespeare's tragic vision a remarkable correspondence with his own and therefore frequently related his work to that of Shakespeare. As one of the major twentieth-century critics of Shakespeare, Yeats brings to bear on the subject of his study the weight of his own personality and attitudes. His views on Shakespeare are valuable in their own right as insights that have a critical importance quite independent of any light that they may shed on Yeats's attitudes toward his own art. His fine awareness of nuances in Shakespeare, which appears in his view of death as he saw it experienced by Shakespeare's heroes, finds elaboration in the distinction that he drew between personality and character. Personality, to Yeats, denoted an emphasis on a single passionate aspect of the hero, a change of state from ignorance to knowledge, and true death could only be experienced by one who possessed personality. Character, on the other hand, was no more than a depiction of the individual during the drab moments of his existence.

41   *Ex,* p. 299; *Boiler,* pp. 35, 25. See also *E&I,* p. 254, where Yeats sees Shakespeare, in his tragic heroes, combining sorrow and ecstasy "when the last darkness has gathered about them." Yeats was, of course, familiar with Nietzsche's exuberance at destruction: see above p. 62, n. 15.

42   *Ex,* p. 296; *Letters,* p. 832.

6

Personality and Character in Shakespeare

The poet's eye, in a fine frenzy rolling,
Doth glance from heaven to earth,
   from earth to heaven;
And as imagination bodies forth
The forms of things unknown, the
   poet's pen
Turns them to shapes, and gives to
   airy nothing
A local habitation and a name.
Such tricks hath strong imagination.

    —A Midsummer Night's Dream

Some few remembered still when I was
   young
A peasant girl commended by a song,
Who'd lived somewhere upon that
   rocky place,
And praised the colour of her face,
And had the greater joy in praising
   her,
Remembering that, if walked she there,
Farmers jostled at the fair
So great a glory did the song confer.

    —Yeats, "The Tower"

THE ADMIRATION of the nineteenth century for character, a quality standing for unimpeachable respectability, found fervent expression in much Shakespearean criticism of the age. Yeats recalls that as a schoolboy he had been asked to write an essay on the topic, "Men may rise on the stepping-stones of their dead selves to higher things." His father, furious, denounced the cultivation of such smug self-righteousness, saying that "ideals make the blood thin, and take the human nature out of people." Yeats adds: he "told me not to write on such a subject at all, but upon Shakespeare's lines, 'To thine own self be true, and it must follow as the night the day thou canst not then be false to any man.'" Describing his father's refreshing heterodoxy, he says, "At another time, he would denounce the idea of duty: 'imagine,' he would say, 'how the right sort of woman would despise a dutiful husband'; and he would tell us how much my mother would scorn such a thing." Yeats then states, "All he said was, I now believe right."[1]

As early as 1893, in a lecture entitled "Nationality and Literature," Yeats had distinguished between the "general life" of the common man and the towering personality of the hero who refuses to come to terms with his environment. Yeats declared that in the Elizabethan Age poetry "no longer reflected the general life, but gave us Lear, Hamlet, and Macbeth, making silent isolated colossal characters, dominating the whole life about them, and deafening into silence the general bustle of the world." "At Stratford-on-Avon" is the culmination of his conviction that the hero stands apart from his society. Yeats found corroboration for this view in the values that Shakespeare believed in, as evidenced in his dramatic heroes—"The deeds of Coriolanus, Hamlet, Timon, Richard II had no obvious use, indeed no more than the expression of their personalities." Even though Yeats did not formulate the distinction between character and personality until 1910, clearly the beginnings of this awareness are already present in his ascribing "personality" to Shakespeare's heroes as early as 1901. In 1902, defending his play *The Countess Cathleen* against the charge of its being demoralizing and unpatriotic because it "pictured Irish men and women selling their souls" to the devil, Yeats wrote that he could not "keep from thinking of the experience of other dramatists, for the drama has always been a disturber. The plays of Shakespeare and his contemporaries had to be acted on the Surrey side of Thames to keep the Corporation of London from putting them down by law." He underlines the incompatibility between the artist's vision and the prevalent notion of moral propriety as dictated from the pulpit:

> I am trying to show that it is impossible to write plays in a spirit of sincerity without sometimes putting one's stick into the beehives. The reason is that drama is a picture of the soul of man, and not of his exterior life. We watch Coriolanus with delight, because he had a noble and beautiful pride, and it seems to us for the moment of little importance that he sets all Rome by the ears and even joins himself to her enemies.

1   *Au,* p. 35.

Shakespeare makes a wise hearer forget everything except what he wants him to remember.[2]

By categorically denying "the exterior life" a vital role in determining the form that tragic drama takes, and by choosing to treat it as a "picture of the soul," Yeats establishes an autonomous and aesthetic framework within which it remains suspended.

In "At Stratford-on-Avon" Yeats perhaps deliberately overstated his case because he was assailing critical attitudes that since the eighteenth century had entrenched themselves. (Wordsworth in his "Preface" had had to do much the same thing.) Character criticism, based on Shakespeare's ability to create convincing and lifelike characters, began with Maurice Morgann's *An Essay on the Dramatic Character of John Falstaff* (1777); Coleridge and Hazlitt continued this trend but without perpetrating the extravagances of later critics. That a book like Mary Cowden Clarke's *The Girlhood of Shakespeare's Heroines* (3 vols., 1851–52) could, by the mid-nineteenth century, prove immensely popular is an indication of the growing tendency to view Shakespeare's world, not as a visionary realm, but as a mirror of the actual world. Shakespeare now came to be regarded as a repository of all human wisdom, as a paragon of Victorian virtue and decency. Increasingly he was lauded as God's representative on earth, as an upholder of morality exposing the obliquity of Macbeth and Antony, and of *King Lear* it could be said pontifically that "the majesty of moral law sits as unseen arbiter over the tumultuous strife of passion."[3]

Reacting to such a climate, Yeats sarcastically animadverts on "that singular criticism of Shakespeare, which has decided that *Hamlet* was written for a warning to the irresolute, and *Coriolanus* as a lesson to the proud," and goes on to vindicate Shakespeare's art as being "too full of life" to be concerned with the worldly wisdom that "Nietzsche has called

---

2   *UP*, p. 270; *E&I*, pp. 102–3; W. B. Yeats, "The Freedom of the Theatre," *The United Irishman* (November 1, 1902).

3   Frederick S. Boas, *Shakspere and his Predecessors* (London, 1896), p. 439. See also Hiram Corson, *An Introduction to the Study of Shakespeare* (Boston, 1889); Frederick Gard Fleay, *Shakespeare Manual* (London, 1876); and F. J. Furnivall, Introduction to *The Leopold Shakspere* (London, 1877) for a similar scale of moral and ethical values.

an infirmary for bad poets."[4] (Not many years later, Yeats, as we have noted in chapter 2, saw Shakespeare's creativity as being "rammed with life.") In Germany, preoccupation with Shakespeare as a moral teacher rather than as poet and dramatist was even more evident than in England. Yeats directly refutes the validity of such an attitude toward Shakespeare; A. C. Swinburne, Walter Pater, and Arthur Symons also emphasize the poetic and dramatic qualities in Shakespeare,[5] the result of his imaginative experience of life, and eschew the criticism that made him view his characters with—as Yeats sardonically put it—"the eyes of a Municipal Councillor weighing the merits of a Town Clerk."[6]

The attempt made by numerous nineteenth-century writers to force Shakespeare into the mold of moralist espousing the morality of their age resulted, Yeats believed, in a falsification of the domain of art. Since to such critics the worlds of art and of life constantly overlapped, the extracting of a Victorian brand of morality from the plays of Shakespeare was both easy and inevitable. In 1904, attacking such a confusion of values and insisting on the separateness of art from life, Yeats used Shakespeare's plays as proof of a higher code of morality governing the artist's domain: although the "character who delights us may commit murder like Macbeth, or fly the battle for his sweetheart as did Antony, or betray his country like Coriolanus," no putative set of values can convince us "that the murderer and the betrayer do not deserve our sympathy. We thought so yesterday, and we still know what crime is, but everything has been changed of a sudden; we are caught up into another code, we are in the presence of a higher court." Shakespeare's universe, like that of any great, imaginative writer was, for Yeats, compounded of elements not directly imported from life, but transformed into "the subject of all art [which] is passion," and "character" as a

---

4   W. B. Yeats, "A Canonical Book," *The Bookman* (May, 1903).

5   For a summary of the German critics' views, see Augustus Ralli, *A History of Shakespearian Criticism* (1932; reprinted New York, 1965), II, 91–116. See Swinburne, *A Study of Shakespeare* (London, 1880); Pater, *Appreciations* (London, 1878); Symons, *Titus Andronicus* (1885), *Antony and Cleopatra, Twelfth Night, Measure for Measure*, etc. (1889–90) in *Studies in the Elizabethan Drama* (London, 1920).

6   *E&I*, p. 105.

utilitarian quality of the everyday world could not bear comparison with this heightened vision. Such imaginative writers reveal "the reality that is in our minds," and as the apotheosis of this inner reality, he turns to Shakespeare. "We, who are believers," he declares, "cannot see reality anywhere but in the soul itself, and seeing it there we cannot do other than rejoice in every energy, whether of gesture, or of action, or of speech, coming out of the personality, the soul's image, even though the very laws of Nature seem as unimportant in comparison as did the laws of Rome to Coriolanus when his pride was upon him."[7] As Coriolanus disdained subservience to the laws of Rome when they clashed with his individuality, so can and should the artist flout the crippling laws of realism.

For the realist school of writers, any analysis of character necessarily implied motive. Coleridge's "motiveless malignity" of Iago and the tireless quest of countless critics to find reasons for Hamlet's delay are conspicuous features of nineteenth-century Shakespearean criticism. Yeats, in "At Stratford-on-Avon," asserts a directly contrary point of view that immediately removes the play from the world of simple cause and effect and places it in a context that looks beyond these superficialities:

> Time after time [Shakespeare's] people use at some moment of deep emotion an elaborate or deliberate metaphor, or do some improbable thing which breaks an emotion of reality we have imposed upon him by an art that is not his, nor in the spirit of his.

Yeats is here emphasizing a level of meaning in the plays of Shakespeare overlooked by many of his contemporaries but now made so familiar by twentieth-century criticism that its nonrecognition would seem to us incredible. To Yeats, the play is not a fragment of life, but an arrangement of experience, a pattern that deviates deliberately from the accepted

7 *Ex*, pp. 154–55, 167, 170. See also *Ex*, p. 111, where Yeats denies that he is indifferent to moral issues in art, and explains that what he objects to is "the rough-and-ready conscience of the newspaper and the pulpit in a matter so delicate and so difficult as literature." A few years later, in 1909, Yeats points out that a "moral understanding of life" is presented by great artists who are able to "create a model of a race to inspire the action of that race as a whole," and as examples of this he cites Milton and Shakespeare, who "do it through exceptional individuals" (*Au*, p. 300).

norms of causality. The poet uses "an elaborate or deliberate metaphor," a description that reminds us of his own account of *A Vision:* the communicating spirits, urging him not to become immersed in their revelations, said, "We have come to give you metaphors for poetry," and Yeats later says of the theories set forth in the book, "I regard them as stylistic arrangements of experience comparable to the cubes in the drawing of Wyndham Lewis and to the ovoids in the sculpture of Brancusi."[8] Like many of Yeats's other statements, however, this does not sum up his entire position. So also his dismissal of character and motive in Shakespeare should not be taken to mean a total repudiation of these elements. As with other great artists, he was constantly feeling his way toward an artistic form best suited to his genius and in the process did not hesitate to declare himself boldly.[9]

The symbolic significance of Richard was reiterated by Yeats a few years after his essay "At Stratford-on-Avon." In 1904 he wrote:

> One day, as [Shakespeare] sat over Holinshed's *History of England,* he persuaded himself that Richard II, with his French culture, "his too great friendliness to his friends," his beauty of mind, and his fall before dry, repelling Bolingbroke, would be a good image for an accustomed mood of fanciful, impracticable lyricism in his own mind.

Thus, Richard becomes an expression of Shakespeare's inner state of being, almost a "metaphor for poetry," so that to view him as simply a historical figure would be a gross distortion of what Shakespeare intended. In "At Stratford-on-Avon," Yeats separates Shakespeare's characters into two opposing groups: those who have souls and those who are soulless. Richard is "the vessel of porcelain" and Henry "the vessel of clay." The play becomes for Yeats a battleground for hostile forces, dreamers and poets against materialists. Yet it will be noticed that Yeats too pronounces a moral judgment on Hal when he condemns him for the dismissal of Falstaff and his companions, an observation that demon-

---

8 *E&I,* p. 101; *Vis,* pp. 8, 25.

9 Charles Berryman, *W. B. Yeats: Design of Opposites* (New York, 1967), pp. 66, 77–80, examines in detail Yeats's dialectical approach to various issues, and calls it "dramatic paradox." Berryman restricts himself to the poems, plays, stories, and *A Vision,* but much of what he says would hold good for Yeats's critical writings as well. See also Henn, chapter 7.

strates that no absolute line of demarcation can be drawn between realism and imagination.[10]

Yeats himself was fully aware of this impossibility, and though, in an unpublished essay written in 1915, he had said that Hamlet and Lear "express the dream," and another group expresses its antagonist, a few years earlier, in 1910, he conceded that in tragic art "the real world is not altogether rejected, it is but touched here and there, and into the places we have left empty we summon rhythm, balance, pattern, images that remind us of vast passions." At about the same time he had also come to believe that an easy compartmentalizing was not Shakespeare's method. In an unpublished fragment, written probably in 1913, he said that "nobility struggles with reality, the eagle and the snake," and as an example of this cited the case of Macbeth: "The nobility is never all personal—in Shakespeare where it is often intermixed with reality in the same characters—Macbeth for instance."[11] Yeats's honesty always prevailed over his dogmatism. Having earlier regarded the play as an arena in which contending forces meet in the form of a clash between personalities, Yeats now sees the conflict as raging within a single personage, so that the hero himself becomes the battleground. The play being enacted on the stage is symbolical of the drama taking place within the mind of the hero.

Yeats's theories find expression in his own plays written during this period. In *On Baile's Strand* (1903) and *The King's Threshold* (1904), the opposition between the two types of characters is easily discernible. In *On Baile's Strand*, Cuchulain, the dreamer, is pitted against Conchubar, the pragmatist, even as Fool and Blind Man in the play are shadows of this conflict. So also in *The King's Threshold*, Seanchan and his pupils, the idealists, are confronted by the King and his Court, the realists. But in *Deirdre* (1907), there is greater subtlety. Is Conchubar an unmitigated schemer, or does he possess some sparks of heroic greatness? His last speech with which the play concludes seems to suggest the latter:

10   *Ex,* p. 145; *E&I,* p. 108.
11   Quoted in *Identity,* p. 105; *E&I,* p. 243; quoted in *Man and Poet,* p. 318.

Conchubar. You are all traitors, all against me—all.
                And she has deceived me for a second time;
                And every common man can keep his wife,
                But not the King.
(*Loud shouting outside:* "Death to Conchubar!" "Where is
                Naoise?" etc. *The dark-faced men gather round
                Conchubar and draw their swords; but he mo-
                tions them away.*)
                I have no need of weapons.
                There's not a traitor that dare stop my way.
                Howl, if you will; but I, being King, did right
                In choosing her most fitting to be Queen
                And letting no boy lover take the sway.

Though schemer, coward, and murderer, Conchubar, like Macbeth, is
clearly not all reality; there is in him an element of "nobility that struggles with reality." Yeats may be seen to be broadening the base of the
play's structure to include greater diversity, a feature that he recognized
was fundamental to Shakespeare's art.

                                    II

    During the first decade of the century, Yeats was to insist on the
need for the dramatist's personality to express itself through his work.
In keeping with his belief that poetic drama should be regarded as a
metaphor for the dramatist's vision, he had visualized Richard as an
image of "fanciful, impracticable lyricism" in Shakespeare's mind; this
was the opposite of prose drama, which adhered slavishly to realism and
was devoid of personality. Yeats pleads for an art that is truly creative
and springs from the dramatist's "personal vision" of the world, "and
the greater the art the more surprising the vision." "By extravagance,
by an emphasis far greater than that of life as we observe it" can the
artist express his personal vision of the world, and as an example of
this, Yeats turns to Shakespeare and Sophocles, who "can crowd into a
few minutes the knowledge of years," who "can so quicken, as it were,
the circles of the clock, so heighten the expression of life, that many
years can unfold themselves in a few minutes." These dramatists can
shape life into any artistic form they desire. Defying natural law, they

escape the tyranny of time through their art, even as Yeats, many years later in his Introduction to *The Resurrection,* hinted at the possibility of a spiritual escape from successive rebirths, perhaps attainable only by the saint who can compress into one life several lives, who can exhaust all possible lives by setting, as it were, "the hands of the clock racing."[12] In "The Double Vision of Michael Robartes," the Sphinx, the Buddha, and the dancing girl have

> so wrought
> Upon a moment, and so stretched it out
> That they, time overthrown,
> Were dead yet flesh and bone.

In art (the dancing girl), as in intellectual exploration (the Sphinx) and mystical experience (the Buddha), time ceases to exist as a controlling continuum.

Shakespeare and Sophocles, as artists, create not only new concepts of time, but also characters that are a heightened representation of what we discover within ourselves. "It is always Shakespeare or Sophocles, and not Ibsen, that make us say, 'How true, how often I have felt as that man feels'; or 'How intimately I have come to know those people on the stage.'" The dramatist truly succeeds "when he awakens within us for an instant our own heroism, our own sanctity, our own desire," and as examples of this, Yeats cites "Odysseus and Don Quixote and Hamlet who are with us always." Elsewhere he asserts that the greatness of these universal figures comes home to us because we see ourselves represented in them, "for when the tragic reverie is at its height . . . it is always ourselves that we see upon the stage."[13] Later, as we shall see, he was to change his position slightly and differentiate between the characters of

12   *Ex,* pp. 145, 194–96, 398. The question of time in Shakespeare had been discussed (sometimes ingeniously) by nineteenth-century critics. See, e.g., N. J. Halpin, *The Dramatic Unities of Shakespeare* (London, 1849); Charles and Mary Cowden Clarke, *The Shakespeare Key* (London, 1879); Edward Rose, *Inconsistency of Time in Shakespeare's Plays* (London, 1880). In general, however, it can be said that although the presence of "long time" and "short time" in Shakespeare was admitted in nineteenth-century criticism, the tendency was also to point out that Shakespeare's time sequence was not inconsistent with the actual duration of time. But Yeats of course dismisses the need to justify it at all, implying that the argument is irrelevant in an art that is by its very nature extravagant.

13   *Ex,* pp. 196, 197; *E&I,* pp. 240–41.

comedy (Odysseus, Don Quixote, Falstaff) and the personages of tragedy (Hamlet, Lear, Oedipus).

With the publication of A. C. Bradley's *Shakespearean Tragedy* in 1904, character criticism had found its most notable spokesman since Coleridge. Bradley's tendency to regard Shakespeare's persons as real human beings is too well known to need elaboration. Strongly influenced by the realist prose drama of the nineteenth century, he, despite many excellent insights, failed to discern the fundamental point of divergence between prose and poetic drama. Character and environment in systematic interaction were the twin forces that, for him, determined the direction the play would inevitably take; this solidly respectable approach was fortified by the writings of Mill and Spencer, George Eliot and Thomas Hardy. Bradley's critique is based on a conviction that character analysis is the key to an understanding of Shakespeare's art; that poetic drama is just an extension of prose drama, but written in verse; and that Shakespearean drama is essentially a slice of life in which cause and effect operate predictably.[14]

If Bradley's interpretation of Shakespeare is regarded as generally representative of the trend of his times, Yeats's position was diametrically opposed to this. Whereas Bradley stresses that character is the direct cause of action, Yeats maintains that the tragic hero in his finest moments ascends "into that tragic ecstasy which is the best that art—perhaps that life—can give." We, the audience, too are "carried beyond time and persons to where passion . . . becomes wisdom; and it was as though we too had touched and felt and seen a disembodied thing." In 1910, perhaps deliberately refuting Bradley's theory, Yeats denies that "definite character" is indispensable for tragedy.

> One dogma of the printed criticism is that if a play does not contain definite character, its constitution is not strong enough for the stage, and that the dramatic moment is always the contest of character with character.
> In poetical drama there is, it is held, an antithesis between character and lyric poetry, for lyric poetry—however much it move you when read out of a book—can, as these critics think, but encumber the action. Yet when we go back a few centuries and enter the great periods of drama, character grows less and sometimes disappears, and there is much lyric

14 A. C. Bradley, *Shakespearean Tragedy* (London, 1960), pp. 89–90, 1, 11.

feeling. . . . Suddenly it strikes us that character is continuously present in comedy alone.[15]

This insistence on regarding the play as an organic construct would deprive the Bradleyan thesis of much of its validity, for to abstract motives from poetic drama and analyze them as separate entities would, according to Yeats, destroy the very fabric of the play. Thus, for Yeats, poetic drama, reflecting an inner reality that might never appear on the surface of daily existence, makes no pretence to being a rendering of actual life. It establishes its own world, which may well seem unreal and astonishing.

In 1911, addressing the Dramatic Club of Harvard University, Yeats distinguished between comedy, character, and prose drama on the one hand, and tragedy, personality, and poetic drama on the other; he defined the differences in terms of the kinds of settings appropriate to the two contrasting dramatic modes.

> To express character, which has a great deal of circumstance, of habit, you require a real environment; some one place, some one moment of time; but in tragedy, which comes from that within us which dissolves away limits, there is a need for surroundings where beauty, decoration, pattern—that is to say, the universal in form—takes the place of accidental circumstance.[16]

Since earlier in the address Yeats has been contrasting Shakespeare's tragic heroes with Molière's and Congreve's comic characters, it seems likely that when he deprecates "a real environment; some one place, some one moment of time," he has in mind the Shakespearean paradigm of an indeterminate locale for the settings of poetic drama, along with inconsistencies in time sequence, neither of which disturbed the Elizabethans; unimaginative editors of Shakespeare, determined to make his plays look plausible, however, had imposed on them precise and restrictive settings: "Rome. Caesar's House," "Rome. An Ante-Chamber," and so on.

In the address Yeats describes some of the experiments with a cyclorama conducted by several European producers; he praises their

15 *E&I*, pp. 239–40.
16 W. B. Yeats, "The Theater of Beauty," *Harper's Weekly* (November 11, 1911), p. 11.

efforts to get rid of the picture-frame stage with its crude wings, saying that "all of these methods based upon the curved-back scene aim, I think, to give one a beautiful, realistic effect, reproducing as exactly as possible the sense of the open air." He concludes the address with a courteous bow to those who strive after authentic realism but dissociates himself from this trend, pointing out that he, like Shakespeare and the Japanese dramatists, is a writer of poetic drama.

> In Japan . . . an exterior is only suggested. . . . Being a writer of poetic drama, and of tragic drama, desiring always pattern and convention, I would like to keep to suggestion, to symbolism, to pattern like the Japanese. Yet realism, too, is a legitimate thing, and a necessary thing for all plays that seek to represent the actual environment of a man, and to reflect the surface of life in words and actions. We should not stage Galsworthy and Shakespeare in the same way.[17]

In the same year, 1911, Yeats defined his concept of poetic drama with reference to Shakespeare's tragedies. After dismissing realistic settings with painted backcloths as being "meretricious" and "irrelevant," he quotes Antony's lines,

> Sometime we see a cloud that's dragonish,
> A vapour sometime like a bear or lion,
> A towered citadel, a pendent rock,
> A forkéd mountain, or blue promontory
> With trees upon't, that nod unto the world
> And mock our eyes with air,
>
> [*Antony*, IV, xiv, 3–7]

and says, "I have heard Anthony [sic] speak those lines before a painted cloth that, though it could not make them nothing, left in the memory the sensation of something childish, theatrical as we say." Envisioning a time when the stage would be liberated from the tyranny of realism, he declares that when such a time comes, "Gloster [sic] will be able to fall but from his own height and think that he has fallen from Dover cliff, and Richard's and Richmond's tents can face one another again. We shall have made once more a noble, capricious, extravagant, resonant,

17   Yeats, "Theater of Beauty."

fantastic art." So inferior was prose drama, with its insistence on character, to this extravagant art, that, though Yeats concedes that it may occasionally have the power to move an audience, he argues that this power is actually derived from some faint resemblance that such a scene may have with some great scene out of Shakespeare, with "let us say, the passion of Coriolanus."[18]

In the opening decade of the century, Yeats began to employ a terminology that later developed into a sharp distinction between character and personality. This was a perpetuation of his dichotomy between the dreamers (Richard, Hamlet, Cuchulain) and the realists (Henry, Fortinbras, Conchubar), except that character and personality were broader terms. To exalt the dreamer over the realist would appear less acceptable than to exalt personality over character. Also, *personality* was a richer word, capable of many more connotations than the narrow dreamer; it suggested the individual's soul, whereas *character* implied the Victorian definition of good conduct, an external code of behavior. As was usual with Yeats, he began to test and justify his theory with reference to Shakespeare. Whereas Bradley's exposition of Shakespearean tragedy had concentrated on making the characters appear as human beings who had walked into the play,[19] Yeats stresses their dramatic function and argues that they are inextricably suspended within the framework of the play, and that no attempt is made to give them a dimension outside the play. In a tragedy, the dramatist reveals "only so much of their humanity" as is necessary for the play's design, and Yeats then makes the amazing statement that the heroes of comedy ("Don Quixote and Odysseus") are more real to him than are the heroes of tragedy—"for even Hamlet and Lear and Oedipus are more cloudy. No playwright ever has made or ever will make a character that will follow us out of the theatre as Don Quixote follows us out of the book." And in a footnote to this observation, Yeats states: "I had forgotten

18   W. B. Yeats, Preface, *Plays for an Irish Theatre* (London and Stratford-on-Avon, 1911), pp. ix–xiii; *E&I*, pp. 275–76.

19   A glance at Bradley's list of contents will confirm this: "Events before the Opening of the Action in *Hamlet*"; "Where was Hamlet at the time of his father's death?" etc.

Falstaff, who is an episode in a chronicle play."[20] By renouncing character in tragedy and calling Shakespeare's tragic heroes "cloudy," Yeats made a complete break with the school of character criticism so indisputably holding sway at the time.

Not unexpectedly, Yeats's attitude here resembles that of Dr. Johnson, who regarded Shakespeare's persons as representatives of general humanity—they "act and speak by the influence of those general passions and principles by which all minds are agitated. . . . In the writings of other poets a character is too often an individual; in those of Shakespeare it is commonly a species." Answering complaints that Shakespeare's Romans are not sufficiently Roman and his kings not completely royal, Johnson says that though Shakespeare's stories require Romans and kings, "he thinks only on men." Shakespeare, "knowing that kings love wine like other men, and that wine exerts its natural power upon kings," adds drunkenness to Claudius' other attributes.[21] Similarly, Yeats sees tragedy—particularly Shakespearean tragedy—as "a drowning and breaking of the dykes that separate man from man."[22] For Yeats, individual characteristics disappear and the tragic hero, in his moments of suffering or enlightenment, becomes Everyman. Although Johnson and Yeats are concerned with different levels of Shakespeare's representation of men—Johnson inclining more toward the visible and the natural, Yeats toward the intrinsic oneness of all human experience—it is possible for us to detect a similarity of approach.

Character then, for Yeats, belongs to comedy, not to tragedy. By 1910 this conviction enabled him to say of Falstaff, "How well that man is realised! I should know him were I to meet him on the street." By contrast, the tragic hero remains mysterious. Despite Shakespeare's

---

20 *E&I*, pp. 272–73. Peter Ure, "The Plays," in *An Honoured Guest: New Essays on W. B. Yeats,* ed. Denis Donoghue and J. R. Mulryne (London, 1965), pp. 158–59, seems to have oversimplified Yeats's response to Shakespeare by saying that his admiration is for only the lyrical passages in the plays. In an age when poetic drama was nearly incomprehensible, Yeats—endeavoring to advance its cause—had necessarily to arrange his reactions in order of priorities; but to conclude from this order that any virtue after the first was nonexistent to him would be a misunderstanding of his position.

21 *Dr. Johnson on Shakespeare,* ed. W. K. Wimsatt (Harmondsworth, Middlesex, 1969), pp. 59, 61.

22 *E&I*, p. 241.

elaborate preparation for the arrival of the hero on stage, Yeats felt that "complete definition" of the hero was never achieved, because it was not desired:

> Nor does character ever attain to complete definition in these lamps [Timon, Hamlet, Antony] ready for the taper, no matter how circumstantial and gradual the opening of events, as it does in Falstaff, who has no passionate purpose to fulfill.[23]

Yeats seems here to have in mind the slow unfolding of the situation that, in *Hamlet*, occupies 240 lines before we hear Hamlet speak; in *Timon of Athens*, 97 lines; in *Macbeth*, 110 lines. No comic character in Shakespeare is ever introduced this way to the audience. A legitimate deduction from Yeats's argument would be that, when Falstaff appears for the first time in scene ii of *Henry IV, Part I*, it is an appropriately abrupt appearance; he demands of the prince, "Now, Hal, what time of day is it, lad?" and from this point the audience knows that, though each fresh sally of his wit will be unexpected, he has already attained "to complete definition" in his first question.

Never precise or static, the outline of the tragic hero is constantly expanding, changing, "alluring us almost to the intensity of trance." Emphasizing the impossibility of restricting his contours to a single form, Yeats traces the effect of this deliberate variation: "We feel our minds expand convulsively or spread out slowly like some moon-brightened image-crowded sea." Unlike comedy, which gives us a Falstaff who can be recognized on the street, tragedy contains "devices to exclude or lessen character." Falstaff, with his ebullient wit and "abundant vocabulary," "gives one the sensation of reality," for he is the most highly developed expression of the comic genius, and, by implication, of character portrayal. The heroes of tragedy, however, are embodiments of "passion and motives, one person being jealous, another full of love or remorse or pride or anger," Yeats argues, perhaps thinking of Othello, Romeo, Macbeth, Coriolanus, and Lear, respectively. He declares that Shakespeare, being a writer of tragicomedy, also depicts character, but only in the comic scenes. On the other hand, "when Timon orders his tomb, when Hamlet cries to Horatio 'Absent thee from felicity awhile,'

23 *E&I*, p. 240.

when Antony names 'Of many thousand kisses the poor last,' all is
lyricism, unmixed passion, 'the integrity of fire.' " The cloudy nature
of the tragic hero may be related to what Yeats says of the heroes of
myth and legend (Cuchulain, Finn, Oisin) who "are hardly so much
individual men as portions of universal nature, like the clouds that
shape themselves and reshape themselves momentarily . . . and yet
this but brings them nearer to us, for we can remake them in our image
when we will." The artist "create[s] all things out of himself," but we
who watch the play perform a similar function by creating ourselves
in the likeness of the tragic hero on stage.[24]

The creations of a great dramatist are never drawn out of objective
detachment, but are "pictured from within," Yeats reasons in an article
written in 1902. He continues with the reflection, which was certainly
more startling to some of his contemporaries than to us today, "Shakespeare could not have written the part of Iago unless he had something
even of Iago in him. If he had given himself up to his amorous emotions
he would have been Romeo, if to his hatred of the world he would
have been Timon, if to his Philistinism he would have been Henry the
Fifth, and if to the near ally of his wit he would have been King Lear."[25]
Everything and yet nothing, the persons of drama may be regarded as
facets of their creator. Each possesses an intensity in a particular trait,
which his human prototype lacks, yet each lacks the innumerable traits
that his prototype necessarily possesses.

Richard "is typical not because he ever existed, but because he
has made us know of something in our own minds we had never known
of had he never been imagined." When Timon orders his tomb, or when
Cleopatra sets the asp to her bosom, "their words move us because their
sorrow is not their own at tomb or asp, but for all men's fate."[26] Thus the

---

24 *E&I*, pp. 245, 241, 243; *Ex*, p. 166; *E&I*, p. 240; *Ex*, pp. 18, 20. For
Yeats's metaphor of the artist as Adam naming "the passions and motives of men,"
see *Ex*, p. 242; *Vis*, p. 48; *Letters*, p. 468. In his own work, an example of Yeats's
abnegation of character may be seen in his comment on *Deirdre*: "The absence of
character is like the absence of individual expression in wall decoration. It was acted
with great simplicity; the actors kept very quiet, often merely posing and speaking.
The result was curiously dream-like and gentle" (*Au*, p. 273).
25 Yeats, "Freedom of the Theatre."
26 *Ex*, p. 145; *E&I*, p. 255.

lyrical, poetical persons of Shakespeare are universal or typical, not because they resemble some historical character, but because they are the quintessence of similar lyrical feelings deep within the spectator. Personality can come to the fore in poetic drama, which explores this less traveled region, whereas character belongs in the world that is seen and heard.

III

In 1910, in a letter to his father, Yeats succinctly states, "Juliet has personality, her Nurse has character." He says character and personality are two different things, but adds, "or perhaps different forms of the same thing." By this important modification, he allows for both character and personality in a dramatic creation. Moreover, by regarding "personality as the individual form of our passions," and citing as examples of this statement "Dowson's in his poetry or Byron in *Manfred* or Forbes-Robertson in a romantic part," he makes it clear that it is only through their art that their personality comes out. "We do not necessarily know much about their characters," he points out.[27] The true self of the artist, or his anti-self, both aspects of personality, are revealed in his work, whereas in his life, only his character is apparent to his contemporaries.

Great art, then, is an expression of the writer's personality, which assumes an existence out of the very act of creation; it is not an already existing entity that simply discloses itself in the work of art. It will be recalled that Yeats came to stress the fact that in the process of creating Hamlet and Lear, Shakespeare "found out that he was an altogether different man to what he thought himself." In 1931, concurring with Berkeley's rejection of his early concept of Heaven "as physical pleasure," Yeats likens this concept to Shakespeare's creation of the nurse (in *Romeo*) "from observation, from passive sense-impression"; moving beyond Berkeley's position, Yeats then suggests that a better concept of Heaven would be that of a world of spirits and

---

27 *Letters*, p. 548. For a discussion of J. B. Yeats's views on "personality" and their effect on Yeats, see Joseph Ronsley, *Yeats's Autobiography: Life as Symbolic Pattern* (Cambridge, Mass., 1968), pp. 38–43.

their relations. Each depends on the others for his existence, even as Shakespeare drew "Hamlet, the Court, the whole work of art, out of himself in a pure indivisible act."[28] The artist and his work are indispensable parts of a whole, mutually coexistent. This Shakespearean analogy clearly goes back to the statement he made to J. B. Yeats twenty years earlier, but now Hamlet has been substituted for Juliet. Thus, Hamlet becomes inseparable from Shakespeare, a doctrine consistent with Yeats's theory of the Mask, that the dramatist moves toward an image of himself or his Mask and becomes at certain moments his own opposite.

Yeats's concept of character, as he himself recognizes, comes close to Congreve's (or Ben Jonson's) theory of humors. For Yeats, character is formed from objects and situations impinging on the individual. It is a shaping from without, comparable to the Will and the Body of Fate, which are also extrinsic. By itself, the Will is purely functional and mechanical, and the Body of Fate, like a tablet of wax, passively records the imprint of "the series of events forced upon him from without."[29] Like these two uninteresting partners, character is a process of accretion, and, devoid of passion, fails to touch the roots of human experience.

Since comedy consists of a series of episodes strung together like beads on a string, Yeats says: "Character belongs I think to Comedy," and he justifies this assumption by explaining that a " 'character actor' builds up a part out of observation," but "an 'emotional actor' . . . builds it up out of himself, and in this last case—we always add, if he is not commonplace—that he has personality. Of course Shakespeare has both because he is always a tragic comedian."[30] Continuing the analysis in the terminology of *A Vision*, we find that the remaining two faculties, Mask and Creative Mind, with their innate vitality, counterpoise the dullness of Will and Body of Fate. When they begin to make their presence felt, tragedy is born, for personality, as opposed to character, emerges, and we, the spectators, are caught up in that process of striving to become which is the essence of tragedy and also the challenge of the Mask.

28   *Letters*, p. 741; *E&I*, p. 410. See above pp. 47–48.
29   *E&I*, p. 241; *Vis*, p. 83.
30   *Letters*, p. 549.

Yeats, as we have seen, points out that Shakespeare "was the greatest of modern poets, partly because [he was] entirely true to phase, creating always from *Mask* and *Creative Mind,* never from situation alone, never from *Body of Fate* alone."[31] Reduced to less technical equivalents, Shakespeare's plays do not consist merely of a series of accurately observed, lifelike episodes, which are the limited range of Body of Fate, but are quickened into imaginative life by Mask and Creative Mind. Shakespeare's universality soars above the particulars of time and place. The realistic drama of the twentieth century was, Yeats felt, a slave to its time; removed from that context, it would be unintelligible. Dealing with social ills and with a remedial objective, it could have no appeal once those ills were eliminated.

Personality meant several things to Yeats. Around 1910, when he was grappling with the distinction between personality and character, he associated personality with lyrical intensity. In a letter to his father, he said he believed "that lyric poetry should be personal. That a man should express his life and do this without shame or fear. Ernest Dowson did this and became a most extraordinary poet, one feels the pressure of his life behind every line as if he were a character in a play of Shakespeare's."[32] This statement is ambiguous, and Yeats would certainly have qualified it in any context other than a letter, because whereas the life of a poet may be related to his poetry, the life of a character in a play has no existence independent of the play itself. Nevertheless, what he implies here is consistent within limits: Shakespeare's heroes reveal their deepest preoccupations not once, but repeatedly. The scenes of the play, therefore, are not heterogeneous, but homogeneous.

That Yeats wanted his statement to convey such a meaning is confirmed by his observation, made in 1921 and intended for publication, about W. E. Henley, editor of the *Magazine of Art.* Here Yeats is more deliberate in his assessment, more precise than in the letter to his father.

> He was most human—human I used to say like one of Shakespeare's characters—and yet pressed and pummelled, as it were, into a single attitude,

31   *Vis,* p. 153.
32   *Letters,* p. 548.

almost into a gesture and a speech as by some overwhelming situation.
. . . I meant that he was like a great actor of passion . . . and an actor
of passion will display some one quality of soul, personified again and
again.[33]

Yeats saw personality as the aspect of the hero that the dramatist emphasizes by revealing it in different situations, "personified again and again,"
through all of which it retains its integrity. The hero is "freed from
everything that is not a part of that action," the action being "an eddy
of life purified from everything but itself."[34] The entire play becomes,
then, for Yeats, a testing ground for this particular quality that he calls
personality, and the dramatist's intention is to expose the hero to varied
situations so that his personality is revealed.

Traditional critics of Shakespeare would regard, for example, the
rashness of Lear in act I as a symptom of senility, or his undefeated pride
in later acts as a sign of his nobility, and thus deduce his character in
the round, to borrow E. M. Forster's terminology. Yeats, however, would
repudiate such analysis and insist that Lear's personality is his "rage
under the lightning," and all else is secondary. Similarly, "the last words
of Shakespeare's people . . . gather up into themselves the energy of
elaborate events, and they put strange meaning into half-forgotten things
and accidents, like cries that reveal the combatants in some dim battle."[35]
The distinctive attributes of the tragic hero are present, but narrowed,
intensified, heightened, and the battle is "dim," because the hero, though
recognizable, fades away into all humanity. By emphasizing the seeming
irrationality of the hero's actions, Yeats endeavors to move drama away
from the realm of causality to a realm in which the personality of the
hero, unpredictable and unaccountable by conventional standards of
behavior, rather than the clash of character, as Bradley asserts, provides
the thrust that propels the play forward. In short, Yeats must have found
much that he could agree with in the work of critics like G. Wilson
Knight and L. C. Knights.

33 *Au*, pp. 76–77. Jerome Hamilton Buckley, *William Ernest Henley* (Prince-
ton, 1945), pp. 148–52, gives an account of Henley's personality and notes that
Yeats compared him with a Shakespearean character.
34 *Ex*, pp. 153–54.
35 *Boiler*, p. 35; *E&I*, p. 307.

IV

In 1919, in his open letter to Lady Gregory, Yeats briefly but forcefully enunciates his position. He maintains that Shakespeare's concern was with a single point in time in his hero's life; and that point was located at the intersection of two forces, emotion and intellect:

> Shakespeare set upon the stage kings and queens, great historical or legendary persons about whom there is nothing unreal except the circumstances of their lives which remain vague and summary, because he could only write his best—his mind and the mind of his audience being interested in emotion and intellect at their moment of union and at their greatest intensity.

He argues that Shakespeare deliberately eschews "intricacy and detail" in the delineation of Lear and Cordelia and devotes his drama to the depiction of Lear's agony, so that "Shakespeare's groundlings watched the stage in terrified sympathy." He then points out caustically that the modern audience, interested in character traits, concerns itself with "Lear and Cordelia the real millionaire and the real peeress, and seeks to make them charming by insisting perpetually that they have all that wealth can buy."[36] Scorning the obsessive class consciousness of his age, Yeats in fact would deny that Shakespeare chose kings and queens to be the heroes and heroines of his plays because he felt they could boast of possessing an innate loftiness of soul—Bradley's reckoning—but, rather, that their being kings or queens was incidental or inessential to Shakespeare, whose attention was focused on the universal in them. For Yeats, even petty and vindictive Paudeen, of the poem "Paudeen," has in his soul the potential to rise above his class: "There cannot be, confusion of our sound forgot, / A single soul that lacks a sweet crystalline cry."

Bradley devotes much of his skill to proving that Lear's division of the kingdom on the basis of his daughters' protestations of love for him "is not at all incredible," and he concludes with the following faintly pompous assertion:

> The first scene, therefore, is not absurd, though it must be pronounced dramatically faulty in so far as it discloses the true position of affairs

36 *Ex,* pp. 245–46.

only to an attention more alert than can be expected in a theatrical audience or has been found in many critics of the play.[37]

But clearly, for Yeats, any attempt to establish the plausibility of a play like *King Lear,* no matter how well intended, would be inane. In a closely reasoned examination of the nature of tragedy and comedy, Yeats asserts:

> Tragedy is passion alone, and rejecting character, it gets form from motives, from wandering of passion; while comedy is the clash of character. . . . In practice most works are mixed: Shakespeare being tragicomedy.

In this remarkable probing may be detected many of Yeats's earlier attitudes, now brought together. (Yeats long before had insisted that, judged by utilitarian standards, Bolingbroke, Fortinbras, and Aufidius, all of them full of energy, would certainly make better rulers than Richard, Hamlet, and Coriolanus, and elsewhere points out that Shakespeare was no "British Benthamite," in spite of Dowden's efforts to make him one.) Yeats goes on to say that "joy is of the will which labours, which overcomes obstacles, which knows triumph. The soul knows its changes of state alone, and I think the motives of tragedy are not related to action but to changes of state."[38] From this observation, it is clear that Hamlet's much-discussed "delay" would have no relevance for Yeats, since the substance of tragedy lies, not in the energy or the activity displayed by the hero, but, rather, in his "changes of state," which manifest themselves perhaps in the nexus of external events, but nevertheless owe their significance, not to these events, but to the hero's own personality.

If the twentieth-century critic of Shakespeare has become more aware of symbolic patterns in the plays and less preoccupied with lifelike character portrayal, the reason for this shift in sensibility can perhaps be traced through Craig and Granville-Barker to Yeats and Wilde.[39] Yeats regrets that "Mr. Benson did not venture to play the scene in

37   Bradley, pp. 249, 251.
38   *Au,* pp. 286, 143.
39   Wilde's exaltation of art over life did not fail to make an impression on Yeats, though Yeats did not allow his flamboyant style to overpower him. "Life imitates art rather than art life," Wilde announced (see Richard Ellmann, "The

Richard III where the ghosts walk as Shakespeare wrote it" but remained a slave to realism. Shakespeare's art, being unabashedly imaginative, "brings us near to the archetypal ideas themselves, and away from nature, which is but their looking-glass," Yeats asserts.[40] Tragedy, then, for Yeats, has an existence distinct from life. In tragedy, therefore, the hero's personality is revealed through a particular situation, and it would not be legitimate to speculate on the possibilities of his conduct outside that tightly knit construct.

Passion in tragedy was, for Yeats, its greatest distinguishing feature from comedy, for "comedy is passionless," he tells us.[41] Yeats's relationship with Shakespeare was personal, as that of other recognized critics of Shakespeare could not be, for they, working their way toward a Shakespeare rationale, were necessarily analytic. It was this analytic attitude that Yeats disapproved of in Rossi's book on Swift, but at the same time, he readily acknowledged that the book did have its own kind of merit: "It is not my Swift though it is part of the truth and may well be the beginning of a more profound Swift criticism." Rossi's book failed to come to grips with the passion "that Swift served," and Yeats concludes: "Passion is to me the essential. I was educated upon Balzac and Shakespeare and cannot go beyond them."[42] Swift, Balzac, and Shakespeare

Critic as Artist as Wilde," in *The Poet as Critic,* ed. Frederick P. W. McDowell [Evanston, 1967], p. 53; see also Ellmann, *Eminent Domain: Yeats among Wilde, Joyce, Pound, Eliot, and Auden* [New York, 1967], chapter 2). And Yeats remembered Wilde's aphorism about Hamlet's melancholy well enough to quote it twenty years after Wilde's death: "The world has become sad because a puppet was once melancholy" (*Au,* p. 83).

40 *E&I,* pp. 101–2.

41 *Ex,* p. 249. As early as 1899, Yeats had maintained that every great writer—Homer, Dante, Shakespeare—had used "all knowledge, whether of life or of philosophy, or of mythology or of history" simply to declare "the exaltation of his senses," and he went on to say, "I believe too that the difference between good and bad poetry is . . . in the volume and intensity of its passion for beauty, and in the perfection of its workmanship" (*Literary Ideals in Ireland* [Dublin, 1899], pp. 36–37). It should be noted that Yeats lays equal emphasis on "workmanship"; he does not advocate a gush of emotion but its control—what he later came to call an "image," a term that designated precision and distinctness coupled with intensity. Cf. T. S. Eliot's "objective correlative."

42 *Letters,* p. 791. Yeats's revulsion against the passionless anti-theater that had begun to make itself heard in the twenties is evident in his remarks on Alfred Jarry's *Ubu Roi,* which he saw in Paris (*Au,* p. 210). See *Ex,* pp. 112–13, and *Boiler,* pp. 34–35, for Yeats's disgust with drama that presents a distortion of values.

apprehend the truth through passion, and Yeats would count himself among them.

If the trend of modern Shakespearean criticism is recognized as the continuation of a break away from realism toward an understanding of the symbolic significance of the plays, then Yeats's contribution, which began even before his early essay "The Celtic Element in Literature," in which he stresses the symbolic importance of Shakespeare's imagery, must be acknowledged to be of supreme significance. Bradley himself proved a deserter of the realist school with his refreshingly imaginative study of fire symbolism in *Coriolanus* (1912). Masefield presented his Romanes Lecture, *Shakespeare and Spiritual Life,* in 1924, and thereafter the movement was well under way.

7

Shakespearean Echoes in Yeats's Early Plays

> If our modern poetical drama
> has failed, it is mainly because, always
> dominated by the example of Shakespeare,
> it would restore an irrevocable past.
>> —Yeats, *Four Plays for Dancers*

SEVERAL of Yeats's plays are permeated by the ideas set forth in *A Vision,* where he propounded his theory of alternating historical cycles, of the alternating succession of the primary or the objective mind and the antithetical or subjective mind, each moment of change being accompanied by a destructive overthrow of the values of the previous age. In his Introduction to *The Resurrection,* Yeats wrote:

> For years I have been preoccupied with a certain myth that was itself a reply to a myth. I do not mean a fiction, but one of those statements our nature is compelled to make and employ as a truth though there cannot be sufficient evidence. When I was a boy everybody talked about progress, and rebellion against my elders took the form of aversion to that myth. I took satisfaction in certain public disasters, felt a sort of ecstasy in the contemplation of ruin.

Yeats had, as early as 1901, visualized Shakespeare as one who "cared little for the State, the source of all our judgments, apart from its shows and splendours, its turmoils and battles," and concluded that "the world was almost as empty in his eyes as it must be in the eyes of God." The "tragic joy" of the poem "The Gyres," that Yeats repeatedly emphasized, is, for him, a part of Shakespeare's attitude of heroic indifference toward the overthrow of civilizations, also evinced in the Chinamen of "Lapis Lazuli," who stare "on all the tragic scene" with "ancient, glittering eyes" that are gay. Yeats, seeing in Shakespeare his own thought reflected and intensified, imagines him sitting "over Holinshed's *History of England*," creating "the Richard of the play," while "the historical Richard has passed away for ever." "Writers think the world is but their palette, and if history amuses them," it is but the means whereby they express their own private thoughts, Yeats declares. So also could Yeats view the panorama of history with amused and ironic detachment:

> Each age unwinds the thread another age had wound, and it amuses one to remember that before Phidias, and his westward-moving art, Persia fell, and that when full moon came round again, amid eastward-moving thought, and brought Byzantine glory, Rome fell; and that at the outset of our westward-moving Renaissance Byzantium fell; all things dying each other's life, living each other's death.[1]

The opposition between the primary and the antithetical finds its counterpart in individuals as well. In *On Baile's Strand*, Cuchulain is antithetical because he is spontaneous, emotional, imaginative, subjective; Conchubar, on the other hand, stands for the primary because he is objective, shrewd, calculating. Similar contrasts exist between Fool and Blind Man in the play, Seanchan and the King in *The King's Threshold*, Martin and Thomas in *The Unicorn from the Stars*. Cuchulain and Conchubar become for Yeats symbols of "those combatants who turn the wheel of life," and, in keeping with this deceptively simple view of life, he saw in Shakespeare's vision too the conflict of opposites leading to the overthrow of the antithetical and the establishment of the primary. In "At Stratford-on-Avon," Yeats sees mirrored in Shakespeare his own early view of the world, "that there is some one myth for every man, which, if we but knew it, would make us understand all he did and thought. Shakespeare's myth, it may be, describes a wise man who was blind from very wisdom, and an empty man who thrust him from his place, and saw all that could be seen from very emptiness."[2]

1   *Ex*, p. 392; *E&I*, pp. 106, 107; *Ex*, pp. 145, 236; *Vis*, pp. 270–71.
2   *Ex*, p. 393; *E&I*, p. 107.

Thus Yeats contrasts Hamlet with Fortinbras, Richard with Henry, Coriolanus with Aufidius, the first in each pair being subjective, the second, objective.

Yeats's plays *On Baile's Strand* (1903), *The King's Threshold* (1904), *Deirdre* (1907), and *The Hour-Glass* (1913) abound in both situational and verbal resemblances to Shakespeare. Even after 1913, when for a few years Yeats developed a keen interest in the Noh drama of Japan, he continued also to maintain an affinity with Shakespeare. *Purgatory*, his penultimate play (to be considered in detail in the following chapter), is at once astonishingly Shakespearean and un-Shakespearean in design. As such, of all Yeats's plays, it presents the most interesting problem for the investigator, whose natural inclination would be to emphasize the Shakespearean elements it contains. But such treatment would both distort the play and undermine Yeats's own extraordinary originality, which refused to be stifled by Shakespeare's genius. Whatever is Shakespearean in this play has been alchemized into a Yeatsian compound that loses none of its individuality.

II

The lonely hero in splendid contrast to the rabble was an impression from Yeats's boyhood that was reinforced by images from Shakespeare. Since his understanding of Shakespeare went directly counter to the popular trend of Shakespearean criticism in his time, it is not difficult to perceive his own peculiar interpretation of Shakespeare reflected in certain of his own plays, and it may therefore be more correct to speak of parallels than of influence. Yeats started *On Baile's Strand* at Coole Park in July, 1901, three months after his visit to Stratford.[3] Perhaps it is in this play that Yeats's powerful response to Shakespeare, as reflected in "At Stratford-on-Avon," can, for the first time, be distinctly seen. Although it is true that in early plays such as *The Countess Cathleen* (1892) and *The Shadowy Waters* (1900) certain Shakespearean strains may be detected, they are as yet too faint to be isolated. The countess is perhaps a distant cousin to Portia in *The Merchant of Venice*. Both

3 *Letters*, p. 353.

women retrieve a seemingly hopeless situation. So also, *The Shadowy Waters* seems to look back at *The Tempest* in its opening scene; and the power of music that Forgael wields over his mutinous sailors (48–55, 300–317) may be compared to Ariel's intervention when Caliban, Stephano, and Trinculo hatch their conspiracy against Prospero (III, ii, 115–43). In the play *Mosada,* first published in 1886, a Moorish lady is sentenced to death for summoning spirits to give her news of Ebremar, the man with whom she had fallen in love three years earlier. Ironically, Ebremar, now a fanatical monk who heads the Inquisition, unsuspectingly insists on her being burned at the stake. Mosada, the lady, prefers to die by her own hand; a little before the end of the play she sucks poison from her ring and is on the point of death when Ebremar enters her dungeon: "She sleeps— (*Starting.*) Mosada— / Oh, God!—awake! thou shalt not die. She sleeps, / Her head cast backward in her unloosed hair. / Look up, look up, thy Gomez is by thee." But it is too late. Mosada dies and Ebremar maintains an iron composure when the monks enter to take her body away. "You're pale, my lord," the First Monk remarks, and "His lips are quivering," another observes aside, but Ebremar curtly replies: "I am not well. / 'Twill pass." Then, "Your hood is threadbare—see that it be changed," he brusquely orders one of them. Already Yeats's heroes are beginning to display the heroic self-restraint that he admired in Shakespeare's heroes. Like Shakespeare's early tragedy, *Titus Andronicus,* Yeats's *Mosada* is melodramatic, but it shows promise of better things to come. It is of course possible to detect faint overtones of *Romeo and Juliet* in the play: the manner of Mosada's death; her discovery by Ebremar; and the shadow of Fate that lies heavy on her from the play's opening. But these touches are slight. Yeats has not as yet truly entered and appropriated for himself Shakespeare's world. He is still only a visitor.

With *On Baile's Strand,* however, a significant change in Yeats's dramatic art becomes apparent. The first version of the play owes its ideology to the theory of the clash of opposites that Yeats had so emphatically outlined in his essay: "To pose character against character was an element in Shakespeare's art, and scarcely a play is lacking in characters that are the complement of one another."[4] In addition, Yeats's play, displaying evidence of an effort to break away from the purely lyrical subjectivism of *The Shadowy Waters,* and simultaneously shunning objective realism, seems to be an embodiment of the kind of self-determining and autonomous world of art that Yeats had discovered in the Shakespearean cycle at Stratford.

The supreme moment in Yeats's play is the defeat of the hero, when, to the amazement of the other characters and the audience, he rushes out, battles the waves, and is overcome by them: a gesture that is an explosion of his personality, as it were, into an act at once futile and heroic. In order to better relate the play to Yeats's concept of heroism as corroborated by Shakespeare, certain salient attributes that Yeats detected in Shakespeare's Richard may be seen in Cuchulain. When he appears, Cuchulain is appropriately engrossed in dreamy romanticism, and the audience is left in no doubt that his competence as an administrator or a ruler is highly questionable. The oath of allegiance Conchubar seeks to impose on him is an attempt to tame his wild spirits, to curb his untrammeled fancy. Conchubar, an older man, is Cuchulain's opposite, crafty, efficient, and practical. Cuchulain, full of the joy and the gaiety of life, refuses to submit to Conchubar's behest and displays traits that Yeats had attributed to Richard: "contemplative virtue," "lyrical fantasy," "sweetness of temper," and "dreamy dignity."[5] When Conchubar complains that Cuchulain's "fancy / Runs as it were a swallow on the wind" and prevents him from cooperating in defending the country from aggression, Cuchulain's reply is full of airy disdain for the High King's stodginess:

> Run to the stable
> And set the horses to the chariot-pole,
> And send a messenger to the harp-players.
> We'll find a level place among the woods,
> And dance awhile.
>
> [361–65]

Yeats skillfully differentiates between the language of Cuchulain

4 *E&I,* p. 108.
5 *E&I,* p. 106.

and that of Conchubar: Cuchulain's speech is replete with adjectives
and adverbs, with similes and metaphors drawn from air and sky:

> Nestlings of a high nest,
> Hawks that have followed me into the air
> And looked upon the sun, we'll out of this
> And sail upon the wind once more.
>
> [355–58]

Later he describes himself as "one that lives like a bird's flight from
tree to tree" and adds,

> If the wild horse should break the chariot-pole,
> It would be punished.
>
> [375; 441–42]

Contemptuous of the pragmatism that Conchubar personifies, Cuchulain
describes himself thus:

> The High King there has promised me his wisdom;
> But the hawk's sleepy till its well-beloved
> Cries out amid the acorns, or it has seen
> Its enemy like a speck upon the sun.
> What's wisdom to the hawk, when that clear eye
> Is burning nearer up in the high air?
>
> [476–81]

Conchubar, on the other hand, is guarded in his speech and indulges
in no such strange flights of fancy.

The contrast that Yeats underlines is probably an echo of that
between Richard and Bolingbroke: whereas the one is a self-conscious
lyrical poet, the other is like a brusque "Municipal Councillor," Yeats's
description of the kind of man Shakespeare was not.[6] Cuchulain too
resents having to "sit at the council-board / Among the unshapely
bodies of old men" (218–19), an interesting excoriation of administrative
ability that Yeats applied to both Shakespeare's Bolingbroke and his
own Conchubar. Many years later, in a letter to Ezra Pound, he cautioned him against becoming an administrator. "Do not be elected to
the Senate of your country. I think myself, after six years, well out of
that of mine. Neither you nor I, nor any other of our excitable profes-

6 *E&I*, p. 105.

sion, can match those old lawyers, old bankers, old business men, who, because all habit and memory, have begun to govern the world."[7] The vanquishing of Cuchulain by Conchubar and of Richard by Henry was but the blueprint for the growing alienation of the artist in the modern world.

Again, Cuchulain's submission to Conchubar is comparable to Richard's relinquishing of the crown to Bolingbroke; both regard their subordination as a gift that they offer, not as something wrested from their grasp; Cuchulain says: "I never gave a gift and took it again" (440) and Richard enacts his abdication as if he were a donor:

> I give this heavy weight from off my head
> And this unwieldy sceptre from my hand,
>
> . . . .
>
> With mine own hands I give away my crown.
>
> [IV, i, 204–7]

The astonishing and strangely abrupt reversal of Cuchulain's ardent friendship with the Young Man is perhaps the most extraordinary feature of the play. To complain, as some commentators on the play have done, that there is "an uncontrolled ambiguity" underlying this sudden change in Cuchulain's attitude is simply to name what Yeats deliberately intends as an integral feature of the play.[8] A search for a motive would be in vain, for there is no motive except that which Yeats saw exemplified in some of Shakespeare's plays: "It also is an essential part of [Shakespeare's] method to give slight or obscure motives of many actions." The sudden cry of "Witchcraft" (610), raised by Conchubar and the other kings when Cuchulain resists the King's attempt to thwart the growing friendship between him and the Young Man, is admittedly not designed to explain Cuchulain's about-face, but is intended to remain slightly inexplicable and nonrealistic. Likewise Yeats had seen in Richard's unpredictable moods a dramatic technique that defied rationalistic assessment. Cuchulain, like Richard, is clearly not a simple transplant

7 Vis, p. 26. Pound, however, disagreed. "If a man don't occasionally sit in a senate / how can he pierce the darrk mind of a / senator?" (Canto LXXX), he growled back at Yeats, after Yeats had been dead for nearly ten years.

8 See, e.g., Leonard E. Nathan, The Tragic Drama of William Butler Yeats (New York, 1965), p. 121.

from the real world. Oblivious of this important principle, several critics
deduce Richard's character from his actions only, but Yeats stands against
making such pronouncements on a dramatic character: "You cannot
know a man from his actions because you cannot watch him in every
kind of circumstance."[9] Modern Shakespearean scholarship, which has
rejected the search for a plausible motive as the key to unlock all dramatic problems, has, of course, completely vindicated Yeats's stand.[10]
By emphasizing, not plausibility, but underlying emotion, Yeats lifts
poetic drama out of the context of life and firmly establishes it in the
context of art. Undoubtedly, he sees a self-begotten unity in prose
drama too, but because it employs the language of common speech it
cannot assert its autonomy with the same authority as poetic drama.

In his short essay, "The Emotion of Multitude" (1903), Yeats
refers to Shakespeare's carefully contrived scheme whereby both Hamlet
and Laertes lose their fathers, so that within the context of their common
bereavement the lofty dignity of Hamlet's father is parodied by Polonius,
a comic and pompous bore. Likewise, in *On Baile's Strand,* the Fool
and the Blind Man re-enact the Cuchulain-Conchubar conflict but now
in terms of common humanity. The Blind Man's stroke of genius with
which the play concludes: "The ovens will be full. We will put our
hands into the ovens" (803–4) is surely—considering the boldness with
which the grandeur of Cuchulain's death is rounded off with this bur-
lesque—in the same class as certain of Shakespeare's stunning juxtaposi-
tions of the sublime and the ridiculous (e.g., the porter scene in *Macbeth*). Like Cuchulain, the Fool is credulous enough to be constantly
duped by the Blind Man. Yeats called Cuchulain "the fool—wandering,
passive, houseless and almost loveless." His acts, like those of the Fool,
who is situated at Phase 28 in *A Vision,* "are aimless like his thoughts;
and it is in this aimlessness that he finds his joy." The swift and
unaccountable destruction of his son is as aimless as is his fight with
the sea, which, though a tremendous gesture of defiance, remains ineffectual. It is a demonstration of what Yeats saw befalling all of Shake-

---

9 *E&I,* pp. 101, 103.
10 See, e.g., Peter Ure, Introduction, *Richard II,* New Arden ed. (London,
1956).

speare's heroes: "the defeat that awaits all, whether they be artist or saint."[11]

But despite the close structural resemblances between the two plays, it would be a mistake to conclude that Yeats patterned his work on Shakespeare's *Richard II*. *On Baile's Strand* is in certain ways a statement of attitudes that he felt he shared with Shakespeare. As Virgil was a powerful presence in Dante's mind during the writing of his great work, so was Shakespeare regarded by Yeats as his ally throughout the stormy times that accompanied the founding of the Irish National Theatre. That Yeats never allows his theory to get out of hand and dominate the play is seen in the admirable control he exercises in the portrayal of Conchubar. It would have been easy for him to overemphasize the theory of opposites by making Conchubar despicable, but he is careful never to allow this to happen. Also, though lyrical and capricious, Cuchulain is not ineffectual as is Richard. He is always the man of action, unlike his Shakespearean counterpart, who, hearing of Bolingbroke's increasing menace to the throne, reassures himself with the fatalistic thought that "heaven still guards the right" (III, ii, 62). Such passivity would be alien to Cuchulain.

Thus Yeats, even while putting into practice the theory of the clash of diametrically opposed personalities, was preparing for the next position in his development. No sharply defined boundaries were to be allowed (it may be recalled that he had cited Macbeth, who is neither altogether noble nor altogether sordid, as an example of this), and the conflict not only was to be external, but, more important, it was to rage within the bosom of the hero as well. Cuchulain's fight with the sea is, in fact, already a symbolic expression of this inner opposition. Instead of attacking Conchubar, he attacks the waves, and although these may well have been a surrogate for Conchubar in his mind, they are also clearly an objectification of the rage that he turns against himself. As Lear recognized the tempest on the heath to be an external manifestation of an inner turmoil ("This tempest in my mind / Doth from my senses take all feeling else / Save what beats there" [III, iv,

11   *E&I*, pp. 215–16; *Letters*, p. 425; *Vis*, p. 182; *E&I*, p. 106.

12–14]), so does Cuchulain's battle with the waves represent a psychological condition of schizophrenic mania.

The self-destruction of the hero, a motif at once Greek and Shakespearean, symbolizes on a cosmic scale the defeat of an antithetical civilization by a primary one. "A civilisation is a struggle to keep self-control," Yeats says, and goes on to liken it to "some great tragic person, some Niobe who must display an almost superhuman will or the cry will not touch our sympathy."[12] Cuchulain, like Shakespeare's heroes, whose superhuman self-restraint Yeats repeatedly extolled, trembles violently when he learns of his terrible crime but will not break down: he rushes out, madly battles the waves, and is overwhelmed by them.

A further example of an early Yeats play which reflects certain Shakespearean patterns that Yeats admired and isolated is *The King's Threshold.* An attempt to identify Yeats's debt to Shakespeare may, at times, seem too much like the strenuous maneuverings of Horatio, Marcellus, and Barnardo to surround the ghost of Hamlet's father. Yet these maneuverings may well be legitimate, for, though the ghost "faded on the crowing of the cock," it returned the following night and once again asserted its chthonic presence, demanding attention and recognition.

III

The King's Threshold was first acted in 1903 and published in 1904. The play is a variation on the theme of perpetual conflict between what Yeats calls "government," or deadly organizational ability and all that this connotes, and the artistic vision embodied in the poet Seanchan. *On Baile's Strand* had shown an imaginative warrior subjugated by a scheming king, but in *The King's Threshold,* instead of shunning the council table as Cuchulain did, Seanchan is resolute in asserting the ancient right of the poets to be included as members of the government. The poet here preserves his consciousness of artistic superiority but also claims a share in the day-to-day affairs of state; although he disdains bureaucracy, he is not repelled by it either. Already, therefore, a perceptible shift from the clear line of demarcation that separated the noble from the ignoble is evident.

12 *Vis,* p. 268.

If *On Baile's Strand* is in some respects a reflection of *Richard II*, *The King's Threshold* is rich in overtones from *Hamlet*. Yeats had regarded *Richard II* as a demonstration of the clash between the artistic temperament and the pragmatic. In his essay "At Stratford-on-Avon," he had included Hamlet in this category too, by conceding that Fortinbras would have made a better ruler than Hamlet, but his views on Hamlet thereafter were never as simply defined as they were on Richard. Even in this essay he calls Richard "that unripened Hamlet," which suggests that he already saw Hamlet as a further development or a complication of the elements that went into Richard's composition. Subsequently, in the 1920s, as has been noted, Yeats openly discounted the widely prevalent analysis of Hamlet as an ineffectual dreamer and insisted on his being recognized as a man of action though weighed down by "hesitations of thought" about "certain persons on whom his attention is fixed."[13] Seanchan too has more impulses in his makeup than had Cuchulain. Certain thematic similarities between *Hamlet* and *The King's Threshold* may therefore be traced.

Considering the former play first, we note that Hamlet upholds the right of the artist against the pragmatists who exercise authority and wield power. He eloquently defends the players against the crassness of Polonius, who feels that they, being inferiors, should know their proper place. Resenting Hamlet's glowing tribute to their profession—"the abstract and brief chronicles of the time"—Polonius mutters: "My lord, I will use them according to their desert," and Hamlet, enraged, retorts, "God's bodkin, man, much better" (II, ii, 502–3). Turning to *The King's Threshold*, we find that Polonius' counterpart there is the Mayor. Flunkey to the King, he, like Polonius, busily operates as the King's emissary to Seanchan; officious and nearly senile, he approaches Seanchan with a fulsome speech, but with a memory no better than Polonius' ("What was I about to say? By the mass, I was about to say something. Where did I leave?" [II, i, 50]). He forgets the words and his speech breaks down ignominiously: "but what comes after that? Something

---

13 *E&I*, p. 108; *Boiler*, pp. 33–34. Yeats seems to have in mind here Hamlet's "Of thinking too precisely on th' event" (IV, iv, 41); also his "the native hue of resolution / Is sicklied o'er with the pale cast of thought" (III, i, 85–86).

about the King" (247–48). When he does remember the second half
and delivers it with parrot-like fidelity, it becomes clear that the speech
is a complete muddling of issues, yet he has the temerity to ask Seanchan
to be "reasonable" (261). Seanchan, in reply, turns on him with unconcealed rage:

> Reason, O reason in plenty. Yet you have yellowy
> white hair and not too many teeth. How comes it
> that you have been so long in the world and not
> found reason out?
>
> [265–68]

Hamlet, equally incensed by Polonius' crude attempts to fish out his
secret, anatomizes him with the same ruthlessness:

> old men have grey beards, that their
> faces are wrinkled, their eyes purging thick
> amber and plum-tree gum, and that they have
> a plentiful lack of wit, together with most
> weak hams.
>
> [II, ii, 194–97]

Deaf and blind to artistic excellence, both the Mayor and Polonius
have at least one dubious qualification: they make no pretensions to
artistic taste. The Mayor frankly declares: "I never understood a poet's
talk more than the baa of a sheep" (319–20), and Polonius, not to be
outdone, had interrupted the First Player's fiery speech on Pyrrhus and
Priam—a speech that visibly stirred Hamlet—with the bored observation:
"This is too long," whereupon Hamlet rebuked him with justifiable
venom: "It shall to the barber's with your beard. Prithee, say on. He's
for a jig or a tale of bawdry, or he sleeps" (II, ii, 474–76). Obsequi-
ousness is congenital to both the Mayor and Polonius; both of them
understand that the King's greatness is his prerogative to cut off their
heads: the Mayor piously observes, "And hadn't he the right to? And
hadn't he the right to strike your master's head off, being the King?
Or your head, or my head! I say, Long live the King! because he didn't
take our heads from us" (344–47). Polonius, with the same zeal, though
in a different context, had invited the King to "take this from this
(*pointing to his head and shoulder*)," if his diagnosis of Hamlet's
malady was not the right one (II, ii, 155).

When the Mayor's servility to the King has tried Brian's patience to its utmost, and he seizes him unceremoniously, the Mayor's cry of "Help! Help!" (378) echoes Polonius' cry, "What, ho! help, help, help!" while crouching behind the arras (III, iv, 22). The Mayor, being "the King's man" as he unashamedly calls himself, is only too eager to adopt any ruse whereby Seanchan may be prevailed on to relent in his merciless harassment of the King. As Polonius had conceived of the scheme to "loose my daughter to him" (II, ii, 161), using her as a decoy to uncover Hamlet's secret, so the Mayor is eager to use the woman Seanchan loves to serve the King's interests.

> But I'll go find the girl that he's to marry.
> She's coming, but I'll hurry her, my lord.
> Between ourselves, my lord, she is a great coaxer.
> . . . O, she's the girl to do it;
> For when the intellect is out, my lord,
> Nobody but a woman's any good.
>
> [412–17]

The Mayor is ubiquitous; he loves activity and feeds his soul by plotting traps and stratagems. Hamlet, well aware of a similar propensity in Polonius, had sent him packing when he wanted to confide in Horatio, ordering Polonius to "bid the players make haste" (III, ii, 41); and for an epitaph over his body, said, "Thou find'st to be too busy is some danger" (III, iv, 32).

Yeats's involvement with Shakespeare in *The King's Threshold*, however, goes deeper than the kinship between the Mayor and Polonius. Since Seanchan, as we have seen, defends the same values as Hamlet does, there are moments in the play when his attitude distinctly coincides with that of Hamlet. One such moment occurs when Seanchan's condemnation of the charms that women employ to lure men to their doom is nearly as scathing as Hamlet's denunciation of Ophelia's use of make-up. Seanchan gibes:

> You're fair to look upon.
> Your feet delight in dancing, and your mouths
> In the slow smiling that awakens love.
>
> .   .   .   .
>
> Go to the young men.

> Are not the ruddy flesh and the thin flanks
> And the broad shoulders worthy of desire?
> Go from me!
>
> [598–606]

Hamlet's dismissal of Ophelia was no less charitable. He too had regarded her as being little better than a whore and had upbraided her for painting her face, for jigging, ambling, and lisping (III, i, 139–45).

Again, Seanchan's death is depicted in imagery that is recognizably kin to Hamlet's heroic end. Yeats was greatly stirred by Hamlet's "Absent thee from felicity awhile," and he often cites the line as an example of supreme tragic ecstasy. In *On the Boiler* (1939), he declares that "the arts are all the bridal chambers of joy" and gives, as examples of this, Hamlet's death, "Cleopatra's last farewells, Lear's rage under the lightning," and Oedipus' end. In an earlier section of the same work, he points out that though he had sought to revive this now lost quality in drama, his efforts failed to have the success he had anticipated. In a moving passage, itself distinctive for the note of tragic esctasy that it sounds, Yeats admits defeat yet rejoices in a less tangible triumph— the same kind of triumph he had made his Seanchan assert thirty-four years earlier and that he praised in Hamlet's last words. After recounting the success of the Abbey Players and the principles that created this success, Yeats adds:

> Yet the theatre has not, apart from this one quality, gone my way or in any way I wanted it to go. . . . Then I say to myself, I have had greater luck than any other modern English-speaking dramatist; I have aimed at tragic ecstasy and here and there in my own work and in the work of my friends I have seen it greatly played. What does it matter that it belongs to a dead art. . . . I am haunted by certain moments: Miss O'Neill in the last act of Synge's *Deirdre*. . . . These things will, it may be, haunt me on my deathbed; what matter if the people prefer another art, I have had my fill.[14]

When Seanchan dies, his eldest pupil, speaking for himself and his fellow pupils, announces: "King, he is dead; some strange triumphant thought / So filled his heart with joy that it has burst," and he goes on to express abhorrence for the remaining years of their life that they

14 *Boiler,* pp. 35, 14.

will have to endure: "And we who gaze grow like him and abhor / The moments that come between us and that death" (864–68). Horatio, it will be recalled, had, with equal distaste for life, tried to snatch the poisoned cup from Hamlet to kill himself, but Hamlet entreated him to desist from dying—what he called "felicity"—"And in this harsh world draw thy breath in pain, / To tell my story" (V, ii, 326–27).

Both plays conclude with the protagonists exalted to the stature of military heroes. Fortinbras' eulogy over the dead Hamlet is couched in martial diction:

> and, for his passage,
> The soldiers' music and the rite of war
> Speak loudly for him.
> Take up the bodies. Such a sight as this
> Becomes the field, but here shows much amiss.
> Go, bid the soldiers shoot.
>
> [V, ii, 377–82]

After Seanchan's death, the oldest pupil also gives the order for his teacher's body to be taken up, in language strongly reminiscent of Fortinbras:

> Take up his body
> And cry that, driven from the populous door,
> He seeks high waters and the mountain birds
> To claim a portion of their solitude.
>
> [879–82]

And the youngest pupil, insisting on greater ceremony, orders the musicians to play their instruments:

> Yet make triumphant music; sing aloud,
> . . . .
> O silver trumpets, be you lifted up
> And cry to the great race that is to come.
>
> [889, 894–95]

From such a comparison it becomes clear that, though Yeats was writing his own play and not a variation of *Hamlet*, Shakespeare's example was insistently present in his mind. Yeats discovered in Shakespeare his own preoccupation with the conflict between the philistine and the artist, resulting in the latter's triumph at the instant of death.[15] Such a close association not only gave to Yeats the distinction of having Shakespeare's sovereignty as a precedent, but it also served as a consolation for the failure that he thought had attended the Irish Dramatic Movement. Moreover, the rejection of poetic drama by Yeats's age meant the rejection of Shakespeare as well; by identifying the two, he invested his own work with a quality of unquestionable value, its only misfortune being, he felt, that it had made its appearance at the wrong moment in history.

I V

In *Deirdre*, first published in 1907, Yeats continues to shun Shakespearean multiplicity of detail, modeling his work on the Greek pattern of unity of time and place. In 1908 he wrote about the play:

> The principal difficulty with the form of dramatic structure I have adopted is that, unlike the loose Elizabethan form, it continually forces one by its rigour of logic away from one's capacities, experiences and desires, until, if one have not patience to wait for the mood, or to rewrite again and again till it comes, there is rhetoric and logic and dry circumstance where there should be life.[16]

Recognizing that the closely knit texture of *Deirdre* has none of the expansiveness a Shakespearean (or Elizabethan) play possesses, Yeats argues that the advantage is dubious, for this very singleness of purpose can rob it of the poetic qualities it might otherwise have displayed. With an equilibrist's skill, Yeats walks the tightrope with Shakespeare at one end and Greek drama at the other and refuses to throw in his lot with either.

Deirdre begins with the two lovers arriving at King Conchubar's guesthouse and ends with their death; events preceding their arrival are recounted by the First Musician. But though the play is completely

15 In the first version of Yeats's play, at the end, the King revokes the ordinance that had excluded poets from the government (see *Variorum Plays*, p. 309). Yeats rightly realized that for Seanchan to live would be utterly incongruous, perhaps comparable to Nahum Tate's happy ending to *King Lear*. For a detailed examination of the change, see Peter Ure, *Yeats the Playwright* (London, 1963), pp. 31–42.

16 *Variorum Plays*, p. 391.

un-Shakespearean in structure, in its finest moments it echoes Shakespeare's tragic intensity. Shakespeare's Cleopatra in act V of *Antony and Cleopatra* seems to have been a prototype for Yeats's Deirdre. There are several indications within the play itself that make such a supposition plausible; in addition, in his essay "The Tragic Theatre," first published in 1910, Yeats sees these heroines with one great quality in common. After describing the transition in Deirdre (Synge's *Deirdre of the Sorrows*) from grief to "a reverie of passion that mounts and mounts till grief itself has carried her beyond grief into pure contemplation," or what Yeats calls "that tragic esctasy," in the next paragraph of the essay he cites Hamlet, Timon, and Cleopatra as supreme examples of this condition: "when Cleopatra names 'Of many thousand kisses the poor last' all is lyricism, unmixed passion."[17] When the essay was reprinted two years later in *The Cutting of an Agate* (1912), Yeats had noticed his mistake of attributing the line to Cleopatra and correctly gave it to Antony.[18] Yeats's having thought of Cleopatra immediately after his consideration of Deirdre in her state of "tragic ecstasy" is perhaps akin to Hamlet's Freudian slip when talking to the players (see above, pp. 73–74); if so, this may well be suggestive. Does it not indicate his association of Cleopatra with Deirdre's transformation at the end of the play? And though Yeats wrote "The Tragic Theatre" three years after *Deirdre,* his linking of Cleopatra with Deirdre at this later time tends to confirm the presence of such an association even when the play was written.

An examination of Yeats's deviations from Lady Gregory's *Cuchulain of Muirthemne,* the source for the plot of *Deirdre,* suggests that in the later part of the play he steers in the same direction as did Shakespeare in the closing scenes of *Antony and Cleopatra.* In Lady Gregory's narrative, after the death of Naoise, dramatic tension is nonexistent: Deirdre, we are told, "cried pitifully, wearily, and tore her fair hair." She then meets Cuchulain and tells him of her bitter plight. "After that complaint Deirdre loosed out her hair, and threw herself on the

17 W. B. Yeats, "The Tragic Theatre," *The Mask,* III (Florence, 1910–11), 77–78.

18 *E&I,* p. 240.

body of Naoise before it was put in the grave and gave three kisses to him."[19] Yeats's Deirdre is, by contrast, a statue of frozen emotion: "O do not touch me. Let me go to him" (658), she says to Conchubar, when the executioner appears with the blood of Naoise on his sword. And Conchubar is incredulous:

> But why are you so calm?
> I thought that you would curse me and cry out,
> And fall upon the ground and tear your hair.
>
> [665–67]

Banteringly, Deirdre replies, "You know too much of women to think so" (668). We cannot help remembering at this point Yeats's statement that at the moment of tragic ecstasy "all must be cold; no actress has ever sobbed when she played Cleopatra, even the shallow brain of a producer has never thought of such a thing."[20] After Antony's death, Cleopatra faints but quickly recovers, and it is she who urges her ladies-in-waiting to be of good cheer. The scene concludes with Cleopatra's magnificent courage:

> Good sirs, take heart:
> We'll bury him; and then, what's brave, what's noble,
> Let's do't after the high Roman fashion,
> And make death proud to take us. Come, away!
> This case of that huge spirit now is cold.
> Ah, women, women! Come, we have no friend
> But resolution and the briefest end.
>
> [IV, xv, 85–91]

Yeats's Irish queen and Shakespeare's Egyptian empress are comrades across a three-hundred-year gap.

Again, in Lady Gregory's account, after Deirdre's lamentations are over, Conchubar sends a messenger to fetch her to him, but she refuses to accompany the man. Rather, she goes to the strand, and finding a shipwright at work, asks him for his sharp knife in exchange for her golden ring. Then she goes up to the waves and stabs herself

---

19 Lady [Isabella Augusta] Gregory, *Cuchulain of Muirthemne* (London, 1902), pp. 104–43. Yeats several times mentions that this work is the source for his play: see *Variorum Plays*, p. 389; W. B. Yeats, *Plays for an Irish Theatre* (London and Stratford-on-Avon, 1911), p. 224.

20 *E&I*, p. 523.

in the side. When Conchubar arrives to claim her, he finds a corpse. Yeats, in his *Deirdre*, has completely transformed this predictable sequence of events into an incredibly taut scene of dramatic tension between Deirdre and Conchubar. Like Caesar's officers, who know that Cleopatra will try to kill herself (V, ii, 36–39), Conchubar is reluctant to allow her to go out of his sight (722–23). And as Cleopatra has recourse to duplicity in order to take her own life, summoning the old man with the figs into her presence (V, ii, 191–92, 233–74), so Deirdre too must elude Conchubar's vigilance by psychological legerdemain. Her self-possession and superhuman calm are seen in the mask of composure that she assumes while inviting the king to have her searched for a weapon, when all the time, as the audience well knows, she has a dagger concealed under the folds of her gown:

> *Conchubar.* How do I know that you have not some knife,
> And go to die upon his body?
> *Deirdre.*   Have me searched,
> If you would make so little of your queen.
> It may be that I have a knife hid here
> Under my dress. Bid one of these dark slaves
> To search me for it.
>   (*Pause.*)
> *Conchubar.*   Go to your farewells, Queen.
>   [722–27]

Certain it is that there are few pauses in literature more charged with dramatic intensity.

V

The Hour-Glass was begun in 1902 and first acted in March, 1903. The final poetic version of the play appeared in 1913, and it is this version that is considered here. *The Hour-Glass* was conceived at a time when Yeats was a frequent visitor to Stratford, and it seems to bear marks of his close contact with Shakespeare. Yeats wrote to Lady Gregory on June 13, 1902, less than a year after his first visit and three months after his second visit to Stratford, that he had finished a first draft of the play.[21] In plot and setting *The Hour-Glass* is of course

---

21 *Letters*, p. 375.

quite different from anything in Shakespeare; nevertheless there are certain interesting thematic parallels with *King Lear* that come out in the conversations between the Wise Man and the Fool.[22] Like Lear, who, through humiliation and a painful ordeal of unlearning, arrives at the truth, the Wise Man too has to experience the agony of being cast off by those closest to him. First his pupils refuse to believe him when he says that he saw an angel; because of the excellent training he has given them they construe his statement as a demonstration on his part of the need to be skeptical: "He wants to show we have no certain proof / Of anything in the world" (400–401), the First Pupil sagaciously observes to the other pupils. Next, the Wise Man learns that his wife, Bridget, has lost her faith in God because of his tutelage; when he asks her, "Do you believe in God?" she replies evasively, "O, a good wife only believes in what her husband tells her" (462–64). Finally, in despair, he turns to his children, but they too have been indoctrinated by their father's ideas:

> *Wise Man.* Come to me, children. Do not be afraid.
> I want to know if you believe in Heaven,
> God or the soul. . . .
>
> .   .   .   .
>
> *Both Children* (*as if repeating a lesson*). There is nothing
> we cannot see, nothing we cannot touch.
> *First Child.* Foolish people used to say that there was, but
> you have taught us better.
>
> > [519–30]

The Wise Man has created irrevocably his own doom.

So also had Lear found himself undergoing a progressive isolation that was of his own creation: he rejected Cordelia, only to find that his two other daughters would give him the same kind of treatment. At the time of his total loneliness out in the raging storm, only the Fool remains by his side (III, ii). In Yeats's play too, the Wise Man is finally joined by Teigue the Fool, who "comes in with a dandelion" (542). Lear faced by an inexorable storm and the Wise Man faced by imminent death and damnation are accompanied by fools during the dark night of their

---

22 There are obvious similarities between *The Hour-Glass* and Marlowe's *Doctor Faustus.*

soul's journey. Both fools needle their superiors with witty gibes, and in both plays the refrain of "nothing" becomes increasingly portentous as the climax is reached. In *King Lear*, Cordelia's simple "Nothing, my lord" (I, i, 83) is echoed by the Fool when Kent pronounces his mischievous and impertinent little speech to be "nothing":

> *Kent.* This is nothing, fool.
> *Fool.* Then 'tis like the breath of an unfee'd lawyer, you gave me nothing for't. Can you make no use of nothing, nuncle?
> *Lear.* Why, no, boy: nothing can be made out of nothing.
>
> [I, iv, 119–22]

And at the end of the play, Lear's stupendous line, "Never, never, never, never, never" (V, iii, 309), is a resounding negative, a culmination of all the "nothings" that have gone before, a summing up of the entire tragedy.

In *The Hour-Glass*, the Wise Man maintains that Teigue's claim to having seen angels is nothing: "There's nothing but what men can see when they are awake. Nothing, nothing" (210–11). Shortly after this, Teigue leaves, the Wise Man sees the Angel, who has entered silently, and the play begins to move swiftly, even as after the first dramatic moment in the great "nothing" scene between Lear and Cordelia (I, i), that play had rapidly gained momentum. The Angel then gives the Wise Man an ultimatum: he is doomed to Hell, which is "a Lake of Spaces, and a Wood of Nothing" (262), unless he can "but find one soul" who believes in a reality beyond this life (292–98). Toward the close of the play, when Teigue returns, there is some ironic playing on the word *nothing*: the Wise Man eagerly asks him whether he believes in God and the soul, to which Teigue replies,

> So you ask me now. I thought when you were asking your pupils, "Will he ask Teigue the Fool? Yes, he will, he will; no, he will not—yes, he will." But Teigue will say nothing. Teigue will say nothing.
>
> [565–68]

The motif of *nothing* recurs several times before the end, and when the Wise Man dies unredeemed, Teigue exclaims:

Wise Man—Wise Man, wake up and I will tell you
everything for a penny. It is I, poor Teigue the
Fool. Why don't you wake up, and say, "There is a
penny for you, Teigue?" No, no, you will say nothing.
You and I, we are the two fools, we know everything,
but we will not speak.

[625–30]

Is not Teigue's claiming of the Wise Man to be a fool like himself akin
to the Fool's calling Lear a fool?

Dost thou know the difference, my boy, between a bitter
    fool and a sweet one?
Lear. No, lad: teach me.

The Fool then recites a trenchant versicle ridiculing Lear and dubbing
him a fool; it concludes with the Fool pointing to himself and then to
Lear, thus heightening the meaning of his lines:

The sweet and bitter fool
    Will presently appear
The one in motley here,
    The other found out there.
Lear. Dost thou call me fool, boy?
Fool. All thy other titles thou hast given away; that
    thou wast born with.
Kent (Caius). This is not altogether fool, my lord.

[I, iv, 126–40]

For Shakespeare, as for Yeats, the totally negative can become the positive; folly may, in reality, be true wisdom. Yeats's play *Where There Is
Nothing* ends with Paul declaring, "Remember always where there is
nothing there is God" (471–72).

The relationship of *The Hour-Glass* to *King Lear* is, perhaps,
more fundamental than one of influence; it is based on Yeats's having
found in Shakespeare what he himself espoused. Thus, though verbal
resemblances and thematic parallels are interesting, their significance
really derives from the intrinsic communion that Yeats felt he had with
Shakespeare. Both *The Hour-Glass* and *King Lear* suggest that man
can "come into the desolation of reality" only after being shorn of
the trappings with which he invests himself. So Lear tears off his
clothes and decks himself with wild flowers (IV, iv, 1–6); the Wise

Man repudiates his philosophy and empiricism; and both Lear and the Wise Man are reduced to the condition of "unaccommodated man . . . a poor, bare, forked animal" (III, iv, 103–4) face to face with reality. And both Shakespeare and Yeats compare this denuded condition to a shelled peascod: the Fool, pointing to Lear, tells Goneril, "That's a shealed peascod" (I, iv, 183), and the Wise Man, arriving at the same state of exposure to the truth, realizes at last that

> Only when all our hold on life is troubled,
> Only in spiritual terror can the Truth
> Come through the broken mind—as the pease burst
> Out of a broken pease-cod.
>
> [479–82]

Evidently Yeats, like Keats, who sat down to read *King Lear* once again, must many times have tasted "the bitter sweet of this Shakespearean fruit."

VI

Between about 1907 and 1912 Yeats's relationship with Shakespeare (as we noted in chapter 3) fluctuated, and it is not easy to pin him down to any single attitude. Not at all laconic, this relationship seems, in fact, to have been the anvil on which he hammered his own thoughts on poetic drama into unity. During this period Yeats became both critic and apologist for Shakespeare, accusing him of sacrificing unity for stage effect, but also excusing him for his lack of unity on the grounds that, finding himself obliged "to please the common citizen standing on the rushes of the floor," he dissipated the intensity of his art.[23]

In 1916, in his essay "Certain Noble Plays of Japan," Yeats announced his interest in something new and remote. A few years earlier, during the winter of 1913, Ezra Pound had introduced him to Noh drama, describing it as "a drama of masks." Yeats was immediately captivated by its intensity and purity, because he had been searching for a form that would embody these features. Shakespeare possessed intensity and passion in abundance, but Yeats felt that his work lacked

23 *E&I*, p. 227.

purity. In the opening section of the essay Yeats seems to suggest that the Noh form, in which "the music, the beauty of form and voice all come to climax in pantomimic dance," was a sudden revelation for him; but though it was true that prior to 1913 he had been unacquainted with this form of dramatic art, his earlier convictions had, in fact, brought him to a point where he preferred ritual and convention to "a violence of passion indecorous in our sitting-room."[24]

If the period of Yeats's excursion into Oriental waters signified his alienation from Shakespeare, at the same time it enabled him to develop in his *Four Plays for Dancers* a symbolic intensity undistracted by the realistic details that necessarily feature in a Shakespeare play. Yeats states that he wrote these plays for an audience that ideally belonged to a unified civilization, "very unlike ours," and, by implication, very unlike Shakespeare's, which was on the verge of fragmentation.

> In writing these little plays I knew that I was creating something which could only fully succeed in a civilization very unlike ours. I think they should be written for some country where all classes share in a half-mythological, half-philosophical folk-belief which the writer and his small audience lift into a new subject. All my life I have longed for such a country.[25]

The remoteness of this country makes Yeats's plays for dancers correspondingly distant from Shakespeare, yet even here it would be a hasty judgment that pronounced them at total odds with Shakespeare.

For despite his censuring of Shakespeare, he never repudiated him, but continued to enlist his support; at the same time, Yeats justified his leaning toward the Noh by declaring that "the men [the Japanese] who created this convention were more like ourselves [the Irish] than were the Greeks and Romans, more like us even than are Shakespeare and Corneille." Unkind to Shakespeare though Yeats may sound, he is actually likening the Celtic mind to the Japanese only in its emotional response to certain haunted spots, "tomb and wood." In the essay Yeats

---

24 *E&I*, p. 221; Ernest Fenollosa and Ezra Pound, *"Noh" or Accomplishment: A Study of the Classical Stage of Japan* (London, 1916), p. 5. See *Ex*, pp. 64–65, where Yeats mentions his first contact with Noh drama.

25 W. B. Yeats, *Four Plays for Dancers* (London, 1921), p. 106.

laments that Europe, having discarded tradition, had also abandoned "the art of Shakespeare" for the prose drama of the eighteenth century, so that those who, like himself, desired once again an intimate art form were compelled to look to Asia, where tradition was yet preserved. He then denounces the relinquishing of the Elizabethan theater, which had relied on imagination rather than stage properties, as well as the rejection of the Shakespearean soliloquy because it seemed "unnatural" to the modern mind. The detachment from life that the dance drama personified ("instead of the disordered passion of nature, there is a dance") was the equivalent of Yeats's theory of the Mask, the individual's opposite, which he could cultivate assiduously and try to become. The expunging of superfluity from drama in structure, scenery, costume, verse delivery, and acting technique had been Yeats's concern long before his discovery of the Noh. Although this preoccupation culminated in his seizing on the Noh form as an answer to his quest, it did not satisfy him for long, as he himself had anticipated in the statement that he would "record all discoveries of method and turn to something else."[26] Thus, *Purgatory* has neither musicians nor dancers, yet elements from the Noh are clearly discernible. Even a prose play such as *The Words upon the Window-Pane* possesses undertones from the Noh—the dreaming back process in particular.

Yeats's own thought had been tending toward a purification of the theater long before Pound introduced him to the Noh. As early as 1899, in an essay entitled "The Theatre," Yeats was calling for a form of drama "as unlike ordinary plays as possible," to be put "on the stage in some little suburban hall, where a little audience would pay its expenses." "We must make a theatre for ourselves and our friends," he maintained, likening the discipline to "the preparation of a priesthood."[27] Yeats had no illusions of a popular theater materializing but hoped only that poetic drama would gradually extend its influence: it was to be a revolution from within that would overthrow and reform with mounting pressure, not a public revolt instantly winning the approval of the

26 *E&I*, pp. 233, 232, 225, 226, 230, 222.
27 *E&I*, pp. 165, 166, 168.

masses.[28] The tone of this short essay is identical to that of the open letter to Lady Gregory in 1919 ("A People's Theatre"), which suggests that Yeats never really changed his position—as has been suggested—out of disillusionment and despair but was in fact consistently optimistic that poetic drama would be restored to eminence.[29]

In a vigorous essay, "The Play, the Player, and the Scene" (1904), Yeats traces the steady decline of drama from the ancient past to the present. He deplores the decay of flamboyant speech (Falstaff's "abundant vocabulary" was "but little magnified from the words of such a man in real life") and he cites Shakespeare, Calderón, and the Greeks as examples of writers whose speech arose "out of the common life, where language is as much alive as if it were new come out of Eden." Yeats's plea is continuously for a recrudescence of what modernity pronounces unsophisticated. He then points out that although modern stage management has lost "much of its beauty and meaning on the way, from the days of Shakespeare," degenerating into the naturalism of Garrick, in Ireland the "drama of energy, of extravagance, of fantasy, of musical and noble speech" "was established at the Restoration by an actor who probably remembered the Shakespearean players."[30] By emphasizing speech rather than gesture, Yeats evinced his disgust with the modern actor's theatricality that eclipses the importance of the word. "It is not only Shakespeare whose finest thoughts are inaudible on the English stage," he remonstrates. And to curb unnecessary movement, he conceived the unique idea of rehearsing his actors in barrels (mounted on castors) that he could push around with a long pole when a change of position was necessary.[31]

Abhorring the baroque stage settings so marveled at by his age,

28 After *Deirdre* was successfully presented, Yeats wrote to a friend: "I think we are gradually working down through the noisy and hypercritical, semi-political groups to a genuine public opinion, which is sympathetic" (*Letters,* p. 483).

29 See Vinod Sena, "Yeats on the Possibility of an English Poetic Drama," *Modern Drama,* IX (September, 1966), 195–205, and my reply, *Modern Drama,* XI (February, 1969), 396–99.

30 *Ex,* pp. 166, 167, 170. The Smock Alley Theatre in Dublin presented a surprisingly large number of Shakespearean plays during the eighteenth century. See William Smith Clark, *The Early Irish Stage* (London, 1955).

31 *Ex,* pp. 171, 86–87.

Yeats at the same time never favored a total relegation of scenery from his stage. He felt that the right kind of decorative scenery would "give the imagination liberty, and without returning to the bareness of the Elizabethan stage." At the same time, he granted that it was precisely this bareness that elicited some of Shakespeare's finest poetry. In "The Theatre," he inveighs against realistic stage scenery, "meretricious landscapes, painted upon wood and canvas," and contrasts these with the verbal limning of the scene in Banquo's "pendent bed and procreant cradle" as he stands before Macbeth's castle, a description that exercises the imagination of the audience.[32]

In a letter to Frank Fay written in 1904, which Yeats said he considered important, he deprecated the kind of stage management which "knows nothing of style, which knows nothing of magnificent words, nothing of the music of speech," and maintained that "Racine and Shakespeare wrote for a little stage where very little could be done with movement, but they were as we know careful to get a great range of expression out of the voice." Yeats was certainly right in insisting that, for Shakespeare, voice was of tremendous importance, but he allowed himself to be led away by this one aspect because it tallied with his own predominant interest, and he therefore belittled the movement and gesture with which Shakespeare's plays are replete. Although Hamlet warns his actor not to "saw the air too much with your hand," he immediately adds, "Be not too tame neither." Also, as the researches of John Cranford Adams and others have informed us, the stage of the Globe was by no means small or cramped, even when judged by present standards. Yet Yeats is certainly right when he argues that in a scene showing "Lear upon his heath," it is the words and the voice that give to the situation its magnitude of dimension, devices that leave the realistic prose drama of Ibsen and Sudermann far behind.[33]

In the essay "Certain Noble Plays of Japan," Yeats speaks of having "invented a form of drama, distinguished, indirect, and symbolic, and having no need of mob or Press to pay its way—an aristocratic form." Although the implication here is of a fresh departure, in his

---

32 *Ex*, p. 178; *E&I, p.* 169. See also *Ex*, p. 88.
33 *Letters*, p. 441.

"Note on *At the Hawk's Well*," he states his continuing link with Shakespeare in unambiguous terms: "Shakespeare's art was public, now resounding and declamatory, now lyrical and subtle, but always public, because poetry was a part of the general life of a people who had been trained by the Church to listen to difficult words and who sang, instead of the songs of the music-halls many songs that are still beautiful."[34] Yeats's reasoning is that Shakespeare's art, for the Elizabethans, was public because the audience was perceptive, whereas in the twentieth century Shakespeare's art is no longer public. Yeats would include Shakespeare in the twentieth century, among unpopular dramatists like himself, who, writing in an age when sensibilities are hopelessly disparate, could only think to win appreciation from "an audience like a secret society where admission is by favour and never to many." What is important to observe is the great diversity that Yeats attributes to Shakespeare in the phrase "resounding and declamatory, now lyrical and subtle." Some years earlier, in 1904, Yeats had noted the responsiveness of Shakespeare's audience to this range of appeal, for "the groundling could remember the folk-songs and the imaginative folk-life," whereas to a contemporary audience such a familiarity has been irrevocably lost. This range of appeal was possible only in an age when the collective sensitivity of the people to poetic drama was keen enough to respond to a variety of imaginative situations that drew on a common heritage. The inherent unity of the Elizabethan Age—comparable to the Byzantine, which Yeats would have chosen to visit, where "religious, aesthetic and practical life were one"—could, as it were, counterbalance the diversity of Shakespeare's art.[35]

34   *E&I*, p. 221; Yeats, *Four Plays*, p. 88. Arthur Hallam, too, in his essay on Tennyson, had deplored modern fragmentation and maintained that present response to Shakespeare and Milton was far less astute than before: "That first raciness and juvenile vigor of literature . . . is gone, never to return" ("On Some of the Characteristics of Modern Poetry, and on the Lyrical Poems of Alfred Tennyson," *The Writings of Arthur Hallam*, ed. T. H. Vail Motter [New York, 1943], p. 189). Yeats remarked that this was a work on which he had based his principles when he began to write (*E&I*, p. 347; see also Allan Wade, *A Bibliography of the Writings of W. B. Yeats* [London, 1958], p. 312; W. B. Yeats, "Mr. Lionel Johnson's Poems," *Bookman*, XIII, 155).

35   *Ex*, pp. 254, 139–40; *Vis*, p. 279.

Consequently, when Yeats expressed a preference for the "severe discipline of French and Scandinavian drama"[36] as a fitting model for Irish playwrights, rather than the luxuriance of Shakespearean drama, it must be remembered that Yeats's complaint was not directed solely against Shakespeare; it was also directed against his own twentieth-century audience, which could only be captured and held by a dramatic form that was swift, direct, and uncomplicated.

His open letter to Lady Gregory (1919) insistently holds up Shakespeare as an example of a writer who, like Yeats himself, was dedicated to a distilled form of drama concerned with "emotion and intellect at their moment of union and at their greatest intensity." This description could appropriately be regarded as a blueprint for the Noh form that Yeats now espoused, yet Yeats applies it to Shakespeare, indicating that he never really renounced the poetic drama of Shakespeare. In a footnote to the above observations on Shakespeare, Yeats confirms his argument that Shakespeare is unpopular in the twentieth century by stating that he had "read somewhere statistics that showed how popular education has coincided with the lessening of Shakespeare's audience. In every chief town before [popular education] began, Shakespeare was constantly played."[37] Thus, when Yeats asserted that he wanted to create for himself "an unpopular theatre," and that he desired "a mysterious art . . . a mode of drama Shelley and Keats could have used without ceasing to be themselves," he was by no means excluding Shakespeare from this coterie. The "ironical chirruping" that he heard emanating from the gallery of the Lyceum Theatre during the love speeches of Juliet persuaded him to believe that Shakespeare had become unpopular in the twentieth century—as unpopular as the kind of theater he was now promoting among "an audience of fifty."[38] His extraordinary insistence on including Shakespeare among the unpopular

36   *Ex*, p. 80.
37   *Ex*, p. 245. In 1891 Yeats observed ironically: "We still go to see Shakespeare, but then we have made him one of our superstitions" (*New Island*, p. 213). And in 1938 he noted that "there was once a stock company playing Shakespeare in every considerable town" in England (*Boiler*, p. 18).
38   *Ex*, pp. 254, 255; Yeats, *Four Plays*, p. 88; *Ex*, p. 255.

dramatists of the twentieth century, and his reference to statistics in support of this—dubious though they might appear to us—are an indication of his sense of oneness with Shakespeare.

Actually, at no other time in the history of drama, not even when Shakespeare was alive, had Shakespeare's plays been performed as frequently and been seen by so many as in the nineteenth and the early part of the twentieth century. Never before had there been such a spate of books on Shakespeare, both popular and scholarly, as during this period, nor had Shakespeare been taught in schools, not only in the West, but even in distant India; yet Yeats, in his determination to retain Shakespeare's companionship and approval even while launching on a remote Oriental pattern in drama, chose to regard him as a fellow outcast from the popular stage of his time. Even though Yeats's statistics may have been misleading, his emphasis on Shakespeare as a symbolist and not a realist (symbolism being the nucleus of Yeats's own plays, including the *Four Plays for Dancers*) was the starting point for the fresh way of looking at Shakespeare that developed among later critics.

We have already seen that in his address to the Dramatic Club of Harvard University in 1911, Yeats contrasts poetic drama as exemplified in his own plays, in Shakespeare, and in the Japanese theater with realism as exemplified in Galsworthy.[39] Even in the essay "Certain Noble Plays of Japan," Yeats claims Shakespeare as a symbolist, not a realist, arguing that "realism is created for the common people," that "Cleopatra's old man with an asp" was introduced to please the groundlings, "but the great speeches were written by poets who remembered their patrons in the covered galleries." Continuing his argument that poetic and symbolical drama can be intelligible only to an enlightened audience capable of instantly detecting echoes from past literature and tradition, Yeats cites Shakespeare's allusions to "Lethe wharf" (*Ham.*, I, iv, 33) and "Dido on the wild sea banks" (*Merch.*, V, i, 10) as examples of this sophisticated awareness and then goes on to assert that "poets from the time of Keats and Blake have derived their descent

39 W. B. Yeats, "The Theater of Beauty," *Harper's Weekly* (November 11, 1911), p. 11.

only through what is least declamatory, least popular in the art of Shakespeare."[40] The picture of Yeats's Shakespeare that emerges during this period is fascinating but it need not surprise us. Ostensibly abjuring the Western dramatic form with Shakespeare unavoidably its greatest representative, and harking back to an esoteric and highly convention-alized Oriental theater, Yeats at the same time insists that Shakespeare accompany him on this expedition.

Thus, even the fragmentation that Yeats censured in Shakespeare was modified sharply by him to mean the contemporary producer's rendering of his plays that created this condition, and not Shakespeare's art as he had intended it to be represented on his Elizabethan stage. In a letter of 1905 to Frank Fay, in which he describes his distaste for the way in which *The Merchant of Venice* was staged, Yeats shows himself fully aware of the fact that Shakespeare's plays when rightly rendered have an underlying unity that the modern producer, enthusiastic for realism, has sabotaged.

> The Trial scene was moving, but owing to the stage management the rest was broken up. Shakespeare had certainly intended those short scenes

---

40 *E&I*, pp. 227, 228. But Yeats's disparagement of the groundlings here should not be regarded as a fixed attitude. In "The Theatre" (1900) he longs for a simple and unsophisticated audience, like "the audiences of Sophocles and Shake-speare" (*E&I*, p. 167; see also *Ex*, p. 152). He felt that in Elizabethan times even the groundlings had the capacity to respond to poetic drama because "poetry was a part of the general life of a people . . . who sang . . . many songs that are still beautiful" (Yeats, *Four Plays*, p. 88; see also *Ex*, pp. 139–40). "Shakespeare's groundlings watched the stage in terrified sympathy," unlike the modern "British working-man" who is full of hatred for the upper classes (*Ex*, p. 246). In *The Death of Cuchulain* (1939), the Old Man, Yeats's spokesman, looks for an audience "no more in number than those who listened to the first performance of Milton's *Comus*." A few years before this, however, he had hoped to have "an audience of Connaught farmers, or sailors before the mast" to witness his production of *King Lear* (*Letters*, p. 778). Yeats pictured Shakespeare's audience as violent and savage (*Letters*, p. 759), a state that he would not have condemned. A small and select audience, then, was for Yeats a necessity imposed by his age. Yeats must of course have read Robert Bridges' now famous essay on Shakespeare's audience ("On the Influence of the Audience," in *The Works of William Shakespeare*, ed. A. H. Bullen [Stratford-on-Avon, 1907], X). Bridges argues that much of the violence on Shakespeare's stage was due to Shakespeare's having "deliberately played false to his own artistic ideals for the sake of gratifying his audience." Yeats would perhaps have agreed with this, but with reservations.

of his to be played one after the other as quickly as possible and there is
no reason that they should not, if played in this way, keep the sense of
crisis almost as living as in the long scenes.[41]

Yeats's Noh plays are, in spite of his constant acknowledgment
of his awareness of Shakespeare's practice, a distinct departure from
Shakespeare. With the astonishingly beautiful musician's songs that
open and close the plays, the obsession with a single emotion-freighted
situation that involves the preternatural, culminating "in pantomimic
dance," the plays deliberately eschew the multiplicity of detail that a
Shakespeare play invariably embraces. Yeats's great desire was to create
an image that would be totally distinct from realism, that would hold
itself aloof from "a pushing world," and through "verse, ritual, music,
and dance" would seem to "separate from the world and us a group
of figures, images, symbols, [and] enable us to pass for a few moments
into a deep of the mind that had hitherto been too subtle for our habitation." Thus the work of art becomes the antithesis to life as experienced
on its most obvious level. Yet, Yeats would regard a Shakespearean
tragedy too as containing this intensity, but at the same time feel that
it, alas, occasionally admitted elements that tended to weaken its force.
Even though no tragedy of Shakespeare comes to a climax in pantomimic
dance, Yeats declared that he could "hear the dance music in 'Absent thee
from felicity awhile' " and "in Hamlet's speech over the dead Ophelia,"
a response to the concluding scenes of *Hamlet* that would sound most
unusual coming from any poet other than Yeats.[42]

41   *Letters*, p. 465.
42   *E&I*, pp. 221, 224, 225; *Boiler*, p. 35.

8

Echoes in Yeats's Later Plays

Shakespeare showed, through a style full of joy, a
melancholy vision sought from afar.
—Yeats, *A Vision*

Ireland had preserved longer than England the rhythmical utterance of the Shakespearean stage.
—Yeats, "An Introduction for my Plays"

Those images that yet
Fresh images beget.
—Yeats, "Byzantium"

BY THE TIME Yeats came to write his later plays, he had ceased to
regard Shakespeare as a distant and solitary mountain peak.
In 1901 when Yeats recorded his impressions of Shakespeare, his attitude,
though not worshipful, was one of awe and wonder. But toward the
end of his life, Yeats began to feel that he shared with Shakespeare "the
Vision of Evil" that he felt was granted to only the greatest writers.
To Stephen Spender he remarked in 1935 that, in the end, Shakespeare's
mind was "terrible." When Spender asked him to expand on this, he
answered: "The final reality of existence in Shakespeare's poetry is of a
terrible kind."[1] What did Yeats mean by the word *terrible*, and why

---

[1] *Au,* p. 149; Stephen Spender, *World within World* (London, 1951), p.
165.

did he state it twice? In "Easter 1916," written several years earlier, he had emphasized the word with extraordinary power in the thrice recurring line, "A terrible beauty is born." In this juxtaposition of "terrible" with "beauty" we may glimpse something of the terror that his vision encompassed. While in the Municipal Gallery, Yeats saw, in the paintings that surrounded him, not the dead Ireland of his youth, but "an Ireland / The poets have imagined, terrible and gay." For Yeats, this terrible beauty is born of the interaction between historical reality and the artist's quickening breath. What would normally have been reduced to the insignificance of historical record has been transformed into art—a new kind of reality—that can alone portray the final reality of existence. Yeats seems to have felt that Shakespeare's tragic heroes are shown reaching this culminating stage in their development at the moment when the last darkness gathers about them. This critical moment, as we have seen Yeats define it, in chapter 5, is one of the great qualities in Shakespearean tragedy that Yeats embodied in *Purgatory* and *The Death of Cuchulain,* his last two plays.

Through art it becomes possible to explore this reality. In both *Purgatory* and *The Death of Cuchulain* a play within a play is enacted: in the former, an old man and a boy watch helplessly an inexorable scene being unfolded through a lighted window; in the latter, an old man, ostensibly the producer, is rendered ineffectual by the play's asserting its own identity despite his cantankerousness—the musicians interrupt his wrathful outburst against his degenerate times, and the play begins without his permission. Yeats seems to have seen in his own last plays, as well as in Shakespeare's, art pitted against life. The artist's vision impinges on the amorphous stuff of life, and the resultant work carries within itself its own irrefutable standard of veracity, independent of the logic of the possible and the probable, questions that lesser artists necessarily abide by. Thus, the fantastic world of Yeats's last plays—in which an actress, after pretending to be queen, becomes queen in reality, men combat a herne, spirits act and re-enact the past with fearful intensity, and a hero is beheaded by a blind beggar—has much in common with Shakespeare's tragedies, where diverse planes of existence beyond normally experienced reality are explored in terms of equally fantastic events: Hamlet is directed by a ghost, Macbeth by witches; and Gloucester falls from Dover cliff while actually only falling flat on his face. In *Purgatory,* Yeats seems to have reached a similar state of total emancipation from realism.

II

In *The Player Queen* (1922), Yeats depicts the transformation of the individual into his Mask. Human life by itself is trivial, but when the individual struggles to become something that he is not, or desires to be "united to an image" (sc. ii, 479–80), his life becomes meaningful. Not all human beings are thus engaged, for they lack art, the ability to assume a role and ultimately to become that role. In his play, Yeats makes art a means for the attainment of a new state of being: Decima, the actress who is assigned the role of Noah's wife, a harridan, in the play within the play that is never performed, stubbornly refuses to accept this role because she would then have to wear a hideous mask, and "she would drown rather than play a woman older than thirty" (sc. i, 19–20), Nona, her rival, informs an infuriated Prime Minister.

Even though the play is never acted (unlike Hamlet's "The Mouse-trap"), the pressure of its unborn identity is responsible for the un-expected step that Decima takes at the end of *The Player Queen* in trans-forming herself from actress into actual queen, from the realm of art into that of reality. Her refusal to act in the play does not prevent her from being the heroine in the play of her own choice, which she, in a sense, produces herself by ordering the other actors to dance around her. In spite of her flightiness, she respects art—art for her is not a mere game but has a reality of its own that she recognizes by her refusal to accept a part she detests. Thus the autonomy of the imaginative world is emphasized in Yeats's play. Art has to be accorded an independence from life, for it can even display a capacity to transform life. Yeats had said that drama, to be successful, required both artist and audience to accept the authenticity of mythology just as a child believed in the reality of the wooden beasts and birds in his toy Noah's ark.[2]

In *The Player Queen,* Yeats is grappling with a question that he

2 W. B. Yeats, *Four Plays for Dancers* (London, 1921), p. 106.

seems to have felt Shakespeare had addressed himself to in *Hamlet*. Why Yeats called his play *The Player Queen* is easy to see, for Decima, though she becomes queen at the end, in her last touching speech to her erstwhile comrades still regards herself as a player. But the title is also directly reminiscent of the player queen in *Hamlet* who is in turn an artistic counterpart of Gertrude. Both Gertrude and Decima reject their first husbands and find new mates, but whereas for Decima this act is the culmination of the play, for Gertrude it becomes the cause of Hamlet's malcontent and the starting point of the play.

Yeats had seen in *Hamlet* a movement toward the successful attainment of a Mask, and declared that "for many years Hamlet was an image of heroic self-possession for the poses of youth and childhood to copy, a combatant of the battle within myself."[3] The essay in which this statement appeared, "Reveries over Childhood and Youth," was published in 1916; *The Player Queen* was produced three years later, but Yeats had been working on the play since 1907. His essay *Per Amica Silentia Lunae,* published in 1917, is almost wholly occupied with the question of man's identity merging with that of his opposite—his Mask. And in his notes to *The Player Queen* Yeats mentions the connection between the play and the essay: "I began in, I think, 1907, a verse tragedy, but at that time the thought I have set forth in *Per Amica Silentia Lunae* was coming into my head." That *Hamlet* was much in his thoughts during these years is clear from a striking example he gives of man becoming his Mask after death: he recalls what a Brahmin once told him, that "if a man died playing Hamlet, he would be Hamlet in eternity," or, in other words, that the image can project itself so insistently as to obliterate the individual's identity and enforce itself upon him in the afterlife. As the actor playing Hamlet becomes Hamlet after death, so the player queen in Yeats's play becomes a queen in reality. As further evidence of Yeats's involvement with *Hamlet* while *The*

---

3 *Au,* p. 29; see also *Au,* pp. 93, 94. Nietzsche, whom Yeats had read with close attention, also advocates the mask as a weapon worthy of the hero, and, for an example, cites Hamlet: "There are free insolent minds which would fain conceal and deny that they are broken, proud incurable hearts (the cynicism of Hamlet . . .)" (Friedrich Nietzsche, *Beyond Good and Evil,* in *The Philosophy of Nietzsche* [New York, 1954], p. 597).

Player Queen was in the gestatory process, we should note that in 1916 he wrote Lady Gregory of his intention to produce "the whole *Hamlet*" along with "a fine performance of *Player Queen*" and a few other plays. As long after as 1934, in his Introduction to *The Resurrection*, Yeats again spoke of *The Player Queen* as embodying the notion that a man's effort should be directed toward becoming his image.

> Then after some years came the thought that a man always tried to become his opposite, to become what he would abhor if he did not desire it, and I wasted some three summers and some part of each winter before I had banished the ghost and turned what I had meant for tragedy into a farce: *The Player Queen*.[4]

Having seen the close attention Yeats paid to *Hamlet* while writing *The Player Queen*, it now remains for us to trace the possible links that bind Yeats's play to Shakespeare's.

Decima's refusal to act in the play being rehearsed is not unlike Hamlet's refusal to play a part in the specious drama that Claudius wishes to foist on the Court. True, Claudius' "play" is not a formal structure, as is that being produced by the Prime Minister in *The Player Queen*, yet, more insidiously, he seeks to stage a play before a throng of courtiers and with the fanfare of a spectacular appearance, featuring himself and the queen as the chief actors. The others acquiesce in this, but Hamlet alone refuses to play the part the king would like to assign him. Clad in inky black, he is a misfit in that gay drama and does not hesitate to make the others aware of his deliberate recalcitrance. "For they are actions that a man might play" (I, ii, 84) is his scornful dismissal of external forms of grief. Thus does Hamlet scorn the king's visible stage acting and hint at the psychological drama smoldering within his own mind.

Turning to *The Player Queen*, we discover that though Decima is unwilling to play a part in the prescribed drama, she is eager to produce her own play: she orders the other characters in their animal costumes to dance around her while she, as "Queen Decima," has made her choice of one of them for a mate. She likens herself to Queen

4   W. B. Yeats, *Plays in Prose and Verse* (New York, 1928), p. 437; *Myth*, p. 355 (see also *Vis*, p. 222); *Letters*, p. 612; *Ex*, p. 394.

Pasiphae and Queen Leda, thus showing herself ready to don a mask, to unite herself to an image, her opposite (sc. ii, 346–79). Shortly after, she accomplishes this by changing places with the queen; she puts on her "gold brocade and those gold slippers" (the actor in her yearns to dress up) and becomes queen in reality (sc. ii, 645–91). The mask, or art, displaces life.

Similarly, Hamlet produces his own play, "The Mousetrap," a performance highly distasteful to the king because it (a form of art) is capable of bringing reality to light. Claudius' anguished cry of "Give me some light" is, paradoxically and ironically, precisely what has happened, for his guilt has been brought to light. Hamlet's insertion of "some dozen or sixteen lines," his careful instructions to the players on their acting technique, and his jubilance over the success of his production, all mark him as being an accomplished man of the theater. When the king and his Court break up in confusion, Hamlet's first thought is directed toward his stage triumph, not the king's betrayal of guilt—he tells Horatio: "Would not this, sir, and a forest of feathers . . . with two Provincial roses on my razed shoes, get me a fellowship in a cry of players, sir?" (III, ii, 257–60).

Hamlet, in fact, consists of a series of "plays" that suddenly become grim reality: "The Mousetrap," though the most conspicuous, is not the only one. Hamlet sees Rosencrantz' and Guildenstern's mission to have him liquidated in England as a "play" with a "prologue" (V, ii, 29–31), and at the end of *Hamlet* the "play with Laertes" (V, ii, 179) begins apparently as an innocuous sport but ends on quite a different note. However, Hamlet is too astute a producer to allow the king and Laertes to shape the plot, and in his dying speech represents the situation as an "act" in a play (V, ii, 313–14). Thus, in each "play," Hamlet becomes the chief actor who causes the play to sweep on inexorably to a bloody climax, and what seemed an artifact asserts itself as truth.

In *The Player Queen*, after Decima becomes queen, the claim of Septimus over her, as husband, is dismissed as nonexistent. Before becoming queen, she sings a song in which the man asks the woman to "Put off that mask of burning gold" (sc. ii, 223); the woman's reply is an epitome of the play itself: the mask *is* the real person, for the persona and the person are the same, and the heart beneath, irrelevant. The question constantly posed in *The Player Queen* is, Which has greater validity, art or life? One of the characters in the play mysteriously talks of the power that images can develop over human beings: "until they have been fed with the blood they are images and shadows; but when they have it drunk they can be for a while stronger than you or me" (sc. i, 213–16).

In *Hamlet* every character, except perhaps Horatio, is in one way or another wearing a mask, deceiving or being deceived. Hamlet himself is almost continuously acting a part, feigning madness, exposing those who are in turn trying to uncover his secret; Claudius, an archactor, is his true self, if such a state exists, only when he sees Hamlet's play acted. Significantly, it is his confrontation with art that reveals the inner man and tears the mask from his face. Even the ghost is suspect, for "the spirit that I have seen / May be a devil" (II, ii, 572–73), Hamlet grimly speculates. The play teems with these complications that only conceal further complications, and it may be regarded as a phantasmagoria with perpetually shifting outlines, appearance and reality changing places with teasing complexity.

The Player Queen too is replete with situations where a mask or a façade conceals an inner truth, and this motif manifests itself with varying degrees of light and shadow. The two old men who open the play decide to "pretend to be asleep" (sc. i, 37–38); this first hint at the play's theme is reiterated with the arrival of two other men who have a tryst with their mistresses, only to discover, to their chagrin, that the girls have deceived them and will not turn up. But the men are likewise deceiving their wives: one of them declares, "I would not have my wife find out for the world" (sc. i, 82–83). Then, the Prime Minister "has spies everywhere spreading stories" (sc. i, 149–51), and the honesty (or otherwise) of both the queen and the Unicorn are matters hotly debated throughout the play. The struggle between appearance and reality assumes various perplexing forms: Septimus assures everyone that the Unicorn "is chaste" (sc. i, 256–57), yet the queen has been seen "coupling with a great white unicorn" (sc. i, 237–38).

In the midst of these uncertainties, the only event that undisputably does take place is Decima's ascending the throne, but after this point the play again takes on a note of ambiguity. Decima puts on the mask of the sister of Noah, and the play concludes with her identification with this mask: "This mask would well become, this foolish, smiling face!" (sc. ii, 762–63) she says. Is this then the next mask that Decima is going to "become"? The question appropriately remains unanswered, even as *Hamlet* concludes with Hamlet aware of the fact that there will always be those who remain "unsatisfied" (V, ii, 319). Master producer that Hamlet is, he too is defeated by the untidiness of life, and Horatio sums up the condition by promising to recount to Fortinbras and others "Of carnal, bloody and unnatural acts, / Of accidental judgements, casual slaughters" (V, ii, 360–62). Despite the seeming supremacy of art over life, life ultimately prevails, and Hamlet, an artificer, is swallowed up by its turmoil. So also Septimus the poet, whose song "Put off that mask of burning gold" expresses the play's central idea, is discomfited and victimized by his wife and the Prime Minister at the end of *The Player Queen.*

Even though *The Player Queen,* unlike *Hamlet,* is a comedy (though Yeats originally intended it to be a tragedy), the achievement of Hamlet is, in one sense, very close to that of Decima. Both save their countries from disaster. The royal bed of Denmark had become "a couch for luxury and damnéd incest" (I, v, 83), but at the end of the play, national health has been restored, and though Hamlet dies, it is for the advancement of a larger cause. In *The Player Queen,* the country is on the verge of anarchy; the queen is in danger of being lynched for alleged licentiousness, but with the ascension of Decima to the throne, national equilibrium is restored. Yeats sees art as a decisive factor in promoting the well-being, not only of individuals, but of the state as well. In *The Player Queen,* he shows the repercussions of art causing "the devastation of peoples and the overwhelming of cities," for the old civilization gives place to the new.[5]

Although Yeats's play seems to walk in the shadow of *Hamlet,* the protracted difficulty he had with its writing, extending over a

5   *E&I,* p. 158.

period of fifteen years from 1907 to 1922, discloses itself in the play. Unlike *Hamlet, The Player Queen* is too heavily freighted with allegorical machinations to be successful drama. In *Hamlet,* the human situation is never overcome by a theory—and this does not deny the presence of a theory—but in *The Player Queen,* despite its being a brilliant tour de force, too much of the author is present everywhere for it to achieve a life of its own. Unlike "Hamlet and Lear who educated Shakespeare," Yeats's characters in *The Player Queen* are meekly subservient to their creator.[6] It would be idle to speculate on its content had it remained the tragedy Yeats had originally intended it to be, but perhaps one can venture to say that its debt to *Hamlet* might then have been more obvious than appears now.[7]

III

Closely allied to *The Player Queen* is *The Herne's Egg.* Written much later, this play demonstrates another facet of Yeats's theory that human life is successfully lived only if man is united to an image—the theme of *The Player Queen. The Herne's Egg* sets forth warring opposites objectified in the persons of Kings Congal and Aedh, who represent the two halves between which certain types of men oscillate before finally becoming the opposite of what they were originally. Thus "Paul Verlaine alternated between the two halves of his nature with so little apparent resistance that he seemed like a bad child," and, extending the parable to apply to a nation, Yeats declares that "a nation in tumult must needs pass to and fro between mechanical opposites."[8] Kings Congal and Aedh are, then, the two extremities of a single personality struggling toward self-realization.

---

6 *Letters,* p. 741.

7 I am indebted to Charles R. Forker's article, "Shakespeare's Theatrical Symbolism and Its Function in *Hamlet," Shakespeare Quarterly,* XIV (Spring, 1963), 215–29. Other useful articles consulted are Sanford Sternlicht, *"Hamlet:* Six Characters in Search of a Play," *College English,* XXVII (1966), 528–31; John F. Ross, "Hamlet-Dramatist," *Five Studies in Literature,* Univ. of Calif. Publications in English, vol. VIII (Berkeley, 1940); D. J. Palmer, "Stage Spectators in *Hamlet," English Studies,* XLVII, no. 6 (December, 1966), 423–30.

8 *Au,* pp. 205, 216.

King Congal, the protagonist, is, at the play's beginning, intemperate and excitable. In scene i he insists on being told what kind of dog the two rich fleas bought, and King Aedh's answer, elicited by Congal only with the threat of fighting him all day, is in keeping with his own temperament, which, being the opposite of Congal's, is passive and inert: "A fat, square, lazy dog, / No sort of scratching dog." Again, in scene iii, Congal rashly attacks the Herne and in scene iv accuses Aedh of insulting him with a hen's egg, when he had expected to get a herne's egg. Aedh, in reply, attributes Congal's unreasonable choler to drunkenness, while claiming sobriety for himself. Incensed, Congal fights with Aedh and kills him. Through this symbolism, Congal has now truly become his opposite. He has, by vanquishing Aedh, his early timid half, readied himself to next defy the great Herne. Even though he ultimately goes down in defeat before the Herne, it is not an ignominious defeat. Yeats saw the warring of opposites as an important theme in some of Shakespeare's plays; this Shakespearean undercurrent can be found in *The Herne's Egg*.

The antagonism between Kings Congal and Aedh, depicted at the play's opening, is perhaps an overtone of that between Coriolanus and Aufidius. In Shakespeare's play, these two generals, though sworn enemies, are at the same time conscious of a deep-seated affinity for each other. Coriolanus eagerly questions a fellow general about Aufidius' attitude toward him, his rival:

> *Coriolanus.* Spoke he of me?
> *Lartius.*   He did, my lord.
> *Coriolanus.*   How? What?
> *Lartius.* How often he had met you, sword to sword;
>   That of all things upon the earth he hated
>   Your person most; that he would pawn his fortunes
>   To hopeless restitution, so he might
>   Be called your vanquisher.
>
> [III, i, 12–17]

Despite this open belligerence, Coriolanus aligns himself with Aufidius, who welcomes him warmly and even recognizes the compulsive necessity of this apparently paradoxical convergence of opposites as being inevitable: Aufidius says,

and I have nightly since
Dreamed of encounters 'twixt thyself and me:
We have been down together in my sleep,
Unbuckling helms, fisting each other's throat;
And waked half dead with nothing.
[IV, v, 121–25]

Though enemies, Coriolanus and Aufidius have a radical oneness.

Yeats knew Shakespeare's *Coriolanus* very well indeed; he referred to the play several times with keen approbation (see Appendix 2). The lonely hero in splendid contrast to the rabble was an impression that he owed to his father's impassioned reading aloud of *Coriolanus*. Yeats particularly mentions how impressed he was with "the scene where Coriolanus comes to the house of Aufidius and tells the impudent servants that his home is under the canopy": "I have seen *Coriolanus* played a number of times since then, and read it more than once, but that scene is more vivid than the rest, and it is my father's voice that I hear and not Irving's or Benson's." And in 1930 he could speak slightly enigmatically of his communicating with "the living mind of Shakespeare" when reading of Coriolanus among the servants of Aufidius, an allusion that probably takes cognizance of the merging of opposites in Shakespeare's play.[9] Yeats's assimilation of this particular aspect of *Coriolanus* and its expression in his own work appear in *The Herne's Egg*, which he began in 1935.[10] Here he seems to have incorporated, and made more Yeatsian and less Shakespearean, the antagonistic appetency of Coriolanus and Aufidius toward each other in the strangely symmetrical and amusing relationship between Kings Congal and Aedh:

Congal. How many men have you lost?
Aedh. Some five-and-twenty men.
Congal. No need to ask my losses.
Aedh. Your losses equal mine.
Congal. They always have and must.
[sc. i, ll. 1–5]

Later in the play, their final battle results in Aedh's dying at the hand of Congal; the battle, which takes place because of Congal's in-

---

9 *Au*, p. 39; Torchiana, p. 136 (see also above, pp. 114–15).
10 *Letters*, p. 843.

dignation at Aedh's having insulted him with a hen's egg whereas all the others got herne's eggs, is conducted with such prosaic and scarcely lethal weapons as table legs and candlesticks; these improbable weapons are not ineffective, however: Aedh dies "of a broken head" (sc. iv, l. 43). But Congal, though triumphant, with the true magnanimity of the Shakespearean victor who vanquishes his foe, confesses that he

> can weep at his funeral.
> I would not have had him die that way
> Or die at all, he should have been immortal,
>   [sc. iv, ll. 55–57]

and Pat, a soldier in Congal's army, twice declares of Aedh,

> Let all men know
> He was a noble character
> And I must weep at his funeral.
>   [sc. iv, ll. 48–50]

Yeats probably wants to remind us of Aufidius' sudden repentance over the battered body of the dead Coriolanus:

> My rage is gone,
> And I am struck with sorrow. Take him up.
> Help, three o' th' chiefest soldiers: I'll be one.
>   [V, vi, 148–50]

We also recall Antony's lament over Caesar's body:

> Bear with me:
> My heart is in the coffin there with Caesar,
> And I must pause till it come back to me,

and the Second Citizen's exclamation, "Poor soul! His eyes are red as fire with weeping" (*Caesar,* III, ii, 101–11). Octavius Caesar's grief at Antony's death is similar:

> But yet let me lament,
> With tears as sovereign as the blood of hearts,
> That thou my brother, my competitor. . . .
>   [*Antony,* V, i, 40–42]

By subtle hints and suggestions Yeats makes us aware of the Shakespearean atmosphere of heroic seriousness, and he juxtaposes this with his own no less serious—but also ironic—combat between Congal and Aedh.

The Shakespearean parallel of opposites coming together seems to have confirmed and strengthened the Yeatsian hypothesis, even as in his own life Yeats felt that the pattern had validity: George Russell, his opposite, was objective, Yeats subjective; Russell a saint, Yeats a sinner; Russell seeking unity outside himself in Ireland, Yeats seeking it within himself and his circle. After Russell's death Yeats wrote to Lady Dorothy: "AE [Russell] was my oldest friend—we began our work together. I constantly quarrelled with him but he never bore malice."[11] From his own experience and from Shakespeare, Yeats seems to have found reservoirs on which to draw for the dramatic world that his last plays conjure up, a world sometimes deliberately comical, sometimes fierce and pitiless; in one instant echoing a Shakespearean theme, but in the next instant so remote as to render the earlier resemblance bizarre.

IV

After Yeats wrote *Calvary,* the last play in his *Four Plays for Dancers* (1921), his drama develops a new quality, that of tragicomedy. It is true that even in some of his early plays comic elements coexist with the tragic (e.g., Fool and Blind Man in *On Baile's Strand*), but what now appears is a far closer meshing of the two elements so as to make them inextricable. Does this united front that they present result in a confusion of values? Perhaps, yet the same then might be said of the drunken porter's mouthings after the murder of Duncan, of the taunting witticisms of the Fool on the heath with Lear, and of Hamlet's trifling with the grave diggers. These scenes are so integral to Shakespeare's tragic purpose that they cannot be expunged without destroying that purpose.

Yeats's later plays, like Shakespeare's tragedies, explore the domain of tragicomedy, in which grief is enlivened by the comic and laughter is muted by the tragic. Significantly, he began *The Player Queen* in

11 *Letters,* p. 838.

1907 as a tragedy, but it gave him endless trouble, and after struggling with it for six or seven years, he took Pound's advice and "completely transformed the play" into a comedy.[12] *The Herne's Egg* (1938) is a highly serious and disturbing play, yet, like *The Player Queen,* it is permeated with the comic spirit; and does not even *Purgatory* (1939), despite its terrible gloom, admit a solitary ray of grim humor when the Old Man, after stabbing his son to death, vindicates himself with the incredible observation, "I am a wretched foul old man / And therefore harmless" (208–9)?

In *The Death of Cuchulain* (1939), Yeats's last play, the Shakespearean juxtaposition of the tragic and the comic reaches its apotheosis with the Blind Man of *On Baile's Strand* groping to find Cuchulain's neck, preparatory to beheading him with his knife. "I keep it sharp because it cuts my food," he explains to Cuchulain, who is concerned that the knife may be inadequate for the purpose. And when Cuchulain reflects "that the blind / Know everything," the Blind Man modestly replies, "No, but they have good sense," adding with irrefutable logic, "How could I have got twelve pennies for your head / If I had not good sense?" (171–77). Cuchulain has no answer to this overwhelming question. In Cuchulain's situation with the Blind Man, it is possible to catch a glimpse of "the humour of the old man with the basket" who brings to Cleopatra the asp, a scene that Yeats speaks of several times with great approval (see Appendix 2).[13] The Blind Man's briny humor and pedestrian language, brought to bear on Cuchulain at the hour of his death, is an example of Yeats's superb handling of the sublime and the ridiculous as they exist side by side.

By successfully escaping from Shakespeare's domain, Yeats was in a position to declare his own dramatic individuality. Even though *On Baile's Strand* ends with a tremendous gesture of defiance by Cuchulain, comparable to the heroic self-immolation of an Othello, a Brutus, or an Antony, his combat with the waves is not witnessed by the audience, but is described by the Fool (of all persons), and the play concludes—as noted in the previous chapter—with another display of amusing

12 *Man and Masks,* p. 212.
13 *E&I,* p. 244.

trickery at which the Blind Man is such an adept: "There will be nobody in the houses. Come this way; come quickly! The ovens will be
full. We will put our hands into the ovens," he orders the ever-credulous
Fool. Yeats undercuts the heroics, emphasizes the anomalies, the para-
doxes. Irony, understatement, and a bold earthiness come to the fore.
His tragedies are like Nebuchadnezzar's image with head of gold but
with feet of clay and iron.

Shakespeare's heroes, during the last stage of their lives, are not
entangled by fools as are Yeats's heroes. (Lear's Fool, we recall, disappears after Lear is rescued from the heath.) In fact, whereas Shakespeare's comic scenes are distinct from his tragic ones (the porter does
not stagger in while Macbeth is contemplating his bloody hands after
the murder), Yeats's comedy interfuses his tragedy. Both King Congal
in *The Herne's Egg* and Cuchulain in *The Death of Cuchulain* die
attended and assisted by fools, and the assertion of their human dignity
against the vastly superior power of the gods is quiet, unaccompanied
by histrionics. Cuchulain's assassin is a Blind Man who hopes to earn
twelve pennies by beheading him. We have only to think of Hamlet's
death before a crowded court, followed by the arrival of Fortinbras and
his retinue, to visualize the emptiness of Cuchulain's last moments.
King Congal dies attended by the Fool, who informs him that his name
is "Poor Tom Fool" (sc. vi, ll. 1–2). Clearly, Yeats wants his audience
to associate him with Edgar, who tells Lear that his name is "Poor Tom"
(III, iv, 42). Yeats enriches the situation with Shakespearean overtones.
In both plays the kings identify themselves with the fools: Congal
screams, "Fool! Am I myself a Fool?" (sc. vi, l. 116), and Lear moves toward the state of wisdom that his fool represents: "Dost thou call me
fool, boy?" (I, iv, 137) he asks the Fool. Yeats's fools, however, have
an unconscious wisdom, unlike Shakespeare's fools who are consciously
wise. Teigue, in *The Hour-Glass,* is fond of money (like Feste), but he
does not have the craft and the legerdemain that Feste and Touchstone
display. Yeats's fools are not worldly-wise but possess an instinctive wisdom that they share with Shakespeare's fools: both Touchstone and the
Fool of *King Lear* prefer banishment to staying on at Court, and Feste's
song at the play's end is a sad and ironical little commentary on the

failure that has been his life. Yeats locates the fool at Phase 28, seeing him as "but a straw blown by the wind, with no mind but the wind and no act but a nameless drifting and turning." "His thoughts are an aimless reverie" and "his acts are aimless like his thoughts," but "it is in this aimlessness that he finds his joy." Concluding his examination of the fool, Yeats "finds his many shapes on passing from the village fool to the Fool of Shakespeare," and then quotes three lines from William Watson's poem on *King Lear:*

> Out of the pool,
> Where love the slain with love the slayer lies,
> Bubbles the wan mirth of the mirthless fool.[14]

As early as 1890, in his review of Watson's poems, Yeats had described these lines as being the "finest of all";[15] thirty-five years later, in *A Vision,* he remembered them sufficiently well to quote them with only a slight inaccuracy—evidence of the importance that Yeats attached to Shakespeare's concept of the fool, and his own treatment of the subject.

The site and the manner of King Congal's death are as nondescript as the company that attends him. The setting is described as a mountain top illuminated by "the moon of comic tradition, a round smiling face," and the implements employed by the Fool to put him to death are "a cauldron lid, a cooking-pot, and a spit." Undoubtedly, we are in the presence of the anti-theater, or of the theater of the Absurd, in this scene:

> *(He falls symbolically upon the spit. It does not touch him. Fool takes the spit and wine-skin and goes out.)*
> It seems that I am hard to kill,
> But the wound is deep. Are you up there?
> Your chosen kitchen spit has killed me,
> But killed me at my own will, not yours.
>   [sc. vi, ll. 126–30]

Self-depreciation, pathos, and dignity are all here. His colloquial and even laconic "Are you up there?" is a question that no Shakespearean

    14   *Vis,* p. 182.
    15   *New Island,* p. 210. It is likely that Yeats read Lionel Johnson's essay, "The Fools of Shakespeare" (1887), *Post Liminium: Essays and Critical Papers by Lionel Johnson,* ed. Thomas Whittemore (London, 1912), pp. 64–81.

hero would ever have asked, and his rather cheerful, "It seems that I am hard to kill," is certainly a contrast to the cosmic despair of the Shakespearean hero. When Gloucester attempts suicide from a cliff near Dover, he invokes the "mighty gods" (IV, vi, 34), but King Congal's attitude to the Herne, though one of pride and defiance, also contains a vein of playful bantering directed at the Herne's comical looks: in his last spasm, he gibes, "And you up there / With your long leg and long beak" (sc. vi, ll. 148–49). Yeats greatly admired "the last words of Shakespeare's people," but in his own practice was careful not to imitate what, by its very nature, must remain inimitable. Perhaps Seanchan of *The King's Threshold* is the only Yeatsian hero who dies a rhetorical death and, in this sense, comes close to Shakespeare's practice. Although Yeats seems to have deliberately deviated from Shakespeare in the concluding scenes of his plays, there is, at the same time, a fundamental rapport with Shakespeare's tragic sense. That Yeats recognized this is evident from his many references to the exuberant triumph with which Shakespeare's heroes face death. Of the conclusions to Shakespeare's tragedies, Yeats wrote in 1937: "There may be in this or that detail painful tragedy, but in the whole work none," and he then quotes Lady Gregory's comment, "Tragedy must be a joy to the man who dies." The "painful tragedy" that Yeats, nearly thirty years before, had objected to in the blinding of Gloucester has now been absorbed into the joyous harmony of the whole. King Congal can die on a jest because he shares with Shakespeare's tragic heroes "their ecstasy at the approach of death."[16]

Thus, even while establishing his own jurisdiction outside of Shakespeare's territory, Yeats at the same time had no compunction about expropriating the Shakespearean landscape to form a Yeatsian synthesis whenever it suited his purpose. As noted in chapter 2 above, he could see Richard, Coriolanus, and Hamlet as the opposites of Henry, Aufidius, and Fortinbras, respectively: sensitivity of soul pitted against rough-and-ready opportunism. Yet he also gradually came to feel that this bifurcation in Shakespeare's view of the world was not really so obvious, that the opposites did in fact come together and coalesce.

16 *E&I,* pp. 307 (see also p. 254), 522–23, 333.

V

Even though Yeats's ambition had been "to bring again the theatre of Shakespeare," he was equally conscious of the necessity for poetic drama in Ireland during the twentieth century to refrain from continuing the practice of the previous century, which had produced a blank verse that was often a pathetic and feeble travesty of Shakespeare.[17] Eliot too, aware of the danger of drifting into Shakespearean waters and thereby losing his own navigational ability, scrupulously eschewed Shakespearean blank verse in his plays.[18] Yeats, refusing to be intimidated, did not shun blank verse, though he generally avoided the Shakespearean decasyllabic line with its pronounced iambic meter. Even when employing the line, he introduced frequent variations in the number of syllables, thus breaking up the rhythm to conform to normal speech patterns. He had little to do with the long verse paragraph that Shakespeare reveled in, choosing rather to create his effects by a fusing of tragic and comic elements and by a strict economy of language.

The blank verse that Yeats employs for his plays written after about 1904 is a departure from his earlier practice. In keeping with his statement that all his life he had "tried to get rid of modern subjectivity by insisting on . . . contemporary words and syntax," the style is now less musical than formerly; it is staccato, abrupt, almost conversational at times and deliberately un-Shakespearean. The fact that Yeats rewrote *The Only Jealousy of Emer* as *Fighting the Waves,* a prose play, is an indication of the direction in which his efforts to break free from conventional blank verse were tending. Declaring that "an elaborate verse play" was beyond a twentieth-century audience, Yeats added that if he dared, he would "put King Lear into modern English."[19] In this astounding proposal, Yeats pushes the logic of modernity to its extreme

17 *Ex,* p. 252.

18 See T. S. Eliot, "The Poetry of W. B. Yeats," in *The Permanence of Yeats,* ed. James Hall and Martin Steinmann (New York, 1950), pp. 339–40, and A. G. George, *T. S. Eliot: His Mind and Art,* 2d ed. (Bombay, 1969), chapter 13. For a survey of nineteenth-century poetic drama, see Allardyce Nicoll, *A History of Early Nineteenth Century Drama, 1800–1850* (Cambridge, 1930), and E. B. Watson, *Sheridan to Robertson* (Cambridge, 1926).

19 *Letters,* pp. 892, 778. Regarding his revision of *The Wanderings of Oisin,* Yeats said, "I deliberately reshaped my style. . . . I cast off traditional metaphors and loosened my rhythm" (*Au,* p. 45).

position. As an example of his quest for contemporary words and syntax, the following passage from *Deirdre* is typical. Here Deirdre entreats Naoise, her lover, to consent to her going to Conchubar, his jealous rival in love, to placate his wrath against Naoise:

> It's better to go with him.
> Why should you die when one can bear it all?
> My life is over; it's better to obey.
> Why should you die? I will not live long, Naoise.
> I'd not have you believe I'd long stay living;
> O no, no, no! You will go far away.
> You will forget me. Speak, speak, Naoise, speak,
> And say that it is better that I go.
> I will not ask it. Do not speak a word,
> For I will take it all upon myself.
> Conchubar, I will go.
>
> [594–604]

Clearly Yeats is developing a syntax and an idiom that bear his individual stamp. "The syntax of passionate speech" is what Yeats called the aim of all his work.[20] Since the break from the evocative verse of his early plays occurs first in *On Baile's Strand,* which was begun in 1901, a few months after his visit to Stratford, it is possible that the experience of witnessing Shakespeare's plays was responsible for making him increasingly aware of the necessity for contemporary drama to be freed from the bondage of an emasculated blank verse.

Another example of Yeats's use of understatement may be seen in the conclusion to *At the Hawk's Well,* where Cuchulain, finding that he, like the Old Man, has been deceived by Aoife, sets out to encounter her in battle, stating his resolve in the barest minimum of words:

> *Young Man.* The clash of arms again!
> *Old Man.* O, do not go! The mountain is accursed;
>   Stay with me, I have nothing more to lose,
>   I do not now deceive you.
> *Young Man.* I will face them.
>   (*He goes out, no longer as if in a dream, but*

---

20 Quoted by Torchiana, p. 280. For a detailed discussion of this subject see Thomas Parkinson, *W. B. Yeats: The Later Poetry* (Berkeley, 1960), chapter 4; David R. Clark, *W. B. Yeats and the Theatre of Desolate Reality* (Dublin, 1965), pp. 92–100.

shouldering his spear and calling) :
He comes! Cuchulain, son of Sualtim, comes!
[245–49]

Unlike Shakespeare's tragic heroes, such as Othello and Coriolanus, who die with resounding rhetoric on their lips, Yeats's heroes are almost taciturn. In them, action and rhetoric are subservient to the dignity of quiet resolve also present in Hamlet's "Let be," and in Lear's clarity of perception when he says: "I know when one is dead and when one lives. / She's dead as earth. Lend me a looking-glass." In keeping with Yeats's conviction that "the stage must become still that words might keep all their vividness—and I wanted vivid words," his heroes are at the end subdued, their language restrained, austere.[21]

Any comparison of Yeats's syntax with that of Shakespeare must be suspect because of differences inherent in both context and dramatic purpose; nevertheless Cleopatra's reaction to Antony's death may be placed alongside Deirdre's reaction to the news from Conchubar that her husband is dead. Cleopatra's grief is both visible and eloquent:

> The crown o' th' earth doth melt. My lord!
> O, withered is the garland of the war,
> The soldier's pole is fall'n. Young boys and girls
> Are level now with men. The odds is gone,
> And there is nothing left remarkable
> Beneath the visiting moon.
>
> [IV, xv, 63–68]

Deirdre's response to the information that Naoise is dead sounds, by comparison, flat and almost naïve; it comes close to Lear's "Prithee, undo this button."

> O, do not touch me. Let me go to him.
>   *(Pause)*
> King Conchubar is right. My husband's dead.
> A single woman is of no account,
> Lacking array of servants, linen cupboards,
> The bacon hanging—and King Conchubar's house
> All ready, too—I'll to King Conchubar's house.
> It is but wisdom to do willingly
> What has to be.
>
> [658–65]

21 *E&I*, p. 527.

Purgatory, ruthlessly shorn of the ornamentation that cluttered much of the verse of his early plays, displays an amazing conciseness. Here Yeats discards the conventional metrical foot and employs four stresses per line; and while varying the syllabic content of the lines from four to twelve, he makes the octosyllabic line the norm:

> Í stúck hím with a knífe,
> Thát knife that cúts my dínner nów,
> And áfter thát I léft him in the fíre.
>
> [99–101]

Again, in place of the usual stresses providing rhythm, Yeats employs the device of iterating certain key words which impart to the passage an incantatory and distant quality:[22]

> Had loved the house, had loved all
> The intricate passages of the house,
> But he killed the house; to kill a house
> Where great men grew up, married, died,
> I here declare a capital offence.
>
> [72–76]

Shakespeare too had employed this device. Consider the well-known lines from Hamlet's soliloquy:

> To die, to sleep;
> No more; and by a sleep to say we end
> The heartache, and the thousand natural shocks
> That flesh is heir to, 'tis a consummation
> Devoutly to be wished. To die, to sleep.
> To sleep, perchance to dream: ay, there's the rub;
> For in that sleep of death what dreams may come.
>
> [III, i, 60–67]

The impact of the iteration of "house" in Yeats's passage is more immediate than that of "sleep" in Shakespeare's, because Yeats avoids the iambic pentameter that Shakespeare adopts. In lines that contain only four stresses, "house" engaging a stress in each case, the iteration is necessarily more obtrusive than in the lines from *Hamlet.*

A final example from *Purgatory* will corroborate the point. The

22   For a thoughtful discussion of Yeats's use of this device, see William R. Veeder, *W. B. Yeats: The Rhetoric of Repetition* (Berkeley, 1968).

Old Man describes the scene being re-enacted in the empty house:

> The hoof-beat stops,
> He has gone to the other side of the house,
> Gone to the stable, put the horse up.
> She has gone down to open the door.

[130–33]

Because the play deals with recurrence, the poet has intertwined with the fabric of the verse a repetition of certain suggestive words. By the time Yeats had reached this degree of accomplishment in the handling of his blank verse, he had no longer any debts to pay Shakespeare. He had long since paid them all.

VI

If, as Professor Torchiana persuasively argues, *Purgatory* is integral to *On the Boiler*, being a dramatic summing-up of Yeats's declared convictions, then Yeats's repeated references to Shakespeare in the pamphlet are significant and may well be expected to carry over, albeit transmuted, into the play.[23] How closely Yeats identified himself with Shakespeare in these pages may be seen in his enlisting Shakespeare's support for the presentation of his views. After a brief introduction, Yeats castigates the desire of the mayor of Dublin to be "popular among the common people" as reflected in the tawdry architecture of "the Mansion house as it is to-day." Deploring this growing democratic trend, Yeats maintains that, rather than refinement stooping to the level of the vulgar, the direction should be reversed, and he supports this contention by referring to "that old Shakespearean contempt" for the taste of the masses. The decline, Yeats asserts, was present everywhere, flaunting itself not only in a corrupted taste in architecture, but in drama too. "I gave certain years to writing plays in Shakespearean blank verse about Irish kings," he says, "for whom nobody cared a farthing."[24]

But the affinity that Yeats felt with Shakespeare in these last years of his life went much further than a sense of comradeship in belonging to a greater, more gracious time. In the section entitled "Other Matters"

23 Torchiana, pp. 340–52.
24 *Boiler*, pp. 9–10, 15.

of *On the Boiler*, he points out that Shakespeare's tribunal is public, not private, as is Ben Jonson's: in Shakespeare's moral scheme "all are judged as we would have them judged. The wicked should be punished, the innocent rewarded, marriage bells sound for no evil man." That Yeats himself espoused this elemental standard of values is evident from his being happy that his ballads were being sung by the country people as they went about their work, he tells us in the same section. Unlike Dr. Johnson, whose chief complaint against Shakespeare is that "he sacrifices virtue to convenience," that "he seems to write without any moral purpose," and that "he makes no just distribution of good or evil," for Yeats, Shakespeare's moral scheme is no different from that which Everyman would uphold. In a letter to Dorothy Wellesley written five months before *On the Boiler* was published, he had approved of an article by Archibald MacLeish commending him above other modern poets because his language was "public." "That word which I had not thought of myself is a word I want," he declared. And as early as 1916, Yeats had called Shakespeare's art "always public, because poetry was a part of the general life."[25] Throughout his life, though more so toward the end, Yeats seems to have seen in Shakespeare's practice a mirroring of what he himself was attempting to do.

In *Purgatory*, Yeats's feeling of kinship with Shakespeare is insistently present, yet submerged into the dramatic tensions that the play engenders and resolves by its own momentum. *Purgatory* is, perhaps more than any other play of Yeats's, "dominated by the example of Shakespeare" and at the same time escapes furthest from Shakespeare's territorial jurisdiction.[26] In one way it is an epitome of Yeats's varied attitudes toward Shakespeare, which were subject to change, revision, and adjustment as he sought to reduce this protean relationship to something less intransigent. The very dynamism of his relationship with Shakespeare had hitherto defied such attempts, but in *Purgatory* he achieved a measure of rapprochement that, embodied in an incredibly

25 *Boiler*, pp. 32, 35; *Dr. Johnson on Shakespeare*, ed. W. K. Wimsatt (Harmondsworth, Middlesex, 1969), p. 66; *Letters to DW*, p. 163; W. B. Yeats, *Four Plays*, p. 88.

26 W. B. Yeats, *Four Plays*, p. 88.

taut dramatic form, must be regarded as his final stance with reference to Shakespeare.

Purgatory, with its extreme paucity of characters and concentrated symbolic form, is at the other extreme to "Shakespeare's luxuriance," which Yeats had cautioned his fellow dramatists against, and is strictly disciplined on the "unity" of Greek drama, which he cherished so highly. Yet Shakespeare's presence is discernible in the play. Before the play was written, Yeats wrote to a correspondent, "I have a one-act play in my head, a scene of tragic intensity." He went on to say that his recent work had "greater intensity" than anything he had done. We have already seen that Yeats had defined Shakespeare's tragic vision in terms of "emotion and intellect at their moment of union and at their greatest intensity."[27] While successfully shunning the amorphous aspects of Shakespeare's work, Yeats, in *Purgatory,* has captured the Shakespearean intensity that he never ceased to endorse.

In *Purgatory,* four plays of Shakespeare that Yeats responded to forcefully—*Timon of Athens, Hamlet, King Lear,* and *Macbeth*—coalesce to form a pattern that in turn coincides with the intrinsic symbolism of the play. But for all its amazing consanguinity with these plays of Shakespeare, *Purgatory* remains distinctively and uniquely Yeatsian. A glance at the appendixes will show how deeply ingrained *Timon of Athens* was in Yeats's consciousness. A month after Yeats said that *Purgatory* was conceived in his mind, his poem, "An Acre of Grass," was published. Here, the poet seeks identification with "Timon and Lear," old men whose frenzy carries them beyond reason to the apprehension of a reality that exists on the other side of the grave. The dominant images in *Purgatory* are (1) of two sixteen-year-old boys turning patricidal; (2) of a ruined house; and (3) of a tree once green and flourishing, but now blasted.

Timon of Athens contains all three themes, and though not re-current, they are pivotal symbols in the stages through which Timon passes. When forced to leave Athens because of his bankruptcy, he looks back at the walls of the city and pours forth a stream of invective pro-

27 *Ex,* p. 80; *Boiler,* p. 29; *Letters,* p. 907; *Ex,* p. 245.

phetic of the crumbling of hierarchical values in Athens. Timon en-
visions a time when subordinates in every walk of life will rise against
their superiors. He exhorts slaves and fools to "pluck the grave wrinkled
Senate from the bench," debtors to cut their creditors' throats, servants
to plunder their masters. But the crescendo is reached when he screams:

> Son of sixteen,
> Pluck the lined crutch from thy old limping sire,
> With it beat out his brains!
> [IV, i, 13–15]

It is clearly more than a coincidence that Yeats makes sixteen so pronounced a motif in his play:[28] the Old Man was sixteen when he mur-
dered his father; on his disclosing this to his son, the Boy thoughtfully,
or excitedly, says:

> But that is my age, sixteen years old,
> At the Puck Fair.
> [93–94]

In Yeats's play, no senator is plucked from the bench, nor do servants
plunder their masters; Yeats has shorn his plot of the plethora of detail
that Timon enumerates and has swooped down on only one manifestation of decay, and that the most dreadful, thus preserving a unity that
Shakespearean drama, embracing "so much that is irrelevant and heterogeneous,"[29] lacked. Yeats, it is true, comes to Shakespeare, but he meets
him on his own terms.

   Purgatory opens with "a ruined house and a bare tree in the background." In *Timon of Athens,* Flavius, Timon's faithful steward, sums
up the plight of the servants after their master has gone, in a single
unforgettable line:

> All broken implements of a ruined house.
> [IV, ii, 16]

When Timon, earlier, had expelled his parasitical guests from his Bar-
mecidal feast by flinging dishes of water into their faces, he described

   28 But see Torchiana, pp. 359–60, for a historical explanation of the Boy's
age. For a political explanation of the Boy's age, see Donald Pearce, "Yeats's Last
Plays: An Interpretation," *ELH,* XVIII (March, 1951), 67–76, and John Heath-
Stubbs, *On a Darkling Plain* (London, 1950), p. 205.
   29 *Vis,* p. 294.

the ruin that would shortly overtake Athens in the figure of a burning house:

> Burn, house! sink, Athens! henceforth hated be
> Of Timon man and all humanity!
>
> [III, vi, 97–98]

Like Swift, in Yeats's poem "Swift's Epitaph," whose "savage indigna-tion" had lacerated his breast, Timon foresees the emptiness at the top that is already asserting itself. After Timon abandons his house and goes into the woods, Shakespeare includes a brief scene located in the house, for the purpose of underlining the crumbling of order that follows the decay of a great house (IV, ii). The theme of *Purgatory* is the failure of the individual, the family, and the nation. The age itself rejects a stable society. The Old Man is itinerant, a peddler; his son, a bastard born in a ditch; and the house that once contained "old books and books made fine / By eighteenth-century French binding" (84–85), now an empty shell.

Although the Old Man's sottish father had cut down the trees that were loved by the "great people [who] lived and died in this house" (61), one tree survived: the tree that commands our attention at the beginning and the end of the play. The Old Man tells his son to "study that tree," and then asks, "What is it like?" The boy impudently replies, "A silly old man" (15–16). The tree is the Old Man, but more than this as well. If the Old Man, though degenerate, yet retains vestiges of past aristocratic excellence because of his mother ("some / Half-loved me for my half of her" [80–81]), so does the tree, though shorn of its "green leaves, ripe leaves, leaves thick as butter" (22), yet preserve something of its old identity. Timon too describes his impending end in the imagery of a tree about to be felled. He invites the senators, who hope to prevail on him to return and save Athens, to participate in his own destruction by hanging themselves from the branches of the tree before "my tree hath felt the axe" (V, i, 209). *Timon of Athens* seems to have been present, perhaps unconsciously, in Yeats's mind when he was writing *Purgatory*, but *Hamlet*, *King Lear*, and *Macbeth* also insinuate them-selves into Yeats's play, thus enlarging its boundaries.

The Old Man remembers the atmosphere of bonhomie and

jocularity that prevailed when the house in which he was born stood. He asks,

> Where are the jokes and stories of a house,
> Its threshold gone to patch a pig-sty?
>
> [10–11]

Likewise Hamlet recalls the wit and humor that once emanated from the mouth of Yorick the jester: "Where be your gibes now? your gambols? your songs? your flashes of merriment that were wont to set the table on a roar?" He then recites:

> Imperious Caesar, dead and turned to clay,
> Might stop a hole to keep the wind away.
> O, that that earth, which kept the world in awe,
> Should patch a wall t'expel the winter's flaw!
>
> [V, i, 195–98]

Both Hamlet and the Old Man are disturbed by the same thought, the loss of joy and laughter; and both remember past greatness now reduced to the ignominy of patching a pig-sty in the one case, of patching a wall in the other.

But there are more than fleeting verbal echoes of *Hamlet* in *Purgatory.* Thematically, Yeats's play is a concentration of one element in *Hamlet.* As the most opprobrious curse in Timon's tirade, that of the sixteen-year-old son slaying his father, assumes a dominant role in *Purgatory,* so from *Hamlet* there is one echo immediately recognizable. The Old Man is, in more ways than one, Hamlet's counterpart. As Hamlet is more shaken by his mother's venery (in her marrying a man far inferior to her first husband) than by his uncle's guilt, so the Old Man's avowed desire is to expiate the crime his mother committed in having married beneath her. He kills his son, the Boy, to alleviate the load of anguish he believes his mother carries in knowing that her act was responsible for the dissemination of "pollution" witnessed in her grandson. So also had Hamlet gone to his mother's chamber, aware of his urge to kill her for having succumbed to her lust (III, ii, 365–67). But this "frailty" of hers is not the sole disrupter of Hamlet's mind; his revulsion is also directed against himself for being a product of his mother's degeneracy:

> O, that this too too solid flesh would melt,
> Thaw, and resolve itself into a dew!
>
> [I, ii, 129–30]

Similarly, the Old Man in *Purgatory* condemns his mother for marrying "a groom in a training stable" and declares that her mother was right in ostracizing her:

> Her mother never spoke to her again,
> And she did right.
>
> [53–54]

Lechery and drunkenness obsess the Old Man's thoughts:

> This night she is no better than her man
> And does not mind that he is half drunk,
> She is mad about him.
>
> [134–36]

Hamlet too exacerbates his disgust for his mother's corruption by conjuring up a scene of her and his drunken uncle in bed together:

> Let the bloat King tempt you again to bed;
> Pinch wanton on your cheek, call you his mouse.
>
> [III, iv, 181–82]

Moreover, when the ghost of Hamlet's father appeared in Gertrude's chamber, she was so imperceptive as to be incapable of seeing or hearing anything. In *Purgatory,* the Boy, surrogate for the Old Man's mother, is equally obtuse. Hamlet informs his mother vehemently that he looks "On him, on him! Look you how pale he glares!" but she remains outside this experience. "To whom do you speak this?" she asks.

> *Hamlet.* Do you see nothing there?
> *Queen.* Nothing at all: yet all that is I see.
> *Hamlet.* Nor did you nothing hear?
> *Queen.* No, nothing but ourselves.
> *Hamlet.* Why, look you there! Look, how it steals away!
>   My father, in his habit as he lived!
>   Look, where he goes, even now, out at the portal!
>
> [III, iv, 129–35]

Likewise the Old Man of *Purgatory* urges his son to see and hear what is to him so plainly discernible, but the Boy, initially, remains insentient:

> *Old Man.* Listen to the hoof-beats! Listen, listen!
> *Boy.* I cannot hear a sound.
> *Old Man.* Beat! Beat.
>
> This night is the anniversary
> Of my mother's wedding night,
> Or of the night wherein I was begotten.
> My father is riding from the public-house,
> A whiskey-bottle under his arm.
> (*A window is lit showing a young girl.*)
> Look at the window; she stands there
> Listening, the servants are all in bed,
> She is alone, he has stayed late
> Bragging and drinking in the public-house.
> *Boy.* There's nothing but an empty gap in the wall.

> [114–25]

Both Gertrude and the Boy dismiss the spectacles witnessed by Hamlet and the Old Man as being the products of madness. Gertrude declares,

> This is the very coinage of your brain.
> This bodiless creation ecstasy
> Is very cunning in,

> [III, iv, 136–38]

and the Boy is equally brusque with his father:

> You have made it up. No, you are mad!
> You are getting madder every day.

> [126–27]

And as Hamlet is uneasily conscious of his own hovering between sanity and madness when he tells Rosencrantz, "My wit's diseased" (III, ii, 298), so does the Old Man recognize that the purgatorial scene he alone witnesses, but cannot interrupt, establishes his abnormality: "And that's a proof my wits are out" (146), he declares.

Yeats's play stands on its own, yet dimly in the background *Hamlet* looms large, and when Yeats was writing the play, the consciousness of how Shakespeare had handled the subject must have been stridently present in his mind. As Hamlet, though producer and playwright himself, shows by his spirit of resignation in the last act of the play that he gives his bow to the Other Director who shapes our ends, so the

Old Man of *Purgatory* resigns himself to the grace of God for the release of his mother's soul from its dream.[30]

Purgatory probes the soul's experiences after death, the reliving of transgressions "not once but many times" (220), a phenomenon that Yeats on two occasions seeks to prove valid by turning to *Hamlet.* "When Hamlet refused the bare bodkin because of what dreams may come, it was from no mere literary fancy," Yeats assures us—an explanation of Hamlet's line, "For in that sleep of death what dreams may come" (III, i, 66), that perhaps no Shakespeare commentator has ever suggested. For Yeats, Hamlet's reluctance to commit suicide is occasioned by his dread of the dreaming-back process, the theme of *Purgatory.* Again, seeking to establish the links that bind human life on earth with the activities of the dead, who exercise an unseen control on us, the living, Yeats declares that "the world is a drama where person follows person," so that Polonius is not disproved, though "Hamlet seems to kill him." Yeats here chooses to view the afterlife through a metaphor that he develops from *Hamlet,* and of his own play, *Purgatory,* he wrote in a letter, "I have put there my own conviction about this world and the next."[31]

Gloucester's diatribe against the degeneracy of the age, while denouncing his legitimate son Edgar to his bastard son Edmund, is perhaps one of the sources for *Purgatory*—a source embedded in Yeats's own familiarity with *King Lear.* As Gloucester interprets "eclipses in the sun and moon" to be ominous portents of a chaotic state in which "the bond [is] cracked 'twixt son and father" (I, ii, 95, 100), so the Old Man directs his son's attention to the eclipse enshrouding the house which is now an empty shell:

> The moonlight falls upon the path,
> The shadow of a cloud upon the house,
> And that's symbolical.
>
> [13–15]

At the beginning of the play, Lear's demands are excessive, gro-

30 I am indebted to Wendy Coppedge Sanford, *Theater as Metaphor in Hamlet* (Cambridge, Mass., 1967), p. 21, for the idea of the Other Director in *Hamlet.*

31 *Myth,* pp. 354–55; *Vis* (1925), pp. 171–72; *Letters,* p. 913.

tesque. "Which of you shall we say doth love us most?" (I, i, 47), he demands of his daughters, thus creating a situation in which possible sisterly accord is riven by rivalry—the paradox being that this rivalry is not over the father's love for them, but over the expression of their love for the father, a situation at once unnatural and absurd. Lear's relationship with his daughters lacks tenderness.[32] He does not know what it is to give, but only to exchange on the basis of "merit":

> Which of you shall we say doth love us most?
> That we our largest bounty may extend
> Where nature doth with merit challenge.
> [I, i, 47–50]

Gloucester's diagnosis, "The King falls from bias of nature: there's father against child" (I, ii, 101–2), is sound.

Purgatory too sets forth a violent antagonism between father and child and, like *King Lear,* concludes with some kind of reconciliation between them. As Lear at the play's end enters carrying the dead Cordelia in his arms (V, iii, 257), a gesture symbolic of the tender solicitude of a father for his helpless infant and a total contrast to his attitude of extorting affection at the play's beginning, so also the Old Man of *Purgatory,* after stabbing his son to death, is moved by the sight of his son's helplessness and sings a snatch from the lullaby that he once sang to his son when the boy was a baby:

> Hush-a-bye baby, thy father's a knight,
> Thy mother's a lady, lovely and bright.
> [195–96]

In the midst of horror there is the possibility of redemption. Both Lear and the Old Man are at last able to see their children as they knew them in their pristine state; they have moved from aggression to tenderness.

What the Old Man mutters after stabbing his son,

> I am a wretched foul old man
> And therefore harmless,
> [208–9]

32 I am indebted to Professor C. L. Barber for this insight (*"Hamlet* and *King Lear:* The Use of Tragic Form," lecture at Northwestern University, March 7, 1969).

reminds us of Lear's lines,

> I am a very foolish fond old man,
> Fourscore and upward, not an hour more nor less;
> And, to deal plainly,
> I fear I am not in my perfect mind.[33]
>
> [IV, vii, 60–63]

Immanent in their childishly pathetic self-denigration is the truth of self-realization being reached through paradox: the Old Man, after murdering his son, professes to being "harmless"; Lear, after giving his age as "fourscore and upward," immediately adds, "not an hour more nor less." What do these sharp contradictions signify? Perhaps that the breaking down of the forts of reason ("I fear I am not in my perfect mind," Lear confesses) is a necessary prelude to recovery.[34] (It is worth noting that Yeats spoke of the later Strindberg "as mad and as profound as King Lear.") [35] Lear's salvation is obtainable only through a change of mind: his arrogance and vanity must give place to humility before such a change is possible. In like manner, the Old Man at the end of *Purgatory* realizes that his mother's release and the alleviation of his own misery can be accomplished only through the intervention of divine grace:

> O God,
> Release my mother's soul from its dream!
> Mankind can do no more. Appease
> The misery of the living and the remorse of the dead.
>
> [220–23]

The Old Man, like Lear, has isolated himself from his offspring. Both, in their dreadful loneliness, have destroyed what is nearest to them, only to discover that the act is meaningless. Like Lear who told Goneril,

---

33 F. A. C. Wilson, *W. B. Yeats and Tradition* (London, 1958), pp. 159–60, has taken note of these resemblances.

34 See B. Rajan, "Yeats and the Absurd," *Tri-Quarterly*, no. 4 (1965), pp. 130–37. Professor Rajan points out that "Yeats knows, like Shakespeare, that the poor forked animal, stripped of all pretences and driven into the storm, has in him a certain ineradicable residue of dignity."

35 W. B. Yeats, "The Need for Audacity of Thought," *The Dial* (February, 1926), p. 119.

> But yet thou art my flesh, my blood, my daughter;
> Or rather a disease that's in my flesh,
> Which I must needs call mine: thou art a boil,
> A plague-sore, or embossed carbuncle,
> In my corrupted blood,
>
> [II, iv, 216–20]

the Old Man, by recognizing the pollution that his son would disseminate if allowed to live, acknowledges the corruption his own flesh harbors:

> I killed that lad because had he grown up
> He would have struck a woman's fancy,
> Begot, and passed pollution on.
>
> [205–7]

A few years before writing *Purgatory,* Yeats had considered the deterioration of the race with reference to a poem by the Irish poet Brian Merriman in which bastardy is commended, provided this could insure "fine," "handsome," and "vigorous" children being born. Yeats quotes Merriman's lines advocating the abolition of marriage so "that such children may be born in plenty" and then adds, "The bastard's speech in *Lear* is floating through his mind."[36] The wife in Merriman's poem "who gave herself up to every sort of dissipation"; the young girl in *Purgatory* who marries a groom; her murderous son and vicious grandson; Edmund in *King Lear,* who disdains legitimate offspring begotten "within a dull, stale, tiréd bed" and boasts that bastards are conceived "in the lusty stealth of nature" (I, ii, 1–23) —all these have, for Yeats, a powerful attraction. As in "Oil and Blood" the vampires "full of blood" are more significant to the poet than are the "bodies of holy men and women" that exude "miraculous oil," so the dual crime of *Purgatory* has a certain dark allure for Yeats. He repeatedly affirmed that the greatest art sprang from the "Vision of Evil," as he called it, and regarded Shakespeare, Villon, Dante, and even Cervantes (but not Shelley, Ruskin, Wordsworth, and Morris) as exponents of this "preoccupation with evil."[37]

36 *Ex,* pp. 284–85. Cf. Yeats's section "Tomorrow's Revolution," in *Boiler,* p. 16, where he discusses heredity and eugenics in the light of a situation in which "the principal European nations are degenerating in body and in mind."

37 *Ex,* p. 275 (see also *Au,* pp. 149, 165, 186, 196; *Letters,* p. 680; *Vis,* pp. 144–45); "Shakespeare and Homer sang original sin," Yeats wrote in 1932 [quoted in *Identity,* p. 271]).

Both Lear and the Old Man move toward self-realization and by this development assume tragic dimensions. But the Old Man has one more grim lesson to learn. When he tries to reassure himself nonchalantly that he will easily get the blood off the blade of the knife he, like Lady Macbeth, little realizes that the stain is indelible:

> When I have stuck
> This old jack-knife into a sod
> And pulled it out all bright again,
> And picked up all the money that he dropped,
> I'll to a distant place, and there
> Tell my old jokes among new men.
>   (*He cleans the knife and begins to pick up money.*)
> Hoof-beats! Dear God,
> How quickly it returns—beat—beat—!
>
> > [209–16]

With equal confidence had Lady Macbeth assured her husband that all trace of the deed could be erased:

> A little water clears us of this deed.
> How easy is it then! Your constancy
> Hath left you unattended. (*Knock.*) Hark! more knocking.
>
> > [II, ii, 67–69]

The hoof beats of *Purgatory,* the knocking of *Macbeth:* both are clamorous reminders—one from the realm of the spirit world, the other from the realm of the natural world—that expiation for sin cannot be short-circuited. Yeats's tribunal, like Shakespeare's, is public.

In *On the Boiler* Yeats complains of "the difficult transition from topic to topic in Shakesperean [sic] dialogue" and of "the Elizabethan plot broken up into farce and spectacle." In *Purgatory* there is no transition from topic to topic because the topic is only one: the sudden, swift, and horrifying action of the Old Man stabbing his son thrice in rapid succession. "No Elizabethan had the Greek intensity," Yeats declared, and *intensity* is the word that best denotes *Purgatory.* "Intensity is all," he wrote in 1938, a quality embodied in *Purgatory,* which has a singleness of purpose that is never allowed to flag.[38] The past and the present, the dead and the living are held together in a mesh whose

---

38 *Boiler,* pp. 28–29; *Letters,* p. 906.

grip never relaxes, and the play moves forward with an inexorableness that establishes Yeats as a dramatist in his own right as much as Shakespeare was in his.

Direct References to Shakespeare

DIRECT references to Shakespeare are arranged chronologically. (Shakespeare and Yeats are abbreviated to S and Y throughout.)

1890

"In Victor Hugo's *Shakespeare* occur these sentences" (*New Island,* p. 204).
"Or lights on an epigram comparing Marlowe and S" (*New Island,* p. 208).

1891

"Poetry and romance" become strange "when not sanctioned by long usage, as with S" (*New Island,* p. 134).
"We still go to see S, but then we have made him one of our superstitions" (*New Island,* p. 213).
Y noticed that though Taylor knew plays of S by heart, he knew nothing of poetry or painting (*Man and Poet,* p. 86).
"He had not many books—a Shakespeare" (W. B. Yeats, *Collected Works,* VII, *John Sherman* [Stratford-on-Avon, 1908], 195).

1893

"Dante, who revealed God, and S, who revealed man" (*UP,* p. 266).
"Homer, Aeschylus, Sophocles, S . . . were little more than folk-lorists with musical tongues" (*UP,* p. 284).
"Could he [Shelley] have been as full of folk-lore as was S" (*UP,* p. 287).
"S and Keats had the folk-lore of their own day" (*UP,* p. 288).
Blake's admiration for S mentioned (*The Works of William Blake,* ed. E. J. Ellis and W. B. Yeats [London, 1893], I, 23).[1]

---

1 For the distribution of work between Yeats and Ellis, see Yeats's note in Allan Wade, *A Bibliography of the Writings of W. B. Yeats* (London, 1958), p. 224.

1894

Y contrasts the realism of Zola and others with "the imaginative method of . . . Kaladasa [sic], of Sophocles, of S" (*UP*, p. 322).

"When writers have begun to draw on them [folk tales] as copiously as did Homer, and Dante, and S, and Spenser" (*UP*, p. 328).

1895

"S [remained] an Elizabethan Englishman when he told of Coriolanus or of Cressida" (*UP*, p. 360).

"If it drove them to read Goethe and S and Milton" (*UP*, p. 384).

"Young ladies from Alexandra College gather in little groups and read S" (*UP*, p. 384).

1896

Y contrasts Robert Bridges with S (*E&I*, pp. 200–201).

"M. Verlaine talked of S, whom he admired" (*UP*, p. 398).

Disagreeing with Richard Garnett (author of *William Blake* [London, 1896]) for implying that Blake could have been clear and not cryptic if he so chose, Y argues ironically that this "is as though one should say, 'the songs of S are very clear, let us therefore trouble no more over the mystery of Hamlet'" (*UP*, p. 402).

1897

"S in the orange of the glory of the world" (*Myth*, p. 268).

1898

"S shattered the symmetry of verse and of drama" (*E&I*, p. 192).

1899

"All great poets [Dante, Homer, S] speak to us of the hopes and destinies of mankind" (*Literary Ideals in Ireland: A Controversy between John Eglinton and W.B.Y. in the Saturday Issues of the Daily Express* [Dublin: May, 1899]).

"I believe, too, that though a Homer or a Dante or a S may have used all knowledge" (*Literary Ideals*).

"Y answered that even in S's time people were beginning to talk of the decline of language" (George Moore, *Hail and Farewell: Ave* [New York, 1914], p. 56).

1900

"One bull is all that remains of S's talk" (*E&I*, p. 153).

"S, who is content with emotional symbols" (*E&I*, p. 162).

"The audiences of Sophocles and of S and of Calderon were not unlike the audiences I have heard listening in Irish cabins to songs in Gaelic" (*E&I*, p. 167).

1901

"At Stratford-on-Avon" (*E&I*, pp. 96–110).

S, "the most extravagant of poets" (W. B. Yeats, "At Stratford-on-Avon," *The Speaker* [May 11, 1901], p. 159).

"I feel that I am getting deeper into S's mystery than ever before" (*Letters*, p. 349).

"My father is delighted with my second article on S" (*Letters*, p. 352).

Hyland is afraid that a play by the Irish National Theatre "might keep people away from Benson's S performances" (*Letters*, p. 355).

"Perhaps Greek masterpieces rather more than S, for S is seen . . . not unendurably ill done" (*Ex*, p. 76).

"S being the only great dramatist known to Irish writers has made them cast their work too much on the English model" (*Ex*, p. 78).

"Greater need of the severe discipline of French and Scandinavian drama than of S's luxuriance" (*Ex*, p. 80).

"Compare it with the only fragment that has come down to us of S's own conversation" (*Ex*, p. 81).

"Though their dying may not be like the dying S spoke of" (*Myth*, p. 116).

Y criticizes John Eglinton for commending a book that regards "S and the Greek tragedians" as "bad art," and Mrs. Beecher Stowe as "good art" (W. B. Yeats, "John Eglinton," *The United Irishman* [November 9, 1901]. Quoted in Colton Johnson, "W. B. Yeats's Prose Contributions to Periodicals: 1900–1939" [Ph.D. diss., Northwestern University, 1968]).

1902

Marlowe and S still at school when Spenser was writing poetry (*E&I*, p. 359).

"S, with his delight in great persons" (*E&I*, p. 365).

"He should have been content to be, as Emerson thought S was, a Master of the Revels to mankind" (*E&I*, p. 368).

"I have come here for the S Cycle" (*Letters*, p. 366).

Conversation with Joyce on folklore and literature; Homer, S, etc., mentioned (*Identity*, p. 88).

"The plays of S and his contemporaries had to be acted on the Surrey side of Thames to keep the Corporation of London from putting them down by law" (W. B. Yeats, "The Freedom of the Theatre," *The United Irishman* [November 1, 1902]. Quoted in Johnson, "Yeats's Prose Contributions").

"S makes a wise hearer forget everything except what he wants him to remember" (i.e., we do not judge S's characters by conventional standards of morality) (Yeats, "Freedom of the Theatre").

"S's age was interested in questions of policy and kingcraft, and so he and his contemporaries played shuttlecock with policy and kingcraft" (Yeats, "Freedom of the Theatre").

1903

"The plays of S had to be performed on the south side of the Thames" (*Ex*, p. 111).

1904

"The poorest kinds of farce and melodrama have gone [to the small towns] and Shakespearian drama has not gone" (*Ex*, p. 127).

Pascal, Montaigne, S, etc., "had a different meaning when they spoke of thought . . . a reverie about the adventures of the soul" (*Ex*, p. 141).

"S observed his Roman crowds in London" (*Ex*, p. 160).

"The only realistic play that will live as S has lived . . . will arise out of the common life" (*Ex*, p. 167).

Acting styles in Ireland still retain something of "beauty and meaning . . . from the days of S" (*Ex*, p. 170).

School of acting established in Ireland "by an actor who probably remembered the Shakespearean players" (*Ex*, p. 170).

"It is not only S whose finest thoughts are inaudible on the English stage" (*Ex*, p. 171).

"S wrote for a little stage where very little could be done with movement" (*Letters*, p. 441).

1905

Y tells of Bullen's anger at Sidney Lee's failure to mention his (Bullen's) Stratford Shakespeare edition in a speech, and of his threatening to attack Lee "for some theory about S's sonnets" (*Letters*, p. 449).

Y declines Bullen's invitation to contribute an article on S for his edition of S (*Letters*, pp. 456–57).

"S or Sophocles can so quicken . . . the circles of the clock, so heighten the expression of life" (*Ex*, p. 196).

"Rabelais, Villon, S, William Blake, would have known one another by their speech" (*E&I*, p. 301).

1906

"I found in some English review an essay of his [Verlaine's] on S" (*E&I*, p. 270).

"S, Tintoretto . . . nearly all the great men of the Renaissance" were highly subjective (*E&I*, p. 279).

"I read this sentence a few days ago . . . 'Let nobody again go back to the old ballad material of S'" (*E&I*, p. 283).

"That old ballad material of S" can move us as reason cannot (*E&I*, p. 289).

"S seems to bring us to the very market-place. . . . I have come to think of even S's journeys . . . as the outflowing of an unrest" (*E&I*, pp. 296–97).

"Is there any possibility that Jonson meant S not Chapman by the character of Virgil in *The Poetaster?*" (*Letters*, p. 479).

"I haven't read the Elizabethans for fifteen years, except S and Spenser" (*Letters*, p. 479).

The centre of art is found in speech, as in S and Corneille (*Ex*, p. 211).

1907

"S's persons, when the last darkness has gathered about them, speak out of an ecstasy" (*E&I*, p. 254).

Y doubts whether George Moore ever read a play of S (*Au*, p. 245).

"The feeling for fine oratory that made possible the rogues and clowns of Ben Jonson and the Princes of Corneille and of S" (W. B. Yeats, "Notes," *The Arrow* [June 1, 1907]. Quoted in Johnson, "Yeats's Prose Contributions").

1909

S's works are tragi-comedy (*Au*, p. 286).

"That line written, as one believes, of S by Ben Jonson" (*Au*, p. 291).

"Milton and S inspire the active life of England" (*Au*, p. 300).

"S is always a writer of tragi-comedy" (*E&I*, p. 240).

"The last words of S's people, that gather up into themselves the energy of elaborate events" (*E&I*, p. 307).

In a lecture, Yeats spoke of "the old writers as busy with their own sins and of the new writers as busy with other people's" and ranked S on one side and Milton on the other (*Identity*, pp. 55–56).

1910

"The troubled life of Shakespearian drama. . . . S upon whose stage everything may happen, even the blinding of Gloucester" (*E&I*, p. 333).

Homer, S, etc., "define races and create everlasting loyalties" (*E&I*, p. 341).

"Ernest Dowson . . . as if he were a character in a play of S's" (*Letters*, p. 548).

S "is always a tragic comedian" (*Letters*, p. 549).

"I had put S among the old writers" (*Letters*, p. 555).

1911

"S expresses something that is common to all . . . and in all but his supreme moments S is a writer of comedy" (W. B. Yeats, "The Theater of Beauty," *Harper's Weekly* [November 11, 1911], p. 11).

"We should not stage Galsworthy and S in the same way" (Yeats, "Theater of Beauty").

1913

"The Barker productions of S—all examples of the new decorative method" (*Letters*, p. 579).

"The nobility is never all personal—In S where it is often intermixed with reality" (*Man and Poet*, p. 318).

1915

"We read S for his grammar exclusively" (*Au*, p. 34).

J.B.Y. told Y to write an essay on S's lines "To thine own self be true" (*Au*, p. 35).

"In S . . . you will find a group of characters . . . who express the dream" (*Identity*, p. 105).

Dowden "would have thought himself false to S and Goethe . . . did he not discourage us when in the public eye" (Curtis Bradford, *Yeats at Work* [Carbondale, Ill., 1965], p. 361).

1916

"The art of S passing into that of Dryden" (*E&I*, p. 225).

S wrote to please the groundlings, "but the great speeches were written by poets who remembered their patrons in the covered galleries" (*E&I*, p. 227).

"Poets from the time of Keats and Blake have derived their descent only through what is . . . least popular in the art of S" (*E&I*, p. 228).

"The men who created this convention [the Noh] were . . . more like us [the Irish] even than are S and Corneille" (*E&I*, p. 233).

"They had done this . . . not in the interest of S and Milton" (Torchiana, p. 17).

"S's art was public" (W. B. Yeats, *Four Plays for Dancers* [London, 1921], p. 88).

"Our modern poetical drama . . . always dominated by the example of S"
(Yeats, *Four Plays*, p. 88) .

1917

"Dante can return to his chambering and S to his 'pottle-pot'" (*Myth*, p. 333) .
"We can but cry in words Ben Jonson meant for none but S" (*Myth*, p. 360) .

1919

"S set upon the stage kings and queens" (*Ex*, p. 245) .
"Popular education has coincided with the lessening of S's audience" (*Ex*, p. 245) .
"S's groundlings watched the stage in terrified sympathy" (*Ex*, p. 246) .
"S had nothing to do with objective truth" (*Ex*, p. 246) .
"S, more objective than Dante—for, alas, the world must move" (*Ex*, p. 251) .
"You [Lady Gregory] and I and Synge . . . set out to bring again the theatre of S" (*Ex*, p. 252) .
"In Dante there was little shadow, in S a larger portion" (*Ex*, p. 253) .
"The two great energies of the world that in S's day penetrated each other have fallen apart" (*Ex*, p. 258) .
"If you had to choose, would you give up S or Balzac?" (*Ex*, p. 269) .
Modern writers, except Balzac, are "slight and shadowy" when compared with Dante, Villon, S, Cervantes (*Ex*, p. 275) .
"The strength and weight of S, of Villon . . . come from their preoccupation with evil" (*Ex*, p. 275) .
Shaw complains of "S's 'ghosts and murders.'" S, "a great many-sided man" (*Ex*, p. 276) .
"S might mitigate certain theological asperities" in Y's brother-in-law (*Letters*, p. 659) .
"The only authority I can give you is the authority that a Scotsman gave when he claimed S for his own country" (Hone, p. 321) .

1921

W. E. Henley "was most human . . . like one of S's characters" (*Au*, p. 76) .
William Morris' style monotonous, unlike the "language of Chaucer and S" (*Au*, p. 87) .
"Though I preferred S to Chaucer I begrudged my own preference." "Mind and heart began to break into fragments a little before S's birth" (*Au*, p. 117) .

1922

Y angry over being accused of dissuading "people from the study of 'S and Kingsley'" (*Au*, p. 143) .

"He [Dowden] turned S into a British Benthamite" (*Au*, p. 143) .
"S's people make all things serve their passion" (*Au*, p. 174) .
"But we may attribute to the next three nights of the moon the men of S"
     (*Au*, p. 175) .
"S leaned . . . even as craftsman, upon the general fate of men and nations"
     (*Au*, p. 188) .

1924

"And though he called him [Strindberg] the 'S of Sweden' " (*Au*, p. 327) .
"No man can create, as did S, . . . who does not believe . . . that man's soul
     is immortal" (*Man and Masks*, p. 246) .

1925

"Every schoolchild can understand some lines from Milton or S" (*Vis* [1925],
     p. 252) .
S at Phase 20: detailed analysis of S's personality (*Vis*, pp. 151–54) .
"The will imposes itself upon the multiplicity of living images, or events, upon
     all in S" (*Vis*, pp. 156–57) .
"Whereas S showed, through a style full of joy, a melancholy vision sought from
     afar" (*Vis*, p. 166) .
S's location in history examined at length (*Vis*, p. 294) .

1926

Y maintains that genius sometimes gives to the age its character: "if there is
     amongst them a Sophocles or a S . . . they give their character to the
     people" (W. B. Yeats, "A Defence of the Abbey Theatre: A Speech De-
     livered at a Meeting of the Dublin Literary Society on February 23," *The
     Dublin Magazine* [April–June, 1926], pp. 8–12. Quoted in Johnson,
     "Yeats's Prose Contributions") .

1929

"And yet I have no doubt that just such as he [a fiery, emotional individual]
     surrounded S's theatre" (*Letters*, p. 759) .

1930

"If I communicate with the living mind of S. . . . S had for object the creation
     of a mental image" (Torchiana, p. 136) .
"Or had since learned from the plays of S" (*Ex*, p. 291) .

"When I speak of an image of despair I think of . . . many passages in S"
   (*Ex*, p. 295).
"I had been to a school where Pope was the only poet since S" (*Ex*, p. 297).
"I shall take him to S's history plays" (*Ex*, p. 321).
"I should have said not that the living mind of Keats or S but their daimon is
   present. . . . The daimon of S or Keats has, however, entered into a sleep-
   less universality" (*Ex*, p. 332).

1932

Y gave lessons to his daughter from an expurgated S (Hone, p. 432).
"The Passion in S was a great fish in the sea" (*Identity*, p. 267).
"S and Homer sang original sin" (*Identity*, p. 271).
"Shakespearean fish swam the sea" ("Three Movements," *Variorum Poems*,
   p. 485).
"I was educated upon Balzac and S" (*Letters*, p. 791).
"Perhaps S toiled through libraries of works" (Monk Gibbon, *The Masterpiece
   and the Man: Yeats as I Knew Him* [New York, 1959], p. 137).

1934

"My daughter is fifteen and has just discovered S" (*Letters*, p. 821).
"Then she loves tragedies, has read all S's" (*Letters*, p. 828).
"First comes S" (*E&I*, p. 447).
Pound told Y that "S and Dante had corrupted literature, S by his too
   abounding sentiment" (*Variorum Plays*, p. 1310).
Pound denounced Dublin because "I had said that I was re-reading S" (*Variorum
   Plays*, p. 1310).

1935

Lady Gregory "was a Persse—a form of the name S calls Percy" (*Au*, p. 237).
Lady Gregory as a young lady discussed S with an admirer of hers (*Au*, p. 239).
"Blessed be heroic death (S's tragedies) " (*Letters*, p. 832).
"Homer and S were not more in our fathers' minds than they are in ours"
   (*Letters to DW*, p. 25).
"Of all that Y said, I remembered most his words about S. 'In the end,' he said,
   'S's mind is terrible.' When I asked him to expand this, he said: 'The final
   reality of existence in S's poetry is of a terrible kind' " (Stephen Spender,
   World within World [London, 1951], p. 165).

1936

"We need like Milton, S, Shelley, vast sentiments" (*Letters to DW*, p. 58).

"How can I hate England owing what I do to S" (*Letters to DW,* p. 111).

"Considering all I owe to S" (*Letters,* p. 872).

"Nor can I put the Eliot of these poems among those that descend from S" (W. B. Yeats, Introduction, *The Oxford Book of Modern Verse* [New York, 1936], p. xxii).

1937

"Like S, Dante, Milton, vast sentiments" (W. B. Yeats, Preface, *The Ten Principal Upanishads,* trans. Shree Purohit Swami and W. B. Yeats [London, 1937], p. 10).

"Dante and Milton had mythologies, S the characters of English history" (*E&I,* p. 509).

"I owe my soul to S, to Spenser, and to Blake" (*E&I,* p. 519).

"The heroes of S convey to us through their looks . . . their ecstasy at the approach of death" (*E&I,* pp. 522–23).

Frank Fay said that "Ireland had preserved longer than England the rhythmical utterance of the Shakespearean stage" (*E&I,* p. 528).

1938

"Who despised them [the people] with that old Shakespearean contempt" (*Boiler,* p. 10).

"To set certain passages in S above all else in literature" (*Boiler,* p. 14).

"I gave certain years to writing plays in Shakespearean blank verse" (*Boiler,* p. 15).

"There was once a stock company playing S in every considerable town" (*Boiler,* p. 18).

"The difficult transition from topic to topic in Shakespearean dialogue" (*Boiler,* p. 28).

"S and the ballads judge as we would have them judge" (*Boiler,* p. 32).

"His [Jonson's] tribunal is private, that of S public" (*Boiler,* p. 33).

"S is only a mass of magnificent fragments" (*Letters to DW,* p. 194).

"He [Y] several times said to me [Robinson] that the only dramatist he cared for was S" (Lennox Robinson, "The Man and the Dramatist," in *Scattering Branches,* ed. Stephen Gwynn [New York, 1940], p. 72).

Direct References to Shakespeare's Works

DIRECT references to Shakespeare's works and quotations from them are arranged chronologically under separate works listed alphabetically. In many places Yeats uses a Shakespearean phrase (e.g., "my mind's eye," *Ham.*, I, ii, 185) without seeming to relate it to Shakespeare; such references have been omitted. (References in square brackets are to the Shakespeare play or poem under consideration. Shakespeare and Yeats are abbreviated to S and Y throughout.)

ALL'S WELL THAT ENDS WELL

1915

"I had seen him [a professional athlete] described as 'the bright particular star of American athletes'" [I, i, 80] (*Au*, pp. 23–24).

1925

"That 'bright particular star' of S" [I, i, 80] (*Vis*, p. 52).

ANTONY AND CLEOPATRA
1890

"Of William Watson's lines on Antony at Actium" (*New Island*, p. 210).

1903

"If some strange chance put Plutarch's tale of Antony or S's play into his hands" (*Ex*, p. 120).

1904

"Or fly the battle for his sweetheart as did Antony." "If Antony had railed at Cleopatra in the monument." "If we had not seen Cleopatra through the eyes of so many lovers" (*Ex*, pp. 154–55).

"S observed . . . somewhere in his own Stratford, the old man that gave Cleopatra the asp" (*Ex*, p. 160).

1907

"Cleopatra sets the asp to her bosom" (*E&I*, p. 255).

1910

"When Antony names 'Of many thousand kisses' " [IV, xv, 20] (*E&I*, p. 240).

"The humour of the old man with the basket" and "Cleopatra's dying" (*E&I*, p. 244).

Antony's lines quoted: "A vapour sometime, like a bear or lion" [IV, xiv, 3–7] (W. B. Yeats, *Plays for an Irish Theatre* [London and Stratford-on-Avon, 1911], pp. ix–xiii).

1911

Antony "in a supreme moment . . . when he names 'Of many thousand kisses the poor last' " [IV, xv, 20] (W. B. Yeats, "The Theater of Beauty," *Harper's Weekly* [November 11, 1911], p. 11).

1916

"Cleopatra's old man with an asp" (*E&I*, p. 227).

1922

"Cleopatra [going] to her death" (*Au*, p. 164).

1935

"S made his old man with the asp talk 'Somerset' " (*Au*, p. 267).

1937

" 'Of many thousand kisses, the poor last' [IV, xv, 20] . . . no actress has ever sobbed when she played Cleopatra" (*E&I*, p. 523).

"Even the woman he loves is . . . Cleopatra" (*E&I*, p. 509).

1938

"Cleopatra's last farewells" (*Boiler*, p. 35).
"They brought you up to my rooms in a mattress like Cleopatra" (*Man and Masks*, p. 3).

AS YOU LIKE IT

1887

"None ever hate aright / Who hate not at first sight" [III, v, 80] (*Letters*, p. 41).

1903

"But by that hangs a tale" [II, vii, 28] (*Letters*, p. 392).

1906

"His Mistress's Eyebrows" [II, vii, 148] (*E&I*, p. 288).
"A lover is subtle about his mistress's eyebrow" [II, vii, 148] (*Dramatical Poems*, II, *The Poetical Works of William B. Yeats* [New York and London, 1907]. Reprinted in *Variorum Plays*, p. 1294).
"Yet every old man has lived differently through S's seven ages" [II, vii, 138–65] (*Letters*, p. 784).

1937

"And even the woman he loves is Rosalind" (*E&I*, p. 509).

CORIOLANUS

1895

"S [remained] an Elizabethan Englishman when he told of Coriolanus" (*UP*, p. 360).

1901

"The deeds of Coriolanus had no obvious use." "Aufidius was a more reasonable man than Coriolanus" (*E&I*, pp. 102–3).

1902

"We watch Coriolanus with delight, because he had a noble and beautiful pride,
and it seems to us for the moment of little importance that he sets all Rome
by the ears and even joins himself to her enemies" (W. B. Yeats, "The
Freedom of the Theatre," *The United Irishman* [November 1, 1902].
Quoted in Colton Johnson, "Yeats's Prose Contributions to Periodicals:
1900–1939" [Ph.D. diss., Northwestern University, 1968]) .

1903

"That singular criticism of S, which has decided that . . . *Coriolanus* [was
written] as a lesson to the proud" (W. B. Yeats, "A Canonical Book," *The
Bookman* [May, 1903]. Quoted in Johnson, "Yeats's Prose Contributions") .

1904

"Or betray his country like Coriolanus." "If Coriolanus had abated that high
pride of his." "Had Coriolanus not been a law breaker" (*Ex*, pp. 154–55) .
"As did the laws of Rome to Coriolanus" (*Ex*, p. 170) .

1906

"The passion of Coriolanus" (*E&I*, p. 276) .

1915

J.B.Y. reading aloud from *Coriolanus*. "I have seen *Coriolanus* played a number
of times since then" (*Au*, p. 39) .
"Under the canopy . . . i' the city of kites and crows" [IV, v, 37, 41] (*Au*,
p. 95) .

1930

"If I communicate with the living mind of S when I read of Coriolanus"
(Torchiana, p. 136) .

CYMBELINE

1905

"S laid the scene of *Cymbeline* in his own country, but he found the story in
the *Decameron*" (W. B. Yeats, "J. M. Synge's 'The Shadow of the Glen,' "

The United Irishman [January 28, 1905]. Quoted in Johnson, "Yeats's Prose Contributions").

FALSTAFF

1901

"Mr. Weir's admirable, though too benevolent and cleanly Falstaff" (W. B. Yeats, "At Stratford-on-Avon," *The Speaker* [May 11, 1901]).

1903

Speeches of Falstaff as perfect as the soliloquies of Hamlet (*Ex,* p. 108).

1904

"That he made Sir John Falstaff out of a praiseworthy old Lollard preacher" (*Ex,* p. 145).
"When I think of free-spoken Falstaff" (*Ex,* p. 150).
"Falstaff gives one the sensation of reality" (*Ex,* p. 166).

1905

"Whether it be the art of the *Ode on a Grecian Urn* or of the imaginer of Falstaff" (*Ex,* p. 198).
As examples of the world's great theater Y mentions that of Greece, India, "the creator of Falstaff" (*E&I,* p. 303).

1906

"I had forgotten Falstaff, who is an episode in a chronicle play" (*E&I,* p. 273, n. 1).

1910

"Falstaff, who has no passionate purpose to fulfill" (*E&I,* p. 240).

1911

"I realized that when I watched Falstaff on the stage" (Yeats, "Theater of Beauty").

1928

"A heavily-built Falstaffian man" ("The Road at My Door," *Variorum Poems*, p. 423).

1936

"A friend writes 'all bravado went out of English literature when Falstaff turned into Oliver Cromwell'" (W. B. Yeats, Introduction, *The Oxford Book of Modern Verse* [New York, 1936], p. xxvii).

1937

"Unlike that soul of fire / Sir John— / I but raise your finger tip / To my lip" [2 H. IV, II, iv, 230, 236–37] (*Letters to DW*, p. 151).

HAMLET

1889

"When the witching hour has come and ghosts are creeping about" [III, ii, 361] (*New Island*, p. 82).

1893

"Bring me to the test / And I the matter will re-word, which madness / Would gambol from" [III, iv, 141–43] (*The Works of William Blake*, ed. E. J. Ellis and W. B. Yeats [London, 1893], p. i).
"Poetry . . . gave us . . . Hamlet" (*UP*, p. 270).

1894

"For the mystics cannot, or will not, let any quite pluck out the heart of their mystery" [III, ii, 341] (W. B. Yeats, on E. J. Ellis' "Seen in Three Days," *The Bookman* [February, 1894]).

1896

Disagreeing with Richard Garnett (author of *William Blake* [London, 1896]) for implying that Blake could have been clear and not cryptic if he so chose, Y argues ironically that this "is as though one should say, 'the songs of S are very clear, let us therefore trouble no more over the mystery of Hamlet'" (*UP*, p. 402).

1897

"Hamlet, who saw them [the body's will and pleasure] perishing away, and sighed" (*Myth*, p. 274).

1901

"The deeds of . . . Hamlet . . . had no obvious use. . . . Fortinbras was, it is likely enough, a better king than Hamlet would have been" (*E&I*, p. 103).

"Hamlet who saw too great issues everywhere to play the trivial game of life" (*E&I*, p. 107).

"Richard II, that unripened Hamlet" (*E&I*, p. 108).

1902

"Hamlet's objection to the bare bodkin" (*E&I*, p. 369).

Y saw a Board School continuation class play *Hamlet* (*E&I*. p. 382).

1903

Speeches of Falstaff as perfect as the soliloquies of Hamlet (*Ex*, p. 108).

"In *Hamlet* . . . the murder of Hamlet's father and the sorrow of Hamlet are shadowed in . . . Fortinbras and Ophelia and Laertes" (*E&I*, pp. 215–16).

"That singular criticism of S, which has decided that *Hamlet* was written for a warning to the irresolute" (Yeats, "A Canonical Book").

1904

"And will have a little distrust for everything that can be called good or bad in itself" [II, ii, 244] (*Ex*, p. 162).

1905

"Odysseus and Don Quixote and Hamlet are with us always" (*Ex*, p. 197).

1906

"For even Hamlet and Lear and Oedipus are more cloudy" (*E&I*, p. 273).

1909

"I saw *Hamlet* . . . except for the chief 'Ophelia' scenes. . . . I came back for Hamlet at the graveside. . . . I feel in Hamlet . . . that I am in the

presence of a soul lingering on the storm-beaten threshold of sanctity"
(*Au*, p. 318) .

1910

"Character is defined, in Hamlet's gaiety" "When Hamlet cries to Horatio
'Absent thee from felicity awhile' " [V, ii, 326]. (*E&I*, p. 240) .
"Hamlet broken away from life by the passionate hesitations of his reverie"
(*E&I*, p. 242) .

1911

"Hamlet in a supreme moment: 'Absent thee. . . .' " [V, ii, 326] (Yeats,
"Theater of Beauty") .

1912

Y points out that the *Times*'s statement, "Except *The Hour Glass* at the Abbey
Theatre, Dublin, the Moscow *Hamlet* is the only play, we believe, in which
they [Gordon Craig's screens] have been chiefly or exclusively used," is
erroneous (W. B. Yeats, "Stage Scenery" [letter], *Times* [September 13,
1912]. Quoted in Johnson, "Yeats's Prose Contributions") .

1913

"And before his [Millais's] *Ophelia* . . . I recovered an old emotion" (*E&I*,
p. 346) .

1915

"When I was ten or twelve my father took me to see Irving play Hamlet.
. . . For many years Hamlet was an image of heroic self-possession" (*Au*,
p. 29) .
J.B.Y. told Y to write an essay on "S's lines, 'To thine own self be true' " [I,
iii, 78–80] (*Au*, p. 35) .
"Walking with an artificial stride in memory of Hamlet" (*Au*, p. 50) .
"To be able to play with hostile minds as Hamlet played" (*Au*, p. 57) .
"Hamlet had his self-possession from no schooling" (*Au*, p. 57) .
"Hamlet, Lear, let us say, who express the dream" (*Identity*, p. 105) .

1916

"Lethe wharf" [I, v, 33] (*E&I*, p. 227) .

"When for the first time *Hamlet* was being played in London" (*E&I*, p. 229).
Y wants to stage "the whole *Hamlet*" (*Letters*, p. 612).

1917

"When Hamlet refused the bare bodkin. . . ." "If a man died playing Hamlet,
he would be Hamlet in eternity" (*Myth*, p. 355).

1919

"Rosencrantz and Guildenstern . . . could be but foils for Hamlet" (*Ex*, p.
246).

1921

"Yet who would look at Hamlet in the grave scene if Salvini played the grave-
digger?" (*Au*, p. 76).
Wilde's statement that Hamlet invented "the pessimism that characterises modern thought" (*Au*, p. 83).
"Though he called his Hamlet 'fat' and even 'scant of breath,' he thrust between his fingers agile rapier and dagger" [V, ii, 267] (*Au*, p. 87).
"He [Standish O'Grady] could find quarrel in a straw" [IV, iv, 55] (*Au*, p. 133).
"He [Standish O'Grady] knew a trick of speech that made us murmur, 'We do
it wrong, being so majestical'" [I, i, 143–45] (*Au*, p. 133).

1923

The Introduction to *A Vision* "keeps the 'modesty of nature' in mind now"
[III, ii, 16] (*Letters*, p. 700).

1925

"Nor is Polonius disproved when Hamlet seems to kill him" (*Vis* [1925], pp.
171–72).
"If a man died playing Hamlet he would be Hamlet after death" (*Vis*, p. 222).

1928

"Hamlet and Lear educated S" (*Letters*, p. 741).

1930

"Hamlet's 'Absent thee from felicity awhile'" [V, ii, 326] (*Ex*, p. 296).

1931

"Coleridge's contrast between Juliet's nurse and Hamlet . . . S drew . . . Hamlet . . . out of himself" (*E&I*, p. 410).

1934

"My daughter . . . is writing an essay upon Hamlet" (*Letters*, p. 821).
She is trying "to learn all about the poison that killed Hamlet's father" (*Letters*, p. 828).

1935

Of Standish O'Grady, Y says: "Ye do it wrong, being so majestical, / To offer it the show of violence" [I, i, 143–45] (*Au*, p. 257).

1936

"There struts Hamlet . . . / That's Ophelia . . . / They know that Hamlet and Lear are gay / . . . / Though Hamlet rambles" ("Lapis Lazuli," *Variorum Poems*, pp. 565–66).
J.B.Y. called the poets whom Y described in "The Tragic Generation" "the Hamlets of our age" (Yeats, Introduction, *Oxford Book of Modern Verse*, p. x).

1937

"The Countess Cathleen could speak a blank verse which I had . . . almost put out of joint" [I, v, 188] (*E&I*, p. 525).

1938

"Who can forget . . . Hamlet, Lear, Faust, all figures in a peep-show" (*Boiler*, p. 33).
"Hamlet changes the letters and sends Rosencrantz and Gildenstern [sic] to their death. . . . S when he made Hamlet kill the father of Fortinbras in single combat. . . . Hamlet's hesitations are hesitations of thought" (*Boiler*, pp. 33–34).
"Polonius may go out wretchedly, but I can hear the dance music in 'Absent thee from felicity awhile' [V, ii, 326] or in Hamlet's speech over the dead Ophelia" (*Boiler*, p. 35).
"Some people say I have an affected manner, and if that is true, as it may well be, it is because my father took me when I was ten or twelve to

Irving's famous *Hamlet*" (W. B. Yeats, "I Became an Author," *The Listener* [August 4, 1938]).

"What brushes fly and gnat aside? / Irving and his plume of pride" (Yeats, "I Became an Author").

"What brushes fly and moth aside? / Irving and his plume of pride" ("A Nativity," *Variorum Poems*, p. 625).

"Rilke gives Hamlet's death as an example" (*Letters*, p. 917).

"No Hamlet thin from eating flies" ("The Statues," *Variorum Poems*, p. 610).

HENRY IV, PARTS I AND II

1901

"Mrs. Benson was a really admirable 'Doll Tearsheet' last night in Henry IV" (*Letters*, p. 349).

"I have seen this week . . . the second part of *Henry IV*" (*E&I*, p. 96).

"As unjust or as violent as . . . Bolingbroke." ". . . the historical plays from *Henry IV* to *Richard III*" (*E&I*, p. 106).

"And Mr. Benson's Doll Tearsheet which had the extravagance" (Yeats, "At Stratford-on-Avon," *The Speaker* [May 11, 1901].

HENRY V

1901

Detailed discussion of Henry (*E&I*, pp. 96–108).

"I thought Mr. Benson's Henry V nearly as good as his Richard II" (Yeats, "At Stratford-on-Avon," *The Speaker* [May 11, 1901].

1902

"If he [S] had given himself up . . . to his Philistinism he would have been Henry V" (Yeats, "Freedom of the Theatre").

1910

"Henry V, whose poetry, never touched by lyric heat" (*E&I*, p. 240).

HENRY VI

1901

"I have seen this week . . . the second part of *Henry VI*" (*E&I*, p. 96).

"That boy he and Katharine were to 'compound,' 'half French, half English' . . . turns out a saint" (*E&I*, p. 108).

"Those who have been to Stratford have seen . . . Mr. Ash's Jack Cade"
  (Yeats, "At Stratford-on-Avon," *The Speaker*).
"Exaggerate this spirit a little and you have S's Jack Cade" (W. B. Yeats. "John
  Eglinton," *The United Irishman* [November 9, 1901]. Quoted in John-
  son, "Yeats's Prose Contributions").

KING JOHN

1901

"I have seen this week *King John*" (*E&I*, p. 96).
"As unjust or as violent as . . . Prince John" (*E&I*, p. 106).
"Mr. Rodney and Mr. Sweet play Falconbridge [the Bastard] and King John
  with a barbaric simplicity that was entirely admirable" (Yeats, "At
  Stratford-on-Avon," *The Speaker*).

KING LEAR

1890

"Or weaving metaphors for the play of *King Lear*" (*New Island,* p. 208).
"Or perhaps finest of all [William Watson's poems] the following on the play
  of *King Lear:* 'Here love the slain with Love the slayer lies'" (*New
  Island,* p. 210).

1893

"When S compares the mind of the mad Lear to the 'vexed sea'" [IV, iv, 2]
  (*Works of William Blake,* I, 238).
"Poetry . . . gave us Lear" (*UP,* p. 270).
"Characters like Macbeth and Lear . . . cannot be separated . . . from the
  world about them" (*UP,* p. 272).

1894

"Poetry has ever loved those who are not 'piecemeal,' and has made of them
  its Timons and its Lears" (men committed to their convictions) (*UP,*
  p. 345).

1895

"And many another epigram [of Wilde's] . . . rings out like the voice of Lear's
  fool over a mad age" (*UP,* p. 355).

1897

"Lear and Tristan have come out of legends" (*E&I*, p. 182).
"Lear, his head still wet with the thunderstorm" (*Myth*, p. 275).

1902

"If he [S] had given himself up . . . to the near ally of his wit he would have been King Lear" (Yeats, "Freedom of the Theatre").

1903

King Lear "as the history of a whole evil time" (*E&I*, p. 215).
"Lear's shadow is in Gloucester" (*E&I*, p. 215).

1904

"What would such writers [realists] . . . do . . . with Lear upon his heath?" (*Letters*, p. 441).

1905

"The reveries of the common heart, ennobled into some raving Lear" (*E&I*, p. 301).

1906

"For even Hamlet and Lear and Oedipus are more cloudy" (*E&I*, p. 273).
"I find my pleasure in *King Lear* heightened by the make-believe that comes upon it all when the Fool says, 'This prophecy Merlin shall make' " [III, ii, 93] (*E&I*, p. 279).

1910

"S, upon whose stage everything may happen, even the blinding of Gloucester" (*E&I*, p. 333).
Advocating a suggestive stage setting rather than a realistic one, Y observes that "Gloster [sic] will be able to fall but from his own height and think that he has fallen from Dover cliff" (Yeats, *Plays for an Irish Theatre*, pp. ix-xiii. Reprinted in *Variorum Plays*, p. 1300).

1913

"Meanwhile it remains for some greater time . . . to create a *King Lear*" (*E&I*, p. 354).

1915

"Even to-day when I read *King Lear* his [William Pollexfen's] image is always before me" (*Au*, p. 5).
"Hamlet, Lear, let us say, who express the dream" (*Identity*, p. 105).

1919

"Popular commercial art has substituted for Lear and Cordelia the real millionaire and the real peeress" (*Ex*, pp. 245–46).

1921

Wilde said, "What is *King Lear* but poor life staggering in the fog?" (*Au*, p. 80).

1925

"The daughter who served him [Oedipus] as did Cordelia Lear" (*Vis*, p. 28).
"On passing from the village fool to the Fool of S." William Watson's lines on the Fool in King Lear quoted (see above, *King Lear*, 1890) (*Vis*, p. 182).

1926

"The bastard's speech in *Lear* is floating through his mind" (*Ex*, p. 285).
"I think of Strindberg in his Spook Sonata . . . as mad and as profound as *King Lear*" (W. B. Yeats, "The Need for Audacity of Thought," *The Dial* [February, 1926], pp. 115–19).

1928

"Hamlet and Lear educated S" (*Letters*, p. 741).

1930

"The state of irritation into which I was thrown by *King Lear,* which I thought but half visual and badly acted. . . . If I dared I would put *King Lear* into modern English" (*Letters*, p. 778).

1932–33

"*Hysterica passio* dragged this quarry down" [II, iv, 55] ("Parnell's Funeral," *Variorum Poems*, p. 542).

1936

"There struts Hamlet, there is Lear / . . . / They know that Hamlet and Lear are gay / . . . / Though Hamlet rambles and Lear rages" ("Lapis Lazuli," *Variorum Poems*, pp. 565–66).

1937

"He [the poet] is Lear" (*E&I*, p. 509).

1938

"Who can forget . . . Hamlet, Lear . . . all figures in a peep-show" (*Boiler*, p. 33).

"Lear's rage under the lightning" (*Boiler*, p. 35).

1936–39

"Till I am Timon and Lear" ("An Acre of Grass," *Variorum Poems*, p. 576).

"*Hysterica passio* of its own emptiness" [II, iv, 55] ("A Bronze Head," *Variorum Poems*, p. 618).

MACBETH

1889

"A play on King Arthur . . . is announced to follow *Macbeth* at the Lyceum" (*New Island*, p. 70).

1890

"Shakespeare's witches are born of the Teuton gloom" (*UP*, p. 173).

1893

"Poetry . . . gave us . . . Macbeth" (*UP*, p. 270).

"Characters like Macbeth and Lear . . . cannot be separated . . . from the world about them" (*UP*, p. 272).

1899

"To see 'the pendent bed and procreant cradle' of the 'martlet' as one listened to Banquo" [I, vi, 4–8] (*E&I*, p. 169).

1902

"Even on a large stage one should leave the description of the poet free to call up the martlet's procreant cradle" [I, vi, 6–8] (*Ex*, p. 88).

1904

"This character who delights us may commit murder like Macbeth" (*Ex*, p. 154).

1909

"Of Lady Gregory one can say what S or another said, 'She died every day she lived'" [IV, iii, 109–11] (A. Norman Jeffares, *A Commentary on the Collected Poems of W. B. Yeats* [Stanford, 1968], pp. 113–14).[1]

1913

Nobility "is often intermixed with reality. . . . Macbeth for instance" (*Man and Poet*, p. 318).

1934

"They [Lennox Robinson and others] obliterated the offence of their *Macbeth* by a magnificent performance of *The School for Wives*. . . . I am greatly comforted for I rammed them down the throat of my committee and after *Macbeth* I thought my instinct had failed me" (*Ah, Sweet Dancer: W. B. Yeats, Margot Ruddock, A Correspondence,* ed. Roger McHugh [London, 1970], p. 26).

1936

"Who can keep company with the Goddess Astrea if both his eyes are upon the brindled cat?" [IV, i, 1] (*E&I*, p. 488).

1937

"Unity of Being . . . imminent, differing from man to man and age to age, taking upon itself pain and ugliness, 'eye of newt, and toe of frog'" [IV, i, 14] (*E&I*, p. 518).
"She should have died hereafter" [V, v, 17] (*E&I*, p. 523).

 1   See below, *Macbeth*, 1901, Appendix 3.

MEASURE FOR MEASURE

1893

"And the lady who waited for 'the honeyed middle of the night' " [IV, i, 32–34] (*UP,* p. 288).

1908

"Sara Allgood plays Isabella . . . in *Measure for Measure*" (*Letters,* p. 508). "Last May a performance of *Measure for Measure* was given by the Elizabethan Stage Society" (W. B. Yeats, Editorial, *Samhain* [November, 1908], p. 4).

THE MERCHANT OF VENICE

1897

"In S's 'floor of heaven,' 'inlaid with patens of bright gold'; and in his Dido standing 'upon the wild sea banks,' 'a willow in her hand' " [V, i, 57–58, 10–11] (*E&I,* p. 176).

1905

Detailed account of Y's dislike for the way in which *The Merchant of Venice* was staged (*Letters,* pp. 465–66).

1906

"It [the theater of the Celtic Renaissance] must be made for young people who were sufficiently ignorant to refuse a pound of flesh" [IV, i] (*Ex,* p. 210).

A MIDSUMMER NIGHT'S DREAM

1888

"Speculative persons consider him [the Pooka] the forefather of Shakespeare's 'Puck' " (*Irish Fairy and Folk Tales,* ed. W. B. Yeats [New York, n.d.; 1st pub. 1888], p. 100).

1893

Shelley might have followed the example of S "in *The Tempest* and *Midsummer Night's Dream*" (*UP,* p. 287). "There is a world of difference between Puck and Peaseblossom . . . on the one hand and . . . the evil voices of Prometheus on the other" (*UP*, p. 288).

1897

"And is there not such delight and wonder in—'Meet we on hill, in dale, forest, or mead'" [II, i, 83] (*E&I*, p. 177).
"When S wrote in the Greek way—'I know a bank where the wild thyme blows'" [II, i, 249] (*E&I*, p. 177).
"S found his Mab, and probably his Puck . . . in Celtic legend" (*E&I*, p. 185).

1914

"One remembers Robin Goodfellow and his joint-stool" [II, i, 50–52] (*Ex*, p. 59).

OTHELLO

1891

"She was a fascinating coquette, who encouraged him [Clarence Mangan], amused herself with his devotion, and then 'whistled him down the wind'" [III, iii, 266] (*UP*, p. 196).

1893

"They thought no more of Iago but sang of Hatred" (i.e., the dramatic gave way to the lyrical) (*UP*, p. 270).

1902

"S could not have written the part of Iago unless he had something even of Iago in him" (Yeats, "Freedom of the Theatre").

1922

"To carry the heart upon the sleeve" [I, i, 65] (*Au*, p. 214).
Y points out that "there is no relation between Ruskin's cat and Desdemona's guilt . . . Desdemona's guilt is false reasoning" (*Yeats and TSM*, p. 64).

THE PHOENIX AND THE TURTLE

1936

"Ah my dear how it added to my excitement when I re-made that poem of yours to know it was your poem. I re-made you and myself into a single being. We triumphed over each other and I thought of *The Turtle and the Phoenix*" [ll. 36–48] (*Letters to DW*, p. 82).

RICHARD II

1900

"Might we not go to a matinée of *Richard II* which is on again" (*Letters*, p. 342).

1901

Detailed discussion of *Richard II* (*E&I*, pp. 96–108).
"Richard II beating time to the music . . . and his leaning on Bolingbroke" (Yeats, "At Stratford-on-Avon," *The Speaker*).

1902

"When [Spenser] died . . . *Richard II* . . . had . . . been acted" (*E&I*, p. 363).

1904

"The historical Richard has passed away for ever and the Richard of the play lives more intensely" (*Ex*, p. 145).

1936

"We always murmur in the end 'Let us sit upon the ground / And tell sad stories of the death of kings' " [III, ii, 155–56] (*Letters to DW*, p. 59).

1937

"I went to *Richard II* last night. . . . Did S in *Richard II* discover poetic reverie?" (*Letters to DW*, p. 145).

RICHARD III

1901

"I have seen this week . . . *Richard III*" (*E&I*, p. 96).
"Mr. Benson did not venture to play the scene in *Richard III* where the ghosts walk as S wrote it" (*E&I*, p. 101).

"*Richard III,* that monstrous birth and last sign of the wrath of Heaven" (*E&I,* p. 106).

1902

"When he [Spenser] died *Romeo and Juliet, Richard III* . . . had all been acted" (*E&I,* p. 363).

1904

"Who to-day could set Richmond's and Richard's tents side by side on the battlefield?" (*Ex,* p. 150).

1906

"That Richard's and Richmond's tents should be side by side" (*E&I,* p. 280).

1911

"And Richard's and Richmond's tents can face one another again" (Yeats, *Plays for an Irish Theatre,* pp. ix–xiii. Reprinted in *Variorum Plays,* p. 1300).

1925

"False, fleeting, perjured Clarence" [I, iv, 55] (*Vis,* p. 120).

1935

"False, fleeting perjured Ashley" [I, iv, 55] (*Letters.* p. 835).

ROMEO AND JULIET

1893

"Men ceased to write of Romeo and sang of Love" (i.e., the dramatic gave way to the lyrical) (*UP,* p. 270).

1902

"If he [S] had given himself up to his amorous emotions he would have been Romeo" (Yeats, "Freedom of the Theatre").
"When [Spenser] died *Romeo and Juliet* . . . had . . . been acted" (*E&I,* p. 363).

1908

"God save the mark!" [III, ii, 53] (*Ex,* p. 240) .

1909

"It is right that Romeo should not be a man of intellect or learning" (*Au,* p. 288) .

1910

"Juliet has personality, her Nurse has character" (*Letters,* p. 548) .

1915

"And flings herself out of the room when Juliet would be bride" ("His Phoenix," *Variorum Poems,* p. 354) .

1916

The love speeches of Juliet laughed at by an insensate audience (W. B. Yeats, *Four Plays for Dancers* [London, 1921], p. 88) .

1922

"Caring not a straw whether we be Juliet going to her wedding" (*Au,* p. 164) .

1925

Daniel O'Leary's disgust with a sorry production of *Romeo and Juliet* (*Vis,* p. 33) .

1931

"I think of Coleridge's contrast between Juliet's nurse and Hamlet, remember that S drew the nurse from observation" (*E&I,* p. 410) .

1937

"He [the poet] is Lear, Romeo" (*E&I,* p. 509) .

THE SONNETS

1898

"The arts lie dreaming of things to come" [Sonnet 107] (*E&I,* p. 191) .
"Is there not a proverb about rotten lilies smelling the worst?" ["Lilies that

fester smell far worse than weeds," Sonnet 94] (W. B. Yeats, "The Union
of the Gael" *'98 Centennial Assn. of Great Britain and France: Report of
Speeches Delivered at the Inaugural Banquet Held at the Holburn Res-
taurant, London, on Wednesday, 13th April 1898* [Dublin, 1898], p. 8.

1901

Sonnet 66 quoted in full (*E&I*, p. 107).

1905

Y mentions Bullen's anger with Sidney Lee "for some theory about S's sonnets"
(*Letters*, p. 449).

1906

"A studious man will commonly forget after some forty winters" [Sonnet 2]
(*E&I*, p. 278).

1922

"Than S could justify within the limits of a sonnet, his conviction that the
soul of the wide world dreams of things to come" [Sonnet 107] (*Au*, p. 199).

1925

"I have made myself a motley to the view" [Sonnet 110] (*Vis*, p. 152).
"Not even complaining when somebody pirated his sonnets" (*Vis*, p. 153).

1936

"Da Vinci's sitter had private reality like that of the Dark Lady among the
women S had imagined" (Yeats, Introduction, *Oxford Book of Modern
Verse*, pp. xxx–xxxi).

1937

"I kept repeating the sonnet of S's about 'captive good' "[2] [Sonnet 66] (*Letters
to DW*, p. 123).
"I read . . . S, the Sonnets" (*Letters to DW*, p. 124).

2 Dorothy Wellesley prints the quotation as "captain good," but perhaps
Yeats's handwriting was responsible for this.

"Even the woman he loves is Rosalind, Cleopatra, never The Dark Lady" (*E&I*, p. 509).

"Hugh Lane, 'onlie begetter' of all these" ["To The Onlie Begetter of These Insuing Sonnets . . ."] ("The Municipal Gallery Revisited," *Variorum Poems,* p. 602).

THE TEMPEST

1892

Y writes of the mythology of Ireland: "There alone is enough of the stuff that dreams are made on" [IV, i, 156–57] (*New Island,* p. 159).

"To Blake the only real world was the mental world, and the rest was of the stuff that dreams are made of" [IV, i, 156–57] (*UP,* p. 253).

1893

"The Slavonian peasants tell their children now, as they did a thousand years before S was born, of the spirit prisoned in the cloven pine" [I, ii, 277] (*UP,* p. 284).

"As did the one in *The Tempest*" (*UP,* p. 287, n. 14).

1904

"Tree has turned *The Tempest* into a very common and vulgar pantomime" (*Letters,* p. 443).

TIMON OF ATHENS

1894

"Poetry has ever loved those who are not 'piecemeal,' and has made of them its Timons and its Lears" (men committed to their convictions) (*UP,* p. 345).

1900

"Timon hath made his everlasting mansion" [V, i, 213] (*E&I,* p. 156).

1901

"The deeds of . . . Timon . . . had no obvious use" (*E&I,* p. 103).

1902

"If he [S] had given himself up . . . to his hatred of the world he would have been Timon" (Yeats, "Freedom of the Theatre").

1904

"When Timon makes his epitaph" (*Ex,* p. 163).

1907

"Timon of Athens contemplates his own end" (*E&I,* p. 255).

1911

"Timon when he orders his tomb is ourselves" (Yeats, "Theater of Beauty").

1936–39

"Till I am Timon and Lear" ("An Acre of Grass," *Variorum Poems,* p. 576).

TROILUS AND CRESSIDA

1895

"S [remained] an Elizabethan Englishman when he told of . . . Cressida" (*UP,* p. 360).

TWELFTH NIGHT

1924

One of Y's characters, Peter, says: "Like somebody in S, I think nobly of the soul and refuse to admit that the soul of man or nation is as dependent upon circumstances as all that" [Peter is thinking of Malvolio: IV, ii, 49–50] (W. B. Yeats, "Compulsory Gaelic: A Dialogue by W. B. Yeats," *The Irish Statesman* [August 2, 1924], pp. 649–52. Quoted in Johnson, "Yeats's Prose Contributions").

1935

"Barren rascals" [I, v, 70; V, i, 357] (*Au,* p. 273).

THE WINTER'S TALE

1891

"Hawthorne wanted to make one's flesh creep like the little boy in *A Winter's Tale*" [II, i, 25–31] (*New Island,* p. 135).

1921

Wilde said, "Give me *The Winter's Tale,* 'Daffodils that come before the swallow dare'" [IV, iv, 118–19] (*Au,* p. 80).

Shakespearean Echoes in Yeats's Works

SHAKESPEAREAN echoes in Yeats's works are arranged chronologically under separate works of Shakespeare listed alphabetically. With a writer so steeped in Shakespeare as Yeats, Shakespearean echoes are certain to be present. As Yeats detected "the bastard's speech in *Lear* . . . floating through his [the Irish poet Brian Merriman's] mind,"[1] so the diligent investigator may detect numerous Shakespearean reminiscences in Yeats. Nevertheless, I have presented these with considerable caution, while bearing in mind the fact that Shakespeare himself was as great an originator as a confiscator. (References in square brackets are to the Shakespeare play or poem under consideration. Shakespeare and Yeats are abbreviated to S and Y throughout.)

ANTONY AND CLEOPATRA

1907

"For naught's lacking / But a good end to the long, cloudy day" (*Deirdre, Variorum Plays,* p. 374, ll. 466–67). Cf. "Finish, good lady: the bright day is done, / and we are for the dark" [V, ii, 192–93].

"We'll be different; / Imperishable things, a cloud or a fire" (*Deirdre, Variorum Plays,* p. 376, ll. 496–97). Cf. "I am fire and air; my other elements / I give to baser life" [V, ii, 284–85].

1936–39

"There all the golden codgers lay, / There the silver dew, / And the great water sighed for love" ("News for the Delphic Oracle," *Variorum Poems,* p. 611). Cf. "The barge she sat in, like a burnished throne, / Burned on the water. The poop was beaten gold; / Purple the sails, and so perfuméd

---

1 *Ex,* p. 285.

that / The winds were lovesick with them; the oars were silver" [II, ii, 194–97].[2]

AS YOU LIKE IT

1893

"It is, however, wonderful and again wonderful, and no less inexcusable than wonderful" (*UP*, p. 280). Cf. "Oh, wonderful, wonderful, and most wonderful wonderful! And yet again wonderful" [III, ii, 179–80].

1925

"He is full of practical wisdom, a wisdom of saws and proverbs" (*Vis*, p. 110). Cf. "Full of wise saws and modern instances" [II, vii, 155].

1933

"Saving the rhyme rats hear before they die" ("Parnell's Funeral," *Variorum Poems*, p. 542). Cf. "that I was an Irish rat" [III, ii, 166].[3]

1936

"All perform their tragic play, / . . . / Yet they, should the last scene be there" ("Lapis Lazuli," *Variorum Poems*, p. 565). Cf. "And all the men and women merely players. / . . . / . . . Last scene of all" [II, vii, 139, 162].[4]

HAMLET

1890

"I hear it in the deep heart's core" ("The Lake Isle of Innisfree," *Variorum Poems*, p. 117). Cf. "and I will wear him / In my heart's core" [III, ii, 64–65].

1891

"I am at present trying to go sideways like the crabs" (W. B. Yeats, *Collected Works*, VII, *John Sherman* [Stratford-on-Avon, 1908], 260). Cf. "For, your-

2 See *Identity*, p. 284.
3 See Henn, p. 46, n. 2.
4 I am indebted to Professor Roger McHugh for having drawn my attention to this Shakespearean echo.

self, sir, shall grow old as I am, if like a crab you could go backward" [II, ii, 199–200].

1902

"He [Morris] found it enough to hold up, as it were, life as it is to-day" (*E&I,* p. 63). Cf. "Whose end, both at the first and now, was and is, to hold, as 'twere, the mirror up to nature" [III, ii, 18–19].

1904

"Who has a keen eye for rats behind the arras" (*Ex,* p. 143). Cf. III, iv, 23–24.

1908

"A dream is a sort of a shadow" (*The Unicorn from the Stars, Variorum Plays,* p. 651, ll. 74–75). Cf. "A dream itself is but a shadow" [II, ii, 252].

1914

"He is gone, he is gone, he is gone, but come in, everybody in the world" (*The Hour-Glass, Variorum Plays,* p. 639, ll. 638–39). Cf. "He is gone, he is gone, / And we cast away moan" [IV, v, 190–91].

1917

"You should be native here, for that rough tongue" (*At the Hawk's Well, Variorum Plays,* p. 404, l. 96). Cf. "though I am native here / And to the manner born" [I, iv, 14–15].

1918

"Soldier, scholar, horseman, he" ("In Memory of Major Robert Gregory," *Variorum Poems,* p. 327). Cf. "The courtier's, soldier's, scholar's, eye, tongue, sword" [III, i, 147].

1919

"Come, we must have music [*She picks up a lute* . . .]" (*The Player Queen, Variorum Plays,* p. 742, ll. 322–23). Cf. "Ah, ha! Come, some music! Come, the recorders!" [III, ii, 272].

1925

"Cowardice, some silly over-subtle thought / Or anything called conscience once" ("The Tower," *Variorum Poems,* p. 413). Cf. "Thus conscience does make cowards of us all, / And thus the native hue of resolution / Is sicklied o'er with the pale cast of thought" [III, i, 83–85].

1926–27

"As though my sorrow were a scene / Upon a painted wall" ("Human Dignity," *Variorum Poems,* p. 452). Cf. "Or are you like the painting of a sorrow, / A face without a heart?" [IV, vii, 108–9].

1929

"Mad as the mist and snow" ("Mad As the Mist and Snow," *Variorum Poems,* p. 523). Cf. "Mad as the sea and wind when both contend" [IV, i, 7].

1934

"You think to wound her with a knife! She has an airy body, an invulnerable body" (*Fighting the Waves, Variorum Plays,* p. 554, ll. 229–30). Cf. "For it is, as the air, invulnerable" [I, i, 145].[5]

1935

"All is well with AE. His ghost will not walk" (*Letters,* p. 838). Cf. "I will watch to-night: / Perchance 'twill walk again," and, "All is not well. / I doubt some foul play" [I, ii, 241–42; 254–55].

1938

"There is no release / In a bodkin or disease" ("The Man and the Echo," *Variorum Poems,* p. 632). Cf. "When he himself might his quietus make / With a bare bodkin?" [III, i, 75–76].
"Congal. . . . Cut him up with swords.
   Pat. I have him within my reach.
   Congal. No, no, he is here at my side.
   Corney. His wing has touched my shoulder.
   Congal. We missed him again. . . ." (*The Herne's Egg, Variorum Plays,*
   p. 1023, ll. 16–20). Cf.:
"*Horatio.* . . . Stop it, Marcellus.
   Marcellus. Shall I strike at it with my partisan?
   Horatio. Do, if it will not stand.
   Barnardo.   'Tis here!
   Horatio.   'Tis here!
   Marcellus. 'Tis gone!" [I, i, 139–43].

   5 A passage that Yeats seems to have been particularly conscious of: see above, *Hamlet,* 1921 and 1935, Appendix 2.

JULIUS CAESAR

1908

"It was the falling sickness" (*The Unicorn from the Stars, Variorum Plays*, p. 649, ll. 22–23). Cf. " 'Tis very like. He hath the falling sickness" [I, ii, 251].

1922

"The wavering, lean image of hungry speculation" (*Au*, p. 87). Cf. "Yond Cassius has a lean and hungry look: / He thinks too much" [I, ii, 194–95].

1925

"In one the dog bays the Moon" (*Vis*, p. 94). Cf. "I had rather be a dog, and bay the moon" [IV, ii, 26].

1927

"Many times he died" ("Death," *Variorum Poems*, p. 476). Cf. "Cowards die many times before their deaths" [II, ii, 32].

1935

"For ever and for ever" ("Whence Had They Come?" *Variorum Poems*, p. 560). Cf. "Forever and forever, farewell, Cassius" [V, i, 116].

1938

"He was a noble character, / And I must weep at his funeral" (*The Herne's Egg, Variorum Plays*, p. 1027, ll. 86–87). Cf Antony's funeral oration for Caesar [III, ii, 69–103].[6]

KING LEAR

1902

"On finding that her voice is sweet and low" ("Adam's Curse," *Variorum Poems*, p. 205). Cf. "Her voice was ever soft, / Gentle and low, an excellent thing in woman" [V, iii, 273–74].

1916

"In later years [Constance Gore-Booth's] voice became shrill and light, but at

6 F. A. C. Wilson, *W. B. Yeats and Tradition* (London, 1958), pp. 101–2. See also his *Yeats's Iconography* (London, 1960), p. 304.

the time I went up it was low and soft" (Torchiana, p. 186). Cf. "Her voice was ever soft, / Gentle and low, an excellent thing in woman" [V, iii, 273–74].

1922

"Tom the Fool" (*Au*, p. 158). Cf. "he says his name's Poor Tom" [III, iv, 42–43].[7]

1925

"Old lecher with a love on every wind" ("The Tower," *Variorum Poems*, p. 413). Cf. "like an old lecher's heart, a small spark" [III, iv, 107].

1927

"Never, never will he come again" (early draft of "Chosen," *Variorum Poems*, p. 534, in Stallworthy, p. 149). Cf. "Thou'lt come no more, / Never, never, never. . . ." [V, iii, 308–9].

1936–39

"The women that I picked spoke sweet and low" ("Hound Voice," *Variorum Poems*, p. 622). Cf. "Her voice was ever soft, / Gentle and low, an excellent thing in woman" [V, iii, 273–74].[8]

1938

"Intensity is all" (*Letters,* p. 906). Cf. "Ripeness is all" [V, ii, 11].

1939

"What is your name, boy?" "Poor Tom Fool. / Everybody knows Tom Fool" (*The Herne's Egg, Variorum Plays,* p. 1034, ll. 1–2). Cf. "Who's there?" / "A spirit, a spirit: he says his name's Poor Tom" [III, iv, 42–43].

LOVE'S LABOUR'S LOST

1922

"To Joan with her Pot" (*Au,* p. 158). Cf. V, ii, 901, 910.

7 See Stallworthy, p. 239.
8 See J. R. Mulryne, "The Last Poems," in *An Honoured Guest: New Essays on W. B. Yeats,* ed. Denis Donoghue and J. R. Mulryne (London, 1965), p. 135. See also Henn, p. 333.

MACBETH

1895

"Their wine of life has been mellowed in ancient cellars" (*UP*, p. 360). Cf. "The wine of life is drawn" [II, iii, 88].

1901

"To those who die every day they live, though their dying may not be like the dying S spoke of" (*Myth*, p. 116). Cf. "The queen that bore thee, / Oft'ner upon her knees than on her feet, / Died every day she lived" [IV, iii, 109–11].[9]

1904

"They are both stirring the same pot—something of a witches' cauldron, I think" (*Letters*, p. 436). Cf. "Sweltered venom sleeping got, / Boil thou first i' th' charméd pot," etc. [IV, i, 8–9].

1908

"I saw Adam numbering the creatures . . . foul and fair" (*Ex*, p. 242). Cf. "Fair is foul, and foul is fair" [I, i, 11].

1931

"Fair and foul are near of kin" ("Crazy Jane Talks with the Bishop," *Variorum Poems*, p. 513). Cf. "Fair is foul and foul is fair" [I, i, 11].

1933

"Tomorrow and tomorrow fills its thought" (*Letters*, p. 817). Cf. "To-morrow, and to-morrow, and to-morrow, / Creeps in this petty pace" [V, v, 19–20].

1939

"A bastard that a pedlar got / Upon a tinker's daughter in a ditch" (*Purgatory, Variorum Plays*, p. 1044, ll. 89–90). Cf. "Finger of birth-strangled babe / Ditch-delivered by a drab" [IV, i, 30–31].
See also F. A. C. Wilson, *Yeats's Iconography* (London, 1960), p. 223.

9 See above, *Macbeth*, 1909, Appendix 2.

MEASURE FOR MEASURE

1908

"Because he [an actor] believed *The Hour-Glass* to be a problem play" (*Ex,* p. 239). The term "problem play" was first used by Boas in 1896 with reference to *Meas., Ham., All's W.,* and *Troi.*[10]

THE MERCHANT OF VENICE

1891

"And thinking how on such a night as this he had sat with Mary Carton by the rectory fire" (Yeats, *John Sherman,* pp. 259–60). Cf. "In such a night as this / When the sweet wind," etc. [V, i, 1–20].

A MIDSUMMER NIGHT'S DREAM

1935

"Thank the Lord, all men are fools" (*A Full Moon in March, Variorum Plays,* p. 979, l. 27). Cf. "Lord, what fools these mortals be!" [III, ii, 115].

OTHELLO

1907

"And all that's strange / Is true because 'twere pity if it were not" (*Deirdre, Variorum Plays,* p. 351, ll. 109–10). Cf. "She swore, in faith, 'twas strange, 'twas passing strange; / 'Twas pitiful, 'twas wondrous pitiful" [I, iii, 160–61].
See also F. A. C. Wilson, *W. B. Yeats and Tradition* (London, 1958), p. 78.

THE PASSIONATE PILGRIM

1929

"The curtains drawn upon unfriendly night, / That we descant and yet again descant" ("After Long Silence," *Variorum Poems,* p. 523). Cf. "She bade good night that kept my rest away; / And dragged me to a cabin hanged with care, / To descant on the doubts of my decay" [XIV, 1–6].

---

10 See Frederick S. Boas, *Shakspere and His Predecessors* (London, 1896), p. 345.

RICHARD II

1919

"This sentence seemed to form in my head . . . 'Hammer your thoughts into unity'" (*Ex*, p. 263). Cf. "I have been studying how I may compare / This prison where I live unto the world: / . . . / I cannot do it. Yet I'll hammer it out" [V, v, 1–5].

RICHARD III

1925

""The deformity may be of any kind . . . for it is but symbolised in the hump. . . . The eye is fixed upon the sun and dazzles" (*Vis*, pp. 177, 179). Cf. "Unless to see my shadow in the sun / And descant on mine own deformity / And therefore since I cannot prove a lover . . . / I am determinéd to prove a villain" [I, i, 26–30].

ROMEO AND JULIET

1926

"Parting" (*Variorum Poems*, pp. 535–36). Cf. III, v, 1–36.[11]

1938

"A scratch, a scratch, a mere nothing / But had it been a little deeper and higher" (*The Herne's Egg, Variorum Plays*, p. 1037, ll. 90–91). Cf. "Ay, ay, a scratch, a scratch. Marry, 'tis enough" [III, i, 87].

THE SONNETS

1901

"Wisdom and beauty and power may . . . come to those who die" (*Myth*, p. 116). Cf. "Herein lives wisdom, beauty and increase" [Sonnet 11].

1909

"I feel in *Hamlet,* as so often in S, that I am in the presence of a soul lingering on the storm-beaten threshold of sanctity" (*Au*, p. 318). Cf. "To dry the rain on my storm-beaten face" [Sonnet 34].

11 See Hone, p. 433; Stallworthy, p. 143.

THE TEMPEST

1890

"And not a wrack was left to tell of what had been" (*UP,* p. 173). Cf. "And, like this insubstantial pageant faded, / Leave not a rack behind" [IV, i, 155–56].

1937

"They say it is more human / To shuffle, grunt and groan, / Not knowing what unearthly stuff / Rounds a mighty scene" ("The Old Stone Cross," *Variorum Poems,* p. 599). Cf. "We are such stuff / As dreams are made on; and our little life / Is rounded with a sleep" [IV, i, 156–58].

1938

"When sleepers wake and yet still dream, / And when it's vanished still declare, / With only bed and bedstead there, / That heavens had opened" ("Under Ben Bulben," *Variorum Poems,* p. 639). Cf. "That, if I then had waked after long sleep, / Will make me sleep again: and then, in dreaming, / The clouds methought would open" [III, ii, 130–33].

TIMON OF ATHENS

1929

"Bring me to the blasted oak / That I . . . / May call down curses on his head" ("Crazy Jane and the Bishop," *Variorum Poems,* pp. 507–8). Cf. "Be men like blasted woods, / . . . / If thou hat'st curses, / Stay not. Fly. . . ." [IV, iii, 524–27].

TROILUS AND CRESSIDA

1936–39

"Hector is dead and there's a light in Troy" ("The Gyres," *Variorum Poems,* p. 564). Cf. "Hector is dead: there is no more to say" [V, x, 22].

THE WINTER'S TALE

1892

"And dance like a wave of the sea" ("The Fiddler of Dooney," *Variorum Poems,* p. 179). Cf. "When you do dance, I wish you / A wave o' th' sea" [IV, iv, 140].[12]

   12   See Henn, p. 305.

Index